YOUR TOWNS & CITIES IN WORLD WAR TWO

BRIGHTON
AT WAR 1939–45

For Caroline

DOUGLAS d'ENNO is a freelance translator, local historian and journalist who has made an exhaustive study of the impact of both world wars on Brighton. He has also written a comprehensive first volume on Britain's fishermen and their vessels in the First World War (*Fishermen Against the Kaiser*, also published by Pen & Sword). In the course of a career spanning three decades as a translator in public service and in industry, he additionally undertook writing and research, culminating in *The Saltdean Story* in 1985, followed by local history contributions to the *Brighton & Hove Gazette*, the *Evening Argus/Argus* and local/community publications, and in further books, including *The Church in a Garden* (2001), *Foul Deeds and Suspicious Deaths around Brighton* (2004), *Brighton Crime and Vice, 1800–2000* (2007), *Brighton in the Great War* (2016) and *Saltdean from Old Photographs* (2018), as well as a number of 'then and now' pictorial books featuring Brighton, the Brighton area and Sussex. He is the author of two books on the past and present railway stations of Sussex and Surrey respectively. His next book will focus on railway mishaps and accidents in south-east England.

YOUR TOWNS & CITIES IN WORLD WAR TWO

BRIGHTON
AT WAR 1939–45

DOUGLAS d'ENNO

Pen & Sword
MILITARY
AN IMPRINT OF PEN & SWORD BOOKS LTD.
YORKSHIRE - PHILADELPHIA

First published in Great Britain in 2021 and reprinted in 2022 by
Pen & Sword Military
An imprint of
Pen & Sword Books Ltd
Yorkshire – Philadelphia

Copyright © Douglas d'Enno, 2021, 2022

ISBN 978 1 47388 593 6

The right of Douglas d'Enno to be identified as Author of this work has been asserted by him in accordance with the Copyright, Designs and Patents Act 1988.

A CIP catalogue record for this book is available from the British Library.

All rights reserved. No part of this book may be reproduced or transmitted in any form or by any means, electronic or mechanical including photocopying, recording or by any information storage and retrieval system, without permission from the Publisher in writing.

Printed and bound in the UK by CPI Group (UK) Ltd, Croydon, CR0 4YY.
Typeset by SJmagic DESIGN SERVICES, India.

Pen & Sword Books Limited incorporates the imprints of Atlas, Archaeology, Aviation, Discovery, Family History, Fiction, History, Maritime, Military, Military Classics, Politics, Select, Transport, True Crime, Air World, Frontline Publishing, Leo Cooper, Remember When, Seaforth Publishing, The Praetorian Press, Wharncliffe Local History, Wharncliffe Transport, Wharncliffe True Crime, White Owl and After the Battle.

For a complete list of Pen & Sword titles please contact

PEN & SWORD BOOKS LIMITED
47 Church Street, Barnsley, South Yorkshire, S70 2AS, England
E-mail: enquiries@pen-and-sword.co.uk
Website: www.pen-and-sword.co.uk

Or
PEN AND SWORD BOOKS
1950 Lawrence Rd, Havertown, PA 19083, USA
E-mail: Uspen-and-sword@casematepublishers.com
Website: www.penandswordbooks.com

Contents

Introduction 7

Acknowledgements 10

1. **PEACE FOR OUR TIME?** January 1938 – August 1939   12
   Preparations for the unthinkable – General relief, but preparations continue – Our German friends – Treatment of the Jews – ARP readiness – Shelters, gas masks and firefighting equipment – First aid and blackout – Government advice – Freezing yuletide but warming entertainment – Facing the inevitable – The evacuee invasion.

2. **BEFORE THE BOMBS** 3 September 1939 – 14 July 1940   43
   The announcement – The false alarm – A mighty influx – Returnees – Blackout – Aliens – Sandbags and breeze blocks – Shelters (again) – ARP highs and lows – A Civil Defence exercise – The ATS – Local Defence Volunteers stand ready – Eager cyclists – Enlistment – Billets and comforts – Farms and allotments – Food and rationing – Sport and entertainment – Our fishermen at Dunkirk and St Valéry – Impeded access everywhere.

3. **DEATH FROM THE SKIES** 15 July 1940 – December 1942   92
   The first casualties – August visit – Black September – Two October raids – Winter bombs – Attacks in 1941 – Summer, 1942 – October's grim toll – Raid on Rottingdean.

4. **LIFE GOES ON** July 1940 – December 1942   135
   Duel over Brighton – ARP/Civil Defence Services – Shelter shortcomings – Gas mask test failure – The Home Guard – Food production – Mass catering – Defence Area – Curfew – The Army moves in – Saving and fundraising – Targeted saving – Salvage.

5. MORE DEADLY VISITATIONS January 1943 – February 1944   187
The Clinic tragedy – Gloucester Place and Grosvenor Street – Out of the blue – Destruction in Whitehawk – Unlucky Bonchurch Road – Raids in 1944.

6. SEEING IT THROUGH 1943 – 1944   222
'Wings for Victory' – Other savings and causes – 'Holidays at Home' – The ban reintroduced – 'Blackpool Week' – CRIME: Crimes by Canadians – Crimes by British servicemen – Crimes by local civilians – Juveniles misbehaving – Despicable thefts by person(s) unknown – Food production, 1943-44 – Food exhibitions – D-Day, the great crusade.

7. VICTORY YEAR 1945   258
New Year celebrations – Entertainment and sport – Worthy Funds – A resort reborn – VE Day, 8 May 1945 – Thanksgiving – Victory Parade – It's over.

Appendices
1. The Book of Remembrance   273
2. Local Industrial Production   280

Bibliography and Further Reading   286

Index   292

Introduction

On 7 April 2016, local paper *The Argus* printed an interview in its 'Life Argus' feature, conducted by reporter Flora Thompson, relating to my new book, *Brighton in the Great War*. I recall, at the close of our interview and in relation to future plans for books, a vague interest I expressed in the second great conflict of the last century. 'The idea,' I said, 'came to me in the bath. I thought, if I can do a book on what life was really like in Brighton in the First World War, I could look at the Second.'

Five years later, that 'look' has turned into a book. A book which is the first comprehensive volume to describe everyday life and incidents in Brighton in 1939–45. The work involved proved, as I initially feared, to be massive. The pages of the local press were the bedrock of my information and many, many hundreds of these were photographed and distilled.

It seemed reasonable to begin the story with the year 1938 – twelve months of apprehension and preparation, a time when the whole country was living with a fragile peace. Planning for the eventuality of war continued at a more rapid pace during the first eight months of 1939 and due attention has also been paid to that period.

Significant interest in the sufferings of Brighton during the conflict was aroused by a number of books written by local historian David Rowland from 1997 to 2007. These reproduced, among some personal rarities, many of the excellent and readily available photographs of bombardments in this area, especially those to be found in *Brighton & Hove in Battledress, 1939–1945*, published in 1946 by Brighton Herald Ltd. Indeed, selecting the best images in an appropriately managed number proved to be one of the more difficult tasks in preparing this volume.

I am pleased to have been involved with the 'discovery' of the Book of Remembrance, held since 1952 in the parish church of St Peter, Brighton, listing local casualties (civilians and service personnel) and with its relocation in the autumn of 2016 to The Keep, the archive centre serving Brighton and the county of East Sussex. Appendix 1 of this book is devoted to the story and content of this valuable document.

The structure of the present book is chronological, although with the chapters relating to enemy action being kept separate from, and parallel to, those covering everyday life in the town. This has been described by theme, such as 'Food production' and 'Entertainment', but the limitation of space did not allow any one theme to be focused on over the entire duration of the war.

Douglas d'Enno
Saltdean, July 2021

Letter to the *Evening Argus* from a young soldier published on 11 May 1944:

TO BRIGHTON
On the first Sunday in October, 1939, I arrived in Brighton. On the first Sunday in April, 1944, I left. If that was all Brighton meant to me, writing this would be a waste of time. In 1939 a boy came, in 1944 a man left. If at times I have hated you then also I must have loved you. In any case I owe you this tribute.

 The only Brighton I have known is the Brighton of sandbags and sirens, tin hats and water tanks. A town that echoed and re-echoed the sounds of loud-speakers, guns and bombs.

 The Brighton of fairy lights and wonderland I never knew. Therefore you may say I have never seen you at your best. I beg to differ.

 The Brighton that was so firm during the days of Dunkirk, withstood so bravely the Battle of Britain and carried on so steadily during the Nazi terror bombing could never be surpassed in glory by the unreal glitter of Fairylight Brighton. They put out the fairy lights with the black-out, but in your streets to-day shine new lights, the lights of courage and comradeship. They flare so brilliantly through your hours of misery and suffering.

 The Germans have battered and bombed you but they have never broken or beaten you. For allowing me the great privilege of sharing some of the many ordeals you continue to endure, from the bottom of my heart I thank you. I pray that when I return the lights of peace will be shining. Already I feel a pang of regret. For they may build a bigger and better Brighton but they can never make you greater or finer.

           Derrick Laurence, Normanby, Middlesbrough.

Acknowledgements

The following kindly granted a recorded interview in which they recounted their experience of the war, thereby providing much valuable background:

Charlie Coverdale, Sheila Coverdale, Betty Field, June Heasman, John Holden, Geoffrey Kerr, Betty Nutley, Bob Nutley, Pam Piercey, Bernard Sebbage, Violet Simpson, Joyce Stevens, Mary Trimbey, Beryl Tucknott and Charlie Young. I am grateful to Nicky Watts for her transcription of a number of the tapes.

Assistance on various aspects of the war was provided by:

David Cuthbertson (local historian), Helen Day, Marion Devoy, Jennifer Drury (My Brighton & Hove website), Tim Earl (Hove Library), Denis Fielder, Irene Green, Peter Groves (local historian), Penny Harrison (St Mary's Hall Association), Alan Hayes (local historian), Andy Hill, Jane King (Screen Archive South East), Jane Knapp, Mike Laslett (local historian), Sue Lawton, Peter Mercer (local historian), Shona Milton (former archivist, The Keep), Trevor Mitchell (artist), Elia Pugh (Hove Library), David Rose, David Rowland (local historian), Sen Scherbakoff (Brighton Fisheries Museum), David Swallow and Doreen Waite, Don Williams.

I am particularly grateful to local historian and collector of local images, Chris Horlock, for his generous loan of photographic material, his provision of background information and his encouragement and input throughout the course of the project.

Andy Garth, a specialist in local nostalgia items, kindly loaned a number of bound volumes of *The Evening Argus* from the war years and the *Brighton & Hove Herald* for 1938, while local historian Peter Groves kindly supplied important information on selected local manufacturers of munitions and other war-related equipment who are the subject of Appendix 2.

I am greatly indebted to the local and county archive centre The Keep and its staff for granting access to the bound, printed volumes of the local newspapers in their holdings relating to the war years. I similarly acknowledge the freely-available use of the excellent photographic collection of Brighton Royal Pavilion & Museums.

Peter Hines is gratefully acknowledged for his assistance with technical issues, while Carol Homewood ('Brighton Past' website) and Samantha Briffet (*Deans Magazine*) are warmly thanked for their help in connection with marketing and publicity.

Finally, I thank my wife, Caroline, for her forbearance and patience during the years when work on this book dominated my life.

CHAPTER 1

Peace For Our Time?
January 1938 – August 1939

Preparations for the unthinkable

1938. A year of tension, hopes and fears. A year when the country stood on the brink, peering down into the looming abyss of war – a war from which, at the eleventh hour, it was delivered.

The instrument whereby this was achieved – the agreement reached in Munich on 30 September between Britain's Neville Chamberlain, France's Edouard Daladier, Germany's Adolf Hitler and Italy's Benito Mussolini in relation to the planned annexation by Germany of the mainly German-speaking Sudetenland in Czechoslovakia – would ultimately prove to be worthless. Its validity was challenged immediately by Churchill, who declared: 'You were given the choice between war and dishonour. You chose dishonour and you will have war.' In the Commons on 3 October, the First Lord of the Admiralty, Duff Cooper, who had resigned office on account of Munich, expressed the view that the Government had surrendered to brute force and had abandoned a centuries-old principle, the principle that one great power should not be allowed by brute force to dominate the continent of Europe. Chamberlain, he said, 'had spoken to Hitler and Mussolini in the language of sweet reasonableness, while the only language they understood was the language of the mailed fist.'

When in Germany, the premier must have been beguiled by the tumultuous reception he received from the people. Before leaving for his interview with Hitler, he appeared on the balcony of his hotel in response to the cheers of a large crowd waiting outside, a crowd which, for a quarter of an hour, had been vociferously shouting: 'We want Chamberlain.' His appearance was greeted by a storm of cheering, handwaving and clapping. He was again loudly cheered when he returned to the hotel after his discussions.

Few in Brighton or elsewhere in the country were sceptical at the time about the false dawn created by Munich. Praise for Chamberlain and his achievement was on nearly everybody's lips. Two bouquets for Mrs Chamberlain were even sent by Brighton admirers.

The Prime Minister, Neville Chamberlain, disembarks from his aircraft at Heston Aerodrome after returning from his first visit to Munich, 16 September 1938. (IWM 205225257)

Just a few hours after the premier had made his momentous announcement in the House of Commons on 28 September, more than a thousand people gathered at Brighton's Corn Exchange to hear what proved to be speeches of profound thankfulness from the Bishop of Chichester (Dr George Bell), Dr James Reid of Eastbourne (a leading Presbyterian minister) and the Rev. D.W. Langridge (Minister of Union Church).

General relief, but preparations continue

Referring to Chamberlain's 'magnificent initiative', Bishop Bell declared him 'foremost among the human forces making for peace' and 'a real peace man to his fingertips and to the depths of his heart'. He also mentioned how, among Brighton's provisions in preparation for a conflict, all arrangements had been made to receive in the town on the previous morning no fewer than 18,000 children from London. They were to have been met at the railway station and distributed throughout various homes in Brighton, Hove and the surrounding district. There was, he said, some comfort in the thought that the authorities evidently considered the twin towns safe enough. It was not until late in the afternoon of Thursday 29 September that orders were received delaying these arrangements. All had been in readiness, with motor coaches and lorries mobilised for the services of defence and the care of the wounded.

Troop movements had taken place. On the evening of 26 September 1938, mothers, wives and sweethearts gathered in great crowds at the Territorial headquarters in Church Street and Gloucester Road to see off detachments of Territorials leaving in Southdown coaches for Dover, where they were to man the coastal defences. They went with full equipment, including tin hats.

Lorries had been requisitioned to convey tons of kitbags and other materials. Tributes were paid in mid-December, at the Battery's annual dinner and prize distribution, to the efficiency and swiftness with which the 159th Sussex Heavy Battery, RA (TA) had answered the country's call – within nine hours of the crisis mobilisation order.

At a meeting at St Barnabas' Hall, Hove, on 11 October, when addressing a gathering of the church's Youth Fellowship, Brighton's Conservative MP, Sir Alfred Cooper Rawson, emphasised the point that but for Chamberlain's late intervention, the country would already be at war. Peace had been secured, although he did realistically add, 'for how long is purely a matter for conjecture'.

Men of the Territorial Army mobilise in Brighton. (BHIB (Brighton & Hove in Battledress))

Chamberlain's demanding balancing act. (David Low (cartoonist), *News Of The World*, 25.9.38)

A cautionary note had already been struck by the *Sussex Daily News* (henceforth generally *SDN*) on 1 October in its feature 'OUR LONDON LETTER', with the comment that the publication of the Munich peace terms afforded material for somewhat grim reflection. 'Apparently,' stated the writer, 'the Führer and presumably the Duce were prepared to launch Europe on another war over the veriest details of an otherwise agreed settlement.' He also wondered 'how far Mr Chamberlain's separate peace agreement with Herr Hitler holds promise of enduring security'. The paper commented dispassionately on the achievement by stating that the lesson of the previous week had been to increase and improve our defences so that we would be able to meet any challenge facing us. It would be calamitous if we were to relax the measures which had been taken for our protection. In the same issue, the paper reported the reactions of the Mayors of Brighton (Alderman Herbert Hone JP) and Hove (Councillor A.W. HIllman JP). The latter praised Chamberlain's courage, humanity and diplomatic skill and gratefully acknowledged the splendid services of Hove townspeople in carrying out ARP and other necessary preparations, a typical example of which was that in connection with billeting arrangements. Alderman Hone importantly made the point that continued vigilance and preparedness were vital:

> In spite of the more hopeful signs regarding the great crisis through which we are passing, it cannot be said that all danger of emergency has entirely passed. Whilst I fully appreciate and sincerely thank everyone for all the help and assistance given to me by the inhabitants generally, and those particularly connected with Air Raid Precautions work and other emergency measures which have had to be organised, I am advised that we must not at present relax our efforts.

Brighton, for all its rejoicing over the newly-won peace, did not relax its efforts in the slightest. The *SDN* remarked on the immediate sense of relief from the tension, but of course there could be no summary suspension of the air raid precaution operations being carried on after so much preparation. 'The ultimate effect,' it stated, 'remains to be seen.' People in Patcham went one further and rejected the Munich Agreement altogether. A resolution passed at a public meeting held there on the night of 28 September read as follows:

> That this meeting of the people of Patcham does affirm that Chamberlain has betrayed the best interests of the peoples of Europe by negotiating with Hitler, at the expense of Czechoslovakia.
> We demand that this policy shall end, and that Britain shall take her stand with France and the Soviet Union for the defence of Czechoslovakia, believing that this is the way to lasting peace.
> In this grave hour of crisis we send our warm greetings to the people of Czechoslovakia and call upon the people of Britain to stand together for peace and for the cooperation of democratic states.
> Repudiate any Hitler-Chamberlain arrangements. Unite and struggle for the overthrow of the National Government and its replacement by a Government which will defend peace and safeguard the interests of the British people.

On 2 October, Bishop Bell, at a special thanksgiving service for peace held in conjunction with the harvest festival service at Brighton Parish Church, said that the perpetual arming of the nations on a very large scale was only a symptom of a deeper cause – fear, selfishness, greed and the worship of material things that the Bible called idolatry. He expressed these sentiments again on the 12th, in his presidential address at the Dome at the annual meetings of the Chichester Diocesan Council. Laying no blame squarely on Germany for the recent crisis, he declared it was the lack of spiritual faith which lay at the root of the 'antagonisms of the nations, the mutual fear and distrust, and the resort to force'. Churchmen, for their part, should 'Give up that dreadful selfish individualism.' He drew attention to the immediate benefit of Munich, namely that 'millions of lives have been saved from suffering and death'. Everything was owed to one man:

George Bell, Bishop of Chichester (1883-1958). (Bain News Service, publisher/Public domain)

> What sufficient tribute can we pay to the courage and determination of Mr Neville Chamberlain, in face of untold difficulties of every kind, without which we should at this moment have been involved in a terrible war? God has preserved us so far, and by a miracle we have been granted peace. Praise and thanks be to the All Merciful Father.

By now, however, the Sudetenland had been occupied. Paying tribute to the Czech people, he declared:

> It is impossible to forget the desolation of the Czechs, and the bitter sacrifice which they have been compelled to make to the violence of their adversary, or to conceal the gratitude and admiration which we owe them for their fortitude in disaster. I am certain that we should wish everything done by our Government that can be done to support refugees and to relieve their financial distress.

An effort was in fact being made locally. By the time their appeals for the Lord Mayor's fund closed on 5 November, the subscriptions received by the Mayor of Brighton up to noon the previous day totalled £319, and those received by the Mayor of Hove were approximately £245.

Our German friends

Despite the prevailing tension and unfavourable outlook, local Anglo-German relations were warm for most of the year. Hove Councillor H.C. Andrews, founder of the Britannia Youth movement and founder-organiser of the Anglo-German Friendship League which encouraged exchange visits with Germany, arranged, on behalf of the British Legion, for a party of Germans from Wuppertal to visit Hove and other selected locations at the end of January (two years previously a large party of members of the Hove branch had received a warm welcome in Wuppertal). As part of the five-day return visit, the Germans were guests of honour at the annual dinner of the Rottingdean branch of the Legion at the White Horse Hotel on 27 January. The party included high-ranking Nazis, such as *Oberführer* [Senior Colonel] Ruffert, General of Storm Troopers, Wuppertal, *Hauptsturmführer* [Captain] Schroder of the Black Guard, Wuppertal, and *Kreisleiter* [County Leader] Schäfer, a high official of the National Socialist party in Wuppertal.

At the dinner, Colonel Seaburne M. Moens, President of the Rottingdean branch of the Legion, declared that 'An Anglo-German settlement is the key to world peace', later adding, unpatriotically it might be thought, 'Herr Hitler has, to my knowledge, on at least four occasions publicly and with deep sincerity offered the olive branch in certain quarters. It is a tragedy that it has not been accepted up to date in the spirit in which it was offered.' The company of over 120 spent a convivial evening enlivened by German drinking songs, British songs of the trenches, and the traditional 'Sussex by the Sea'. During the rest of their stay, the visitors enjoyed dinner at Langford's Hotel, Hove; a trip to London, where they saw the changing of the guard at Buckingham Palace; one to Bognor Regis, where they were officially received at the Town Hall and where a branch of the Anglo-German Friendship League was formed, with seventy members enrolling, and one to Chichester. They also visited the Royal Pavilion and other places of interest in Brighton; Hove County School for Girls and (an inappropriate choice, surely) the air raid precautions department in Hove.

In 'Munich week', Councillor Andrews received a number of supportive telegrams from Germany, one of which, translated from German and referring to the BBC broadcast of a speech by Chamberlain, read: 'Wireless reception from England wonderful. Your Prime Minister's speech most stirring. Please pray for peace, the same as we are here. Good luck. No war!'

Treatment of the Jews

Councillor Andrews' enthusiasm for the Germans dissipated in November. Disgusted with the 'rotten treatment' meted out to the Jews in Germany, he resigned his presidency of the Hove branch of the Friendship League and severed all connection with its work. This was the month when the Nazis organised a pogrom known as *Kristallnacht* (the 'Night of Broken Glass'), an attack against German and Austrian Jews which included the destruction of synagogues and Jewish-owned stores, the arrest of Jewish men, the vandalisation of homes, and the murder of individuals. Andrews had been busily organising three very big visits for the following year. Now all those visits were off. He received several letters from members of the League tendering their resignation in sympathy with his action as well as messages from all parts of Britain approving of the course he had adopted.

The Jews of Brighton and Hove, meanwhile, were focusing their attention on the plight of Jewish refugees from Germany, particularly the children. The German proscription applied not only to the recognised Jew but to all who could not prove that none of their ancestors, born since 1800, were Jewish. Some 750 people attended a meeting at the Royal Pavilion in late December and raised, there and then, no less than £4,000, which was promptly sent to the National Refugees' Relief Council in London. An appeal was made for offers of hospitality for two or three months for refugee children awaiting their training for work. A Brighton and Hove Jewish Refugee Relief Council was formed.

Speaking at a League of Nations Union meeting held on the evening of 11 November at the Royal Pavilion, the new Superintendent of the Dome Mission, the Rev. G.H. Simpson, declared, 'there has come an era of cruelty and torture'. Alluding to the latest attacks on the Jews in Germany, he said (to applause) one could not read of these happenings without a sense of shame. 'We can believe that there are people in Germany who hate it as much as we hate it (Applause.)' In the following week, a letter was received by the *Brighton & Hove Herald* (henceforth generally the *Herald* or *BHH*) from one David A. Peat of Ditchling, who wrote:

> The callous brutality of the Nazi regime in its treatment of the Jewish people has given a severe blow to the cause of Anglo-German understanding. This is not the work of the German people, for many reports have recorded their amazed dismay; it is the work of a small group of men who seem determined to wreck Mr Chamberlain's efforts for peace.

Christian refugees from Germany elicited sympathy from the Bishop of Chichester. Himself a Rotarian, he made a plea on their behalf at the weekly luncheon of Brighton Rotary Club on 21 December at the Old Ship Assembly Rooms. Much more needed to be done, he urged, in adopting refugee children and finding training for young men and women.

ARP readiness

ARP work proceeded apace in Brighton during 1938. The key players were Squadron-Leader E.L. Ardley, air raid precautions officer for Brighton; Chief Constable Captain W.J. Hutchinson, coordinating officer of the area precautions scheme; and Charles Birch, chief officer of the Brighton fire brigade. All three were speakers at a meeting, attended by close on 200 people, held at Patcham School on the evening of 21 January to explain the town's volunteer air raid precautions service. This was the first of a series of meetings to be held in the various wards of the town. After an address by Ardley, Captain Hutchinson explained the duties and training of Air Raid Wardens and made an appeal for more recruits. Charles Birch then explained the duties which would be required of auxiliary firemen, of whom about 500 were needed.

In March, following developments in the international situation, the Home Secretary, Sir Samuel Hoare, sent a circular telegram to the Mayors of Brighton and Hove stimulating the recruitment of Air Raid Wardens. The week ending 19 March produced an additional 100 volunteers for duty in Brighton and as many as 235 in Hove, where one of the first to enrol was the Bishop of Lewes, the Right Rev. Hugh M. Hordern. A considerable addition to the St John Ambulance and Red Cross units was also recorded, plus recruiting for the Territorials was satisfactory. Of the 500 auxiliary firemen required by Brighton's fire brigade to form an emergency fire service in conjunction with the air raid precautions scheme, eighty-two had been enrolled, of whom sixty-six were already in training. More enquiries from prospective applicants had been received in that same week ending the 19th than in any week since the emergency service had been inaugurated. This was also a week which saw a sudden interest in defensive measures against air raids, resulting in a record number of ninety-seven people visiting the Corporation's gas-proof demonstration room in Market Street on the 17th. Since the opening of the room about a year previously, visitor numbers had exceeded 6,000, including experts from other towns.

For the purpose of air raid precautions, Brighton was divided into forty-two sectors, divided into sub-sectors. Three Wardens were assigned to each sub-sector, which in most cases covered an area with a population of about 500. Between 250 and 260 Brighton Wardens were fully trained locally by the middle of March for general duties, which included assisting in distributing respirators. Garages and some church halls were to be used as ARP posts but not schools or licensed premises. By the end of July, some 536 Air Raid Wardens were fully trained, another sixty-six were undergoing training and twenty-one were awaiting training. Including members of the Red Cross and the St John Ambulance

Brigade, ninety-seven volunteers had already been trained in both anti-gas work and First Aid and seventy-six in one or other of these branches; 226 were under training or awaiting it. By mid-November, there were 655 trained Wardens, 500 other Wardens in course of training, and about 416 waiting to be trained. It was hoped eventually to have 1,800 trained Wardens. Ten instruction classes were being held at the ARP headquarters in Circus Street and another at Withdean Court.

Air raid precautions were considered at a meeting of the Brighton and Hove Chamber of Commerce at the Royal Pavilion on 29 March. One of the matters under consideration was the special responsibilities of employers, who could, for example, cooperate with the local authorities in a variety of ways, including the loan of vehicles. Firms in the building and engineering trades which possessed heavy gear could, it was suggested, organise volunteer rescue and clearance parties among their staffs. One of the most alarming of the ARP problems discussed was that of incendiary bombs, a subject dealt with by Charles Birch (who was also a member of a special Home Office committee). He had made a special study of such bombs and exhibited an example weighing about 2½lbs.

Interior of an Air Raid Wardens' post in Brighton. (Royal Pavilion & Museums, Brighton & Hove)

Nine aeroplanes would be capable of scattering as many as 10,000 of them on Brighton. They were not, of course, weapons of precision, and might be dropped from an aeroplane a dozen at a time.

Six months later, in conjunction with the Fire Brigades' Conference held at the Dome, a dramatic demonstration of an air raid was given to a crowd of many hundreds in the grounds of the Royal Pavilion. A mournful wail gave warning of the approach of aircraft and a few minutes later there were explosions, followed by fires. Two terrific explosions showed what kind of noise high explosive bombs made when dropped. Then another type of HE bomb which exploded in the air with an effect like that of a bursting firework was demonstrated. Next came an example of a 1kg thermite incendiary bomb such as could be carried in thousands by a single aeroplane. The loudspeaker announced that this bomb generated a heat of 2,000 degrees centigrade. An electron bomb, whose object was to start a number of independent fires, sent out a shower of white sparks in all directions. It could not be extinguished with water, although dousing it would help to control it by causing it to burn out more quickly. Next came a mustard gas demonstration, and then the creation of smoke screens was illustrated.

The Circus Street (Board) School (right), ca. 1935. It never re-opened as a school after the war. (Chris Horlock collection)

The clouds of red, black, white and yellow smoke were used partly for purposes of camouflage and partly for giving raiding airmen the erroneous impression that they had hit and set on fire buildings which, in fact, were untouched (a mixture of red and white smoke was particularly effective for this purpose).

On 27 June, Brighton's new air raid precautions headquarters and training centre in the old Circus Street School buildings were opened. The premises comprised the ground and first floors of the Circus Street Schools, taken on a tenancy by the Air Raid Sub-committee for a period of at least two years, at a rental of £200. From this centre the town's entire air raid precautions scheme was to be controlled, and no fewer than 60,000 gas masks were to be stored there. Eight rooms on the two floors included accommodation for storing them and training equipment, a decontamination station fitted with showers, lecture rooms for instruction in anti-gas training, a demonstration room displaying various methods of gas proofing, and clerical offices. E.L. Ardley had an office there.

Anti-aircraft defence in the form of searchlights was well advanced by December. Pending the erection of new drill halls at Brighton and Worthing for the new 70th (Sussex) Searchlight Regiment, Royal Artillery, the headquarters were

Recruits of the new 70th (Sussex) Searchlight Regiment, RA (TA), watch a searchlight demo at their HQ, in the grounds of 'Highcroft', December 1938. The unit was fully embodied in August 1939. (Chris Horlock collection)

located at 'Highcroft', Dyke Road, formerly a private house. Two companies were stationed in Brighton and one in Worthing. The first searchlight demonstration was held at 'Highcroft' on the evening of 15 December and another at night on isolated camping sites at the beginning of June 1939, when thousands of holidaymakers stayed up and occupied vantage points to see the beams sweeping the sky and 'picking up' target aeroplanes. The full strength of some 1,200 officers and men was soon reached and the regiment was divided into three batteries – the 459th and 460th at Brighton and the 461st at Worthing. Intensive work had meanwhile been put in, with individual detachments frequently practising on the Downs above Brighton and Worthing almost every evening of the week, but this last weekend saw the first 'actions' operated under conditions similar to those which might obtain in a national emergency.

All the officers had been appointed, and 300 of the 1,200 NCOs and men had already been recruited a month earlier and full new sets of the latest equipment – powerful searchlights, trailer generating sets, lorries, and sound locators – had arrived and were ready for use.

Shelters, gas masks and firefighting equipment

On the subject of shelters, a letter to the *Herald* from 'E.E.M.', published on 4 June, proposed the use of existing arches and subways, such as those below Brighton Front, by Sussex Square and in Saltdean. These facilities could be 'investigated as a supplement to a more comprehensive scheme, but sheltering in small bodies would be more likely to allay panic than the massing of thousands in one big shelter'. Another suggestion at the time was to use the tunnel leading from Kemp Town Goods Yard. Agreement was given by the Air Raid Precautions Sub-committee on 26 September to the opening to the public as shelters of some of the arches under King's Road and Grand Junction Road and a few under part of Madeira Drive which were owned by the Corporation. In the Air Raid Sub-committee, the air raid precautions officer stated that he estimated the cost of converting and equipping the disused cellars under the kitchens at the Royal Pavilion into a model air raid shelter at £65. The body recommended that the work be carried out for that price, subject to Home Office approval.

The tunnel idea was strongly put forward by one J. Jordan, when he lectured on 'Real ARP for Brighton' at a public meeting of the Left Book Club, held at the Friends' Meeting House, Ship Street, on 11 October. Deeming the Government's ARP schemes to be insufficient, he declared:

Brighton can be made invulnerable against air attack by the construction of a network of tunnels, built 60 feet down in the chalk, with entrances every 100 yards, and a further provision of reinforced concrete shelters on the sea-front and in the low-lying areas.

The whole town should, he thought, be defended by anti-aircraft units on strategic points on the hills (this in fact happened).

Trench-digging began, under the control of the Borough Surveyor, on 28 September at the following locations: Claremont Row, Nelson Street, St John's Lodge Gardens, Oxford Court, Saunder's Recreation Ground, Lewes Road (a picture of work proceeding at the latter location, opposite the Tramway Depot, appeared in the following day's *SDN*), Blaker's Recreation Ground, Preston Drove, Pelham Square, Montpelier Crescent and Powis Square. Approximately 250 men engaged through the local Labour Exchange worked splendidly, despite many of them being unaccustomed to heavy work. They were joined by hundreds of ex-servicemen. The necessary timber, corrugated iron and other materials were acquired immediately. After some procurement difficulties, supplies of sandbags arrived at this time, allowing the protection of the lower Marine Drive – deemed the finest shelter in Brighton, able to accommodate thousands of people – to proceed at once. Ultimately, 100,000 bags were obtained from various sources.

Trenches being dug in Powis Square. (BHIB)

Workmen building a sandbag barrier at the south front of Brighton Aquarium, 2 September 1939. (Royal Pavilion & Museums, Brighton & Hove)

At schools as far apart as Whitehawk and Balfour Road, trenches were prepared in readiness. Built in a straight formation instead of the usual zig-zag, they had seats arranged facing each other so that children and their teachers could be together. By mid-December, Roedean, the famous public school for girls, was ready for air raids. Further to instructions given two days before the crisis by the headmistress, Miss Tanner, it had immediately implemented what were probably the most elaborate and effective air raid precautions adopted by any school in the country. Nearly 1,000ft of refuge trenches, giving shelter to about 270, had been dug at a safe distance behind the school buildings at a cost approaching £2,000. Cut to a depth of 8ft, the trenches were covered by wood, corrugated iron, and earth which formed a roof nearly 4ft thick. In the event of war this roof would be doubled in thickness. Heaped sandbags gave protection to the entrances to the trenches, which were easily accessible from the school. The tunnel from the grounds to the school's private beach would also accommodate 127 scholars and staff, and in wartime each end of the tunnel would be blocked with sandbags and equipped with gas decontamination locks. Electric light and water were laid on in

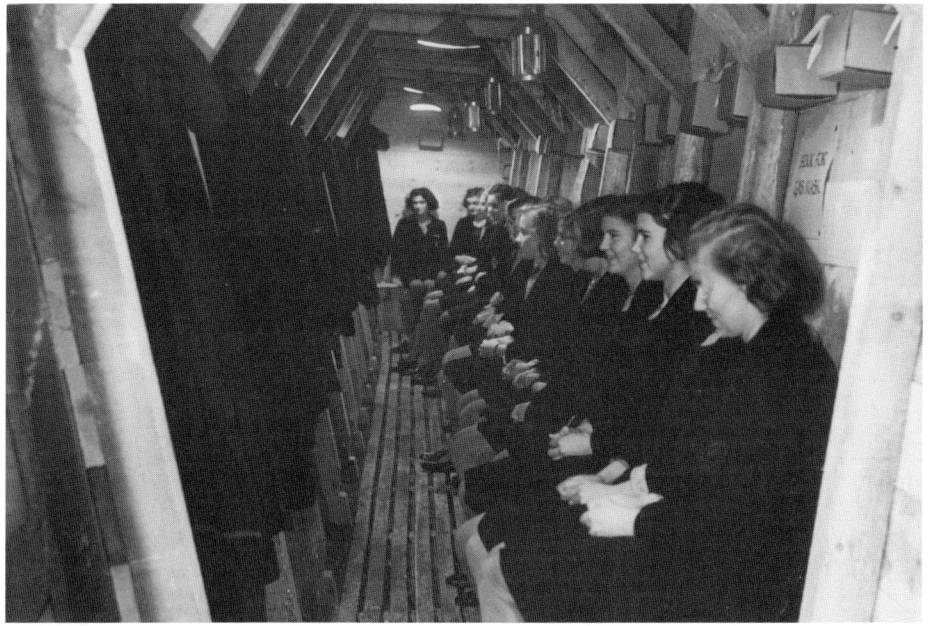

Roedean girls secure in their shelter. (Roedean School archives)

the trenches, and candle lanterns were suspended from the roof as an alternative means of lighting in the event of an electrical failure. In a test alarm carried out in the middle of the night when all the scholars were asleep, the school was emptied in 7¼ minutes.

In *Onward and Upward*, the history of Varndean School for Boys from 1884 to 1975, the authors refer to the,

> constant treks into the trench shelters which had been dug on the north side of the buildings in the autumn of 1939. Equipped with wooden benches but otherwise cramped and dark, the shelters were sometimes occupied all day at the height of the Battle of Britain, lessons being carried on as best as could be. Hutchins [the Headmaster] claimed after the war that the school had learned to move into the trenches in 2½ minutes.

By 1943, however, the aerial threat had changed. The German tactics were now to come in low over the coast, drop their bombs and scoot for home. This meant that the normal air raid warnings could not cope – indeed a special warning of short blasts was introduced – and there was no time to get the school into the trenches. Instead, forms were instructed to take cover under desks or tables. Those who used the Library had a grandstand view down the valley to the sea as the aircraft, looking at that distance like small birds, wheeled over central Brighton and then headed home at sea top level.

A gas mask census of Brighton was carried out in July 1938. The number of people fitted and registered for respirators by the end of that month was reported in the local press as being 15,909. Councillor Bernard Dutton Briant told a *BHH* reporter that the complete stock of respirators was in readiness:

> We shall have our 150,000 gas masks stored in the Preston Road Schools by the end of August. They will remain stored there until our district depots are built. We shall then have 30,000 in each of five depots, covering: central Brighton, the Seven Dials, Withdean, Hollingdean, and East Brighton.

He paid tribute to the four teams – two from the Brighton Hove and Worthing Gas Company and one each from Allen West Ltd and Plummer Roddis Ltd – enrolled for the assembly of respirators. There were thirty members in each team. Half the Municipal Market had been turned into an assembly station, tables, chairs and trestles having been commandeered from Black Rock bathing pool and other places. One ARP Warden from Ovingdean drove into Brighton, collected 500 gas masks for his sector and said he would make his own arrangements for assembling them. Other Wardens followed his example. Several hotels sent down for unassembled masks. Rotarians took their full share in the work of fitting and distributing masks, some keeping at it until the early hours of the morning. 'I know of one Rotarian,' declared A.D. Mackenzie, the President of the Brighton Club, 'who worked the skin off his fingers in putting together gas masks.'

Actual distribution began at the end of September. On the evening of the 26th, tens of thousands were distributed in Brighton and Hove. Unemployed men offered their services in carrying large packages of completed respirators to waiting cars. The appeal in the *SDN* for private cars and vans for speeding up distribution had met with a magnificent response, with offers of help coming from all parts of the borough. Some firms were prepared to lend their entire fleet of vehicles, while private individuals drove to the ARP offices and 'stood by' with their cars. Even street hawkers brought their barrows and volunteered. There was still a need for vehicles at Christmas. A leaflet set out the three categories required, namely improvised ambulances (commercial box vans, offered with a driver, were suitable), vehicles for conveying first-aid parties (a car or light van, also complete with a skilled driver, male or female), and staff and messenger cars (smaller cars than in the preceding category). Drivers likely to be employed in ARP work had to gain experience in driving under blackout conditions and while wearing respirators.

Above: *Councillor H. Hone, Mayor of Brighton, with gas attack trainees, (probably in Brighton Town Hall), 19 March 1938.* (Royal Pavilion & Museums, Brighton & Hove)

Right: *All hands to the (trailer) pump.* (*BHH*, 13.8.38)

In late September, a very substantial supply of equipment for Brighton's auxiliary fire brigade was received from the Home Office, with more on the way. Trailer pumps, hoses, sand containers and scoops, practice bombs, and innumerable other items were included in the list. An exhibition was held in the Corn Exchange in the penultimate week of September in connection with the conference of the British Fire Service. On display were ARP uniforms and costumes in an improved style. Outside the Dome, the latest types of fire engines paraded.

By October, the emergency fire service had a strength of over 220 men.

First aid

In a report submitted in September by the Medical Officer of Health to the Air Raid Sub-committee of the Watch Committee, it was pointed out that large numbers of trained first-aid workers (male and female) were required. First-aid posts had to be established throughout the town (preparations were made for the

ARP trench beside the School of Art (visible in the background), Grand Parade, Brighton, on 17 October 1939 showing the wooden structure within the trench. (Royal Pavilion & Museums, Brighton & Hove)

covering of the bath water at North Road baths in order to provide a first-aid station) so that no casualty suitable for treatment at such posts would have to walk or be carried a greater distance than one mile. Questions concerning the organisation of hospital arrangements for dealing with air raid casualties was now the responsibility of the Ministry of Health.

An early mention of blackout arrangements came in a letter to the *SDN* published on 27 September 1938 from one Olive Middleton-Powell of 24 Wick Hall, Hove, who wrote that she was having thick green curtains made to cover the windows to shut out light and also providing herself with plenty of brown paper, paste, and brushes, besides packets of candles and matches. She also asked whether, in view of air raids in the event of war, it would not be wise to begin precautionary measures at once by making bomb-proof shelters and trenches wherever possible. As it happened, trench digging actually started, under the control of the Borough Surveyor, early on the following day, as mentioned above. At Brighton Station, construction work was carried out to make provision for the reception of schoolchildren and refugees.

Government advice

By mid-October, most householders would have received by post an official Government pamphlet entitled *The Protection of Your Home Against Air Raids*. This included information regarding the use and abuse of respirators, the types of air raid and gas alarms to be employed, the approved methods of handling incendiary bombs, and the lighting restrictions intended to be enforced in wartime. In fact, commented the *BHH* of 15 October, the publication provided 'the answers to a hundred and one questions which were agitating the minds of millions of householders a fortnight ago.' It added:

> The importance of a careful study of this publication cannot be too strongly emphasised; the recommendations made are the result of much careful thought and research, and though some expenditure must of necessity be incurred in putting them into force, they show signs of having been made with due regard to the limits of the average householder's pocket.

Pacifism was not appreciated. The delivery 'under cover of darkness' of a leaflet entitled *Air Raid Precautions. ... A Message to Every Householder* to the home of one Harvard Mentana of 29 Buckingham Road, and to many of his neighbours, prompted him to fire off a letter to *The Times* (published on 11 April). It was apparently, he wrote, sponsored by the Peace Pledge Union.

Its 'wicked propaganda' claimed, inter alia, that 'Air raid precautions are in one sense ineffective, for they are not primarily designed to save your life. Their purpose is to prevent panic, so that the Government can continue the war without being hindered by a panic-stricken population.' And further: 'To decline to take part in air raid precautions is to show that you are not prepared to cooperate in the organisation of war.' Mentana felt it was time that public opinion should be 'aroused generally against an insignificant minority of the misguided, responsible for circulating such dangerous rubbish.'

Construction work was carried out at Brighton Station to make provision for the reception of schoolchildren and refugees.

Freezing yuletide but warming entertainment

Christmas Day 1938 was preceded by the coldest weather for thirty years, with serious dislocation of traffic, the disorganisation of many households and the wholesale closing of schools. Buses had to be withdrawn from the hilliest routes (one casualty was a No. 11 bus which finished up in a front garden in Milner Road and remained there overnight) and taxis did not dare to undertake the climbs. Employment in the building and other outdoor trades was drastically curtailed, with many men being stood off just at the time when they most needed their wages. This was on top of the 7,000 unemployed in the town. Their situation was alleviated by organisations such as the Brighton and Hove Christmas Gift Society, which for the previous eleven years had distributed nearly four tons of groceries to poor families, and donations which included a cheque for £100 received by the Mayor from the committee of the Catholic Truth Society Brighton Conference. An earnest appeal for funds in this 'present regrettable period of depression' on behalf of the unemployed was made in a letter to the local press by social activist Harry Cowley (1890–1971), the Secretary of the Brighton Unemployed Association.

For townspeople not in need, Christmastide entertainment was on offer in abundance. A choice could be made from no fewer than four pantomimes: *Jack and the Beanstalk* at the Theatre Royal, *Snow White and the Seven Dwarfs* at the Hippodrome, *Mother Hubbard* at the Palace Pier Theatre and *The Forty Thieves* at the West Pier. At all the hotels, dinners, dances and other celebrations could be amply enjoyed. The Sports Stadium, SS Brighton, hosted a 'Gigantic New Year's Eve Fancy Dress Carnival'.

There seemed to be little apprehension concerning what 1939 might bring, although Bishop Bell told the *BHH* that he knew 'the dangers which lie ahead in the international field'. The situation was best summed up by Admiral T.P.H. Beamish, speaking on 23 December at the annual dinner of the Rottingdean Conservative Association, held at the White Horse Hotel in the village:

> If Britain's new policy of peace should fail, at any rate, we shall have tried, and history will declare that this country did its best.

Facing the inevitable

There was no let-up in ARP exercises and operations in all their various forms during the pre-war months of 1939. Brighton's first Control Centre exercise took place under the arches on the front in February. Seated in their bomb-proof dugout, ten volunteer hello-girls answered or transmitted almost continuous calls for help. The incoming messages were from Air Raid Wardens in No. 2 Division, telling of raiders' bombs dropped in their sectors. In that month, Warden personnel numbers reached an above-strength level. The Brighton establishment figure was 1,845 and there were altogether 1,888 volunteers, 1,156 of whom had been trained, with 335 under training. Added to these were first-aid personnel, ambulance drivers (volunteers were still needed), rescue parties, decontamination squads and messengers. The total strength was 3,331 against an establishment of 3,172. Not included in these statistics was the important branch of the Auxiliary Fire Service. The town had just over 400 of the 500 volunteers required.

Yet the ARP service never missed an opportunity to add its numbers; when football crowds went out to the Goldstone Ground to watch the Albion's London Combination engagement with Fulham on 4 March, it was announced that instead of the Seven Dials ARP office being closed as usual on Saturday afternoon, it was being kept open until six o'clock especially for them! Three weeks later, Councillor Bernard Dutton Briant was speaking at the opening of the old Kemp Town Railway Station booking office and waiting rooms as an Air Raid Wardens' headquarters for No. 4 Division.

On the organisational front, the appointment of regional commissioners was announced in the spring. The South-Eastern district, which included Sussex, was to be under the control of Sir Auckland Geddes, while Alderman Aldrich and Councillors Dutton Briant and Field were chosen to serve under him as regional dictators (as they were designated) in Brighton. Henry Bertram Johnson of 45 Florence Road was appointed Chief Air Raid Warden for the County Borough. Sir Auckland came to Brighton on 20 May to inspect the ARP services of the Borough on display in Preston Park. He first visited their HQ in Circus Street, the well-protected Report and Control Centre in the King's Road arches,

Enrolment for the ARP service was vigorously promoted. (Author)

the demonstration shelter at the Royal Pavilion and the new report centre in the cellars of Preston Manor, which was virtually a secondary control centre for the northern part of the town and was being subjected to a test for the first time. In an address given on the lawn of the Manor, Sir Auckland praised the progress which had been made in Brighton and said it had to be recognised that 'for the next few months there is nothing in the civic life of this country that is so important as seeing that all the preparations for civil defence, and the other forms of National Service, should be pushed forward with the greatest energy'. Brighton and Hove ARP was, he declared, the best organised in the country.

One form of preparation was testing sirens. When it did take place in Brighton, Hove, Portslade and Southwick, however, at midnight on the night of 1/2 June, it provoked a storm of criticism. The sirens failed to wake most people, and many of those who were awoken complained bitterly. One resident referred to the noise as an 'unearthly din', while another reported, 'My little girl woke up screaming with fear. It took an hour to quieten her down. Why can't they do it at some other time ?' Another resident's wife was in hysterics, thinking the raiders were coming. When the warning was at its height, one Church Road resident, in desperation, threw up

Kemp Town Station – An unlikely headquarters for Air Raid Wardens. (Chris Horlock collection)

his bedroom window and roared into the night: 'For God's sake shut up that damn row!' This provoked roars of laughter from his neighbours. Lights went up in windows, and the whole neighbourhood was aroused. Some keen and enterprising Wardens, believing that the sirens were a 'test raid', leapt out of bed and ran to their stations but on finding nothing happening, returned later to their beds.

Two weeks later, the sirens were tested again as part of a large-scale tactical exercise for Wardens. Conducted in conjunction with a squadron of Hurricane fighters from Tangmere as the enemy, the realistic attack and rescue operations started at 8pm and finished around midnight against the backdrop of a wide-scale blackout. Over 2,000 male and female ARP members took part. The targets were the railway terminus, the barracks, a large factory at Moulsecoomb and the Town Hall (where the charlady arriving the next morning took one look at a dummy that had been used as a casualty and fainted). A fire raging on the Level was dealt with by the AFS. Hundreds of townspeople watched the proceedings, although the authorities later felt that the event, albeit generally successful, had proved to be more of a spectator sport than they would have liked.

On 8 and 9 July Brighton, along with fifteen counties in the south-east of England, cooperated in a blackout and civil defence exercise.

With war becoming an increasingly real possibility, all ARP work forged ahead. Trench digging was accelerated with all available labour and the strengthening of

Trenching the Level. (BHIB)

basements and the sandbagging of vital control centres were speeded up. Many firms allocated their staff members to sandbag filling.

The evacuee invasion

Thoughts turned in official quarters to (inward) evacuation. Mayor Hone was reported on 1 October as saying:

> The survey of houses which it was necessary to undertake in connection with the possible evacuation of children and civilian refugees from London was done to ascertain the accommodation available, and to enable us to make special allowance for householders of advanced age and where sickness existed who should not be expected except in a last resort to carry out the arrangement.

Members of staff of Varndean School for Boys had been recruited early in 1939 to act as Billeting Officers, headmaster Eric Hutchins being appointed Deputy Chief Billeting Officer for Brighton. The team scoured the town, locating suitable households for billeting. At the end of August, the Government announced the start of evacuation and members of staff who were Billeting Officers, together with some forty-eight senior boys who had volunteered to assist, were called back from holiday to man the Area Billeting Centres, including that at Whittinghame College in Surrenden Road, which was known as Red 7.

On Friday, 1 September, under a scheme described in a joint statement to the Press Association by the Ministry of Health and the Secretary of State for Scotland as a 'precautionary measure', which 'does not mean that war is regarded as inevitable', just over 8,000 schoolchildren and their teachers were evacuated from London schools to Brighton, and 1,000 stretcher cases were sent from London hospitals to Brighton – the distribution centre for Sussex – for transport to county hospitals. This intake represented the first batch of over 30,000 children, parents and teachers evacuated to Brighton – the largest evacuation area in the country. Another 20,000 were brought through on Saturday, when emergency hospital arrangements were made for the reception of expectant mothers. The reception of more evacuees was planned for Sunday.

The Mayor of Brighton and Councillor Dutton Briant were in attendance at the station during part of the morning and saw the first ambulance train arrive. Brighton's

A group of evacuated children arriving at Brighton Station, 1-2 September 1939. (Royal Pavilion & Museums, Brighton & Hove)

Two evacuee boys being introduced to a prospective family in Brighton. (Royal Pavilion & Museums, Brighton & Hove)

Chief Constable, Captain W.J. Hutchinson, was in charge of all police arrangements. The public had reportedly responded splendidly to the appeal for their cooperation.

It was at exactly one minute to ten in the morning that the first batch of 900 children from Clapham Junction and the LCC (London County Council) area arrived at the station. Many of them were barely of school age, and looked white-faced and tired but clearly excited at the prospect of an unexpected holiday. The entire organisation at the station was conducted quietly and efficiently. W.O. Dodd, the Deputy Town Clerk and Chief Evacuation Officer, supervised the assembly and transport of the children via a loudspeaker relayed from the emergency office at the station. All motor traffic other than official cars was refused admittance to the station, and the public made the task of the officials easier by keeping clear of the platforms during the periods of arrival. The general waiting room was converted into a first-aid post and auxiliary nurses and VADs (Voluntary Aid Detachment members) were in attendance as required.

On the platform, the children were assembled in groups under the direction of their teachers and were then marched to the fleet of buses waiting outside to transport them to the various centres. Many groups carried banners stating from which school they came. Every child had a label round his or her neck and carried

A re-enactment of Operation Pied Piper at Brighton Station on 3 September 2019. Leading the children of Downs Junior School (formerly Ditchling Road School) is 87-year-old Barry Gooders, who came to Brighton as an evacuee from his home town of Thornton Heath with his brother Gerald 80 years previously. (Author)

a gas-mask container and a parcel of clothes and food. Some had rucksacks on their backs and others had small attaché cases or pillowcases containing their necessary provisions. Porters and bus drivers helped many of them with their packages, while elder brothers and sisters comforted small children and took turns with their baggage. One of the teachers in charge of a group, a Miss Mickleburgh, of Plough Road School, Battersea, told an *SDN* reporter that the children had behaved splendidly throughout the journey, singing their favourite songs to while away the time, playing games and handing round barley sugar sticks and sugar plums. Most of the children imagined that the evacuation was to be a short holiday and were thrilled at the prospect of a visit to the seaside.

At Warmdene School, Patcham, to which the first batch of children was taken by bus for distribution to their several billets, the arrangements were carried out under the supervision of Miss P.W. Warmington, the Head of Varndean School for Girls and billeting officer for the district. Members of the school staff had been recalled on the previous Saturday and had made a complete re-survey of the arranged billets and had secured new ones to replace those which, due to changed conditions in individual families, were not now available. The children were sorted into the necessary groups at the school and were billeted all over Patcham, with the billeting officers following them to their destinations in private cars and giving receipts for their safe custody. By one o'clock there remained only twenty children to be conveyed to their billets.

Distribution centres besides Warmdene included Moulsecoomb School, Whitehawk School, Whittingehame College, Hollingdean Special School, St Luke's School, Warren Farm School, Rottingdean School, Saltdean Lido, the Church of the Good Shepherd, Withdean Tennis Court, Pelham Street School and Middle Street School.

The stretcher cases evacuated from London hospitals to Brighton arrived in six special trains. Dr Rutherford Cramb, Brighton Medical Officer of Health, was in charge of receiving the patients, who were conveyed to hospitals in the town and to all parts of East and West Sussex, specifically Seaford, Chailey, Uckfield, Robertsbridge, West Grinstead, Horsham and Rustington, by a fleet of sixty-six buses, ambulances and commercial vehicles (the Southdown buses were specially converted to carry ten stretcher cases). The first ambulance train, containing 182 patients and six babies, arrived at Brighton at 12.50, just under an hour-and-a-half later than scheduled. Thereafter patients arrived at hourly intervals, the last train being cleared of its load just before eight o'clock. Members of staff from most local hospitals were in attendance on the station platform. The British Red Cross, St John Ambulance Brigade members and VADs, who were in attendance to deal with emergencies and to serve as stretcher-bearers, were supported by several score of volunteers from local businesses who brought the personnel on the reception platform up to over 150. The Sea Scouts also gave useful service as messengers. The Municipal Hospital (today's Brighton General) had evacuated seventy patients from its wards on the Thursday and provided an additional war complement of beds. Its allocation was 200, while that of the Royal Sussex County Hospital was 150. Other receiving Brighton hospitals were the New Sussex Hospital (10), Brighton Sanatorium (25), the Sussex Eye Hospital (30) and the Sussex Throat and Ear Hospital (18).

With the arrival and placement of evacuees a priority, the townspeople cooperated with the authorities by staying at home as much as possible all day on Friday 1 September, the day of Germany's fateful invasion of Poland. Bus services were in any event restricted. Taxis were in great demand and were often unobtainable, particularly while the reception of the evacuees was in progress.

Most householders took advantage of the opportunity to complete the screening of their windows and fanlights. Shopping centres were on the whole comparatively quiet until traffic resumed its normal schedule. London Road was crowded with incoming traffic. Hundreds of cars entered the town during the day bringing whole families with their luggage packed wherever there was room to squeeze it in. Trains to London were crowded as holidaymakers returned home to make room for the thousands of incomers who arrived during the day.

In the evening, food shops experienced their busiest Friday evening's shopping for years. Grocery outlets, particularly those which dealt in tinned foods, were very busy – they were still crowded at closing time. There was a last-minute rush to shops with stocks of blackout cloth and other materials and late orders for mattresses and bedclothes from people in difficulties over the billeting of incomers.

Many businessmen decided not to go to their offices in London and stayed at home to complete preparations for the emergency. Wives and sweethearts thronged Brighton Station to say farewell to the men recalled to the Colours. Telephone and telegraph communications were subjected to long delays, and people making calls from public kiosks were kept waiting outside for as much as two hours and more. People queued up at Brighton GPO to send telegrams. Weather-wise, the day was fine, but Brighton beach, the promenade and the piers were comparatively deserted. There were few bathers.

Scores of aliens reported to the police at Hove and Brighton.

Brighton's Chief Constable announced: 'No industrial hooter or siren shall be used in future except in giving air raid warnings.'

The last dance class at the Regent Dance Hall before war broke out; it was hosted by Renee Burns. (Argus Archive)

The national situation on Saturday, 2 September 1939 was well summed up by the *SDN* of that date:

> War there must be. This fact was made crystal clear by Mr Chamberlain, and the world to-day has to face it. [...] Promises made by Germany were not kept. Decisions were made by Germany, and it was assumed that it was the duty of Poland and other nations to accept these decisions as something from which there was no escape. [...] Never has the world known such arrogance and such disregard for what might be described as the decencies of international life. The Poles were charged yesterday morning with having rejected what they had never seen. This fact will for ever put Germany in a category of diplomacy too gross for a decent world to attempt to live with.
>
> Yesterday's events constitute a collection of grim facts from which there is no escape – German troops crossing the Polish frontier without any declaration of war, open towns being bombed, innocent people being slaughtered. Britain is determined to stop such conduct.

The newspaper rightly referred to 'the war from which there seems now to be no escape'. It came within twenty-four hours.

CHAPTER 2

Before the Bombs
3 September 1939 – 14 July 1940

The announcement

On the morning of Sunday, 3 September 1939, Brighton was bathed in sunshine. All appeared calm and peaceful. But there was tension and expectancy in the air, especially towards 11 o'clock, when premier Neville Chamberlain was due to make his long-awaited announcement to the British people. Virtually everyone with access to a radio set tuned in. Germany, he solemnly declared, had not responded to the British Government's request for an assurance of the immediate cessation of hostilities in Poland, a response due to have been received by 11am. A state of war now therefore existed between the two countries. Chamberlain confessed to the Commons, with a heavy heart, that it was a sad day for all of us:

> Everything that I worked for, everything that I had hoped for, everything that I believed in during my public life has crashed into ruins this morning.

Yet following his announcement, nothing happened. No swarms of enemy aircraft blackened our skies to bomb buildings, installations or the deserted streets. However, an air raid warning siren (in response to the sighting of an aircraft later established as friendly) caused shock and bewilderment. The congregation at St Luke's Church, Prestonville, did not panic; the Second Lesson was not quite finished when the siren went off and it was heard in the church quite clearly. After the close of the Lesson, the vicar (the Rev. E.F. Yorke) announced that a number of the congregation who had not got their gas masks with them or had dependants needing their care at home might wish to leave. During a brief pause, the children of the Sunday School and many of the congregation did so. To the remainder, the appointed preacher, the Rev. H. Lawrence Taylor, gave a brief and apt address from the Communion rails and the service resumed.

The town's first victim was probably 37-year-old waiter Fred Cozens, of North Place, Brighton. He had been found sitting on the pavement near the Pavilion shelters by passer-by Sydney Miller of Freshfield Road, but was unresponsive.

Death was attributed by the RSCH (Royal Sussex County Hospital) pathologist to haemorrhage, probably caused by the man having been excited and in a hurry to get home from the hotel where he worked to tell his wife that war had broken out.

The false alarm

The air raid signal which sounded less than half-an-hour after the declaration of war emptied the town's streets within minutes. A reporter for the *SDN* recorded what he saw:

> I was one of the large crowd at the Brighton Central Station when the warning was given just before 11.30 and noticed that at first no one took it seriously. People simply looked at one another with an air of surprise. The warning was so insistent, however, that it could not be ignored, and at length the voice of Mr W.O. Dodd (Deputy Town Clerk, in charge of arrangements at the Station) came over the loudspeakers announcing that 'This is the air raid warning. Everyone take cover down the steps, please.' Those already in trains were told to lie on the floor, while the evacuation train was held up outside the station. Buses and cars in the vicinity of the station were stopped and were soon deserted. Children engaged filling sandbags for use at the hospitals left their task and disappeared. Many children and others were taken into nearby houses.
>
> Curiously, on the Front the sirens do not appear to have been distinctly heard. Not being aware either of the broadcast or the warning, promenaders strolled on nonchalantly until the fateful word was passed from mouth to mouth. The promenades were then speedily cleared. In some parts of the town, too, the all-clear signal was not heard. When the all-clear warning was given, people streamed out of the shelters and hurried to buses, which with other vehicles became involved in long traffic jams.
>
> The Chief Constable (Captain W.J. Hutchinson) was out in the police van when the warning was given. Over the microphone he urged people to take cover immediately. He then went to the control centre and addressed a similar message over the loudspeakers which had been placed at twelve points. Later, people were advised to carry their gas masks with them wherever they went.

Towards the end of September, the local press cleared up the mystery of that air raid warning. Captain Bernard Laporte, who had just been appointed Assistant

Air Attaché to the French Embassy in London and was on his way to take over the post, was flying in mid-Channel when our ultimatum to Germany expired and his was the unidentified machine which set off the alarm and sent everybody scuttling frantically to their cellars and other shelters.

A mighty influx

The arrival of evacuees had a massive impact on Brighton and this large-scale operation was rarely out of the news, especially during the rest of September. On the 3rd, the first train was – as we saw above – held up outside the station owing to the air raid warning. Fewer than the expected number (900 mothers and children) arrived, but at Hove the number was above schedule. For some unknown reason the last three or four trains came in empty.

The next day, sixteen trains brought 12,000 to the town. One mother brought six children. The *SDN* reported:

> There were mothers with children in their arms; there were girls and boys old enough to realise the meaning of everything that was happening around them. There were little fellows grasping their yellow ration bags and with

A trainload of evacuees arrives at Brighton Station. (BHIB)

their gas masks slung on a string around their shoulders. The first train arrived at the station at 9.30am and the pilgrimage had once more begun. The helpers, the porters, the bus conductors were on the platform to greet them as they streamed from the carriages. This first contingent consisted of the mothers and the young children. Some had had two days' warning that they would be leaving yesterday. They had collected what luggage they could; they had crammed baskets, haversacks and kit-bags with whatever they could carry. Others had had but a few hours' warning that they must leave. They had no time to bring anything with them. They came as they were, thankful only to escape from possible attacks from the air.

A party of 167 children and mothers from the contingent who arrived too late to be sent to their billets, were put up for the night at the Hotel Metropole courtesy of the Manager (Mr J.W. Barnard) and the Assistant Manager (Mr S. Till), who completed the arrangements at twenty-five minutes' notice. The visitors were served with supper, and emergency beds were provided in the Clarence Ballroom. They were given breakfast and lunch the next day before being taken to their billets.

On that day, the foreshore was invaded by the young incomers. 'From Black Rock to Portslade', reported the *SDN*, 'the beaches were thick with boys and girls and their mothers. For many this was the first glimpse they had had of the sea, but they knew how to swim. London does not keep its swimming baths idle.' Those who did not swim, bathe or paddle, made the most of the morning's sand. The stallholders did a roaring trade in toffee apples and ice cream cornets. The main shopping centres were very busy, except for the luxury trades. In Western Road, for example, one might have imagined that it was the height of the season. About 50 per cent of the people were carrying their gas masks.

Evacuation brought many problems, well documented in other books. Some were perhaps unavoidable, as in the case of Mrs May Welsh, of 132 Beaconsfield Villas. Her extreme stress was apparent on 27 November in Brighton Police Court; facing a charge of permitting a light to be shown from her house, she burst into tears, exclaiming:

> I can't stand this worry. I have got fourteen evacuee boys and a prefect and I can't cope with them. They have broken the beds and all the chairs. It was not my fault. I told them not to put the light on but they took a candle into an empty room. When the prefect tells them to be quiet they swear at him and use filthy language. I can't stand it. I have got no income and I have had to sell and pawn everything.

Ministry of Health poster urging more volunteers to accept evacuees in their homes. (*BHG*, 16.3.40)

It emerged from the evidence that she had not applied for the children and also that three weeks earlier she had had twins who were stillborn. She also had a daughter aged 16. The Bench dismissed the case and advised her to make sure all her windows were covered up.

Very occasionally there was a tragedy. On 19 September, Mrs Julia Kathleen Pentecost, aged 49, of Brading Road, was found dying from disinfectant poisoning due to having been worried by having to billet three evacuated schoolgirls. In early July 1940, the death occurred in hospital (cause not stated by the *Gazette*) of one of the first children to be evacuated to Rottingdean on the outbreak of war. Henry Smith, aged 7, younger son of Sergeant Smith of the Irish Guards and Mrs Smith of London, had been living with a Mrs Gaston at New Barn Road. He had been a pupil of Burdett Coutts School, Westminster.

Some evacuees (including mothers) did not stay here long. The *Evening Argus* commented on 19 September that women evacuated from London appeared to be returning home in increasing numbers from South Coast towns, although they were not being encouraged to do so by the local authorities. Many of the women were in excellent billets, and expressed themselves satisfied with their reception, but said that they were returning home with the consent of their husbands. 'It appears,' concluded the paper, 'that many of them have treated the evacuation scheme as an opportunity for obtaining a fortnight's holiday at very little expense.' Some did not like the places to which they were sent. Miss A.C. Tennent, Senior Assistant Organiser of Children's Care Work under the LCC, told a Brighton audience in early December:

> It is a terrible thing to be taken from London and planted down at Woodingdean. You might just as well go to Central Africa; in fact, Central Africa could be more familiar, because you might have seen it on the films. To leave your friends, the fried fish shop and the barrow where you bought things, the social worker and the parson – everything that makes life familiar and comfortable – and go to a place like Woodingdean, where there is nothing but the beauties of nature, is a dreadful experience.

Miss Tennent had been sent down by the LCC to look after the 20,000 children and mothers evacuated from London. When she arrived, she said she found Brighton had made extraordinarily good billeting arrangements and had divided itself for the purpose into eleven areas. The first thing she did was to form a Care Committee in each area and impress on the billeting officers that their great task was to become the friend of every evacuated person in their area. Welfare Centres were opened and every possible type of human problem in due course came up for solution. The mothers were particularly difficult:

> They were lonely and shy and very often they behaved badly – chiefly because of that nervousness and shyness. Then they had the anxiety of not being certain whether the husband would send any money at the end of the week and a further worry of wondering what he was up to in London.

Education and class accommodation were often problematic. The point was made at the meeting of East Sussex County Council's Education Committee on 14 November that, within a few days, almost in a few hours, eighty-seven schools had come down from London and environs, doubling the county's school population. In Allt and Robson's history of Varndean School for Boys, *Onward and Upward*, we read the following recollection of pupil B.K. Parnell of the Lower VIth:

> Varndean was required to take in a school from London – Raine's Foundation Church of England Secondary School, from the East End of London. The two schools could hardly have been more different in their background but their enforced cohabitation could hardly have worked better. The schools shared totally the Varndean facilities, Raine's using the school in the afternoons and Saturday morning, while Varndean used it in the weekday mornings.
> [...] Surprisingly, perhaps, there was little friction between the two sets of boys and Raine's appear to have nourished very warm feelings for their enforced reception. A Raine's Sixth Former wrote: [...] 'We have been treated with extraordinary kindness and unselfishness, both by Varndean School and by our various hosts and hostesses.'

Raine's departed in July 1940.

At a general level, the local press also reported on the issues of the provision of clothing and footwear and difficulties in the feeding of all the new arrivals.

Although dispersal to safe areas had officially been deemed complete in September, nearly 800 additional evacuees from London County Council and Croydon schools arrived in Brighton on 4 November and again during the 7th. They travelled in buses to the Town Hall, which became a distributing centre, and from there were taken to their billets.

Looking back in early January 1940, the *Gazette* considered the Christmas season of 1939 to have been something of an acid test as to whether evacuation was to remain a success or not. It was feared, stated the paper, that when the children returned to their parents for the holidays, the joy of once more being in familiar surroundings and with those they loved would prove so strong that nothing would persuade them to return to their billets, especially since the threat of air raids was not now imminent. The youngsters had been lured back by the Christmas parties staged in the Pavilion and the Intermediate Schools and which overflowed into other schools in outlying districts. Another factor had been that, by and large, the children had grown extremely fond of their billets. A third factor was the part played by the tradespeople of Brighton, who had promptly and generously supported the Christmas treat schemes, financially and otherwise. Finally, the extension, to fathers in London and Croydon, of invitations to take part in the Christmas celebrations in Brighton successfully dissuaded many evacuee mothers with small families from returning for a 'family Christmas' as they had planned.

Returnees

Nevertheless, increasing numbers of evacuees did subsequently go back home. Nationally, the figure was hundreds of thousands by February 1940, whereas in Brighton and Hove a far larger proportion remained than had been the case in most other evacuation areas, a fact which the *Gazette* felt could 'be taken to indicate satisfaction with the conditions under which they are living'. Only 19 per cent of the total number of schoolchildren received in September had returned to the evacuating areas. When the Mayor of Stepney (Councillor F.R. Lewey, JP) visited Brighton on 14 March he thought the Stepney pupils here would agree 'that Brighton was a better place than Stepney'.

Yet on 14 July 1940 (the day before Brighton suffered its first aerial attack), 9,000 London and Croydon schoolchildren left Brighton, Hove and Portslade for 'somewhere in Surrey' under the Government's re-evacuation scheme announced on the 10th. Brighton accounted for 7,000 of them. Little 8-year-old Christine Mills, billeted at Withdean, was a typical example of the disappointment the children felt at leaving foster-parents who had shown them every kindness since the previous September:

I've been very happy in Brighton and I wish I hadn't got to be moved. I'm not looking forward to moving and I would rather go home to Croydon but

London evacuees enjoying their Easter holiday in Brighton. (BHG, 30.3.40)

Mummy and Daddy say I've got to be a good girl and go with all the boys and girls at school. I hope the people where we are going to will be as kind as the auntie and uncle who have been looking after me in Brighton since we came down here last September.

Many children's parents decided to have them home again. A few others would be staying on in Brighton by special arrangement between the foster parents and the billeting officers.

In another development, it was reported at the end of June that 1,700 of Brighton and Hove's own children had been registered for evacuation to the United States and the Colonies, and many more parents were still enquiring about the Government's Overseas Reception Scheme which had been announced a few days earlier. It was open to schoolchildren aged 5–16 but did not include their parents. Offers had been received from Canada, Australia, New Zealand and South Africa to look after children for the duration of the war. Coincidentally, fifty Roedean School girls were on their way to Canada (the country generally preferred across Brighton and Hove) in acceptance of an invitation from the Edgehill School at Windsor, Nova Scotia, which had cabled an offer to look after them for the duration of the war. Other Roedean girls would be going to Canada at a later date when the Government's scheme was in operation. However, the evacuation destination for most of the school was the Lake District, where the Keswick Hotel provided a safe haven from 1940 for some 350 girls between the ages of 11 and 16. Pupils from elsewhere also went north for a time – in March 1941, 120 boys from Varndean School for Boys were voluntarily evacuated to Skipton, Yorkshire; pupils from the Girls' School were sent to Ribblesdale, and children from Balfour Primary School were evacuated to Holmfirth.

Blackout

An important means of passive defence was the blackout, imposed on 1 September 1939 even before war was declared. The importance of ensuring that it was fully enforced was highlighted as early as July 1939 in Public Information Leaflet No. 2 (part of the Air Raid Precautions training literature). Relevant suitable material, whose availability was ensured by the Government, included heavy curtains, cardboard or paint.

Overseeing the blackout by patrolling the streets on the lookout for visible lights was one of the functions of the ARP service.

The streets would always be dangerous – on the evening of the day war was declared, there were not only five accidents in Brighton in which people were injured, but the first blackout death on the town's roads: Benjamin James Tugwell, aged 66, a tailor, of Artillery Street, died after being struck by a car at the bottom of West Street. On the following evening, the local blackout was assessed and although judged as 'good' by Brighton's Chief Constable (Captain W.J. Hutchinson), it was 'still a long way from being perfect'. Everybody, he thought, 'must concentrate on a general effort to make it a success'. A week later, the Mayor (Councillor J. Talbot Nanson, JP), urgently appealed to the townspeople to make the blackout 100 per cent effective – there were still some occupants of flats above ground level who were offending and the open position of such lights was especially dangerous. Brighton evidently took heed, since the blackout on the evening of 14 September was, in Captain Hutchinson's view, the best to date, particularly on the part of householders. A number of motorists took advantage of the new lighting regulations and hand torches were used freely. Unfortunately, torches themselves were found to be dangerous, since they were sometimes flashed by would-be passengers into the eyes of approaching bus drivers.

Only one blackout accident death was reported for Brighton in the figures for October 1939, but a child was killed at the end of the following month, when Joan Knight was hit by a van when running across Elm Grove to join a group of friends. Just over a week later – and in the same road – a runaway trolley bus killed 17-year-old Hector Hutchison, who was wheeling his cycle up the hill in the blackout. Sadly, a further incident involving a bus occurred on 13 January 1940,

A humorous notice issued by Brighton, Hove and District Transport warning against flashing torchlight at a driver's face. (Author)

when 72-year-old Frank Louie Couling was struck in St George's Road, Kemp Town, and died in hospital the following day.

Other effects of the blackout were decreasing church attendances and increased car theft and shopbreaking.

Strict penalties by way of fines were imposed on those transgressing the blackout regulations. In early December 1939, a fine of 10*s* was imposed on Winifred Margaret Lauder of Lower Rock Gardens on account of a light shining all night from a window (a policeman had unsuccessfully attempted to make himself heard at her front door). In February 1940, dentist Alfred Moxley, read a passage from the Acts of the Apostles in his defence but this did not prevent him being fined 40*s* for a light showing from two windows on the ground floor of 12 Old Steine. In June, Homelands Private Hotel in Montpelier Road was fined the substantial amount of £20 (and its Managing Director, Mrs Margaret Meek, was fined 40*s*) due to lights coming from five windows at the rear of the hotel, while the front of the premises in Sillwood Place was 'a fairyland of light', according to the police, who had had a considerable amount of trouble from Homelands for some time. This despite the hotel (which admittedly comprised 135 bedrooms and 350 windows) having spent £250 on blackout precautions. On 8 June, the actress Frances Day permitted a light to be displayed at 1.25am from the bathroom of her flat at Marine Gate and pleaded guilty by letter. In it, she stated in her defence that she always tried 'to be a perfect law-abiding citizen and in the case of blacking-out I drive myself and everybody around me mad with the aim of perfection.' She was fined £3. Fines of £5 each for similar offences were imposed on Elspeth Brocklehurst Phillips of 12 King's Road and Katherine Murphy of 6 Bedford Court.

An unusual source of one transgression was a bonfire which burned at 12.30am on 20 June 1940 – after an air raid warning had been sounded. The offence was committed by a Mrs Ethel Pierce of Loder Road, who had set light to some freshly cut weeds. She was fined 20*s* (£1). On the 30th, an angry crowd gathered outside 7 Royal Crescent, the home of Mrs Grace Amy Willock-Pollen, threatening to smash the windows when a light showed from the property just after 10pm. She told the Bench, who fined her 40*s*, that she thought the blackout time began at 10.18pm (this applied to vehicles but for buildings it was half an hour earlier). Mortified, she declared, 'Nobody is more loyal than I am. My son-in-law is private secretary to the King. I am very sorry; it was a pure mistake.' On the same date, Mrs Evelyn Teague of 75 Ladies' Mile Road, Patcham, received the same fine. In her defence, she stated, 'I was so worried about my poor dear cat', explaining that her daughter had been given a kitten which ran upstairs. She ran after it and during her absence the wind blew the window curtain aside from an open window.

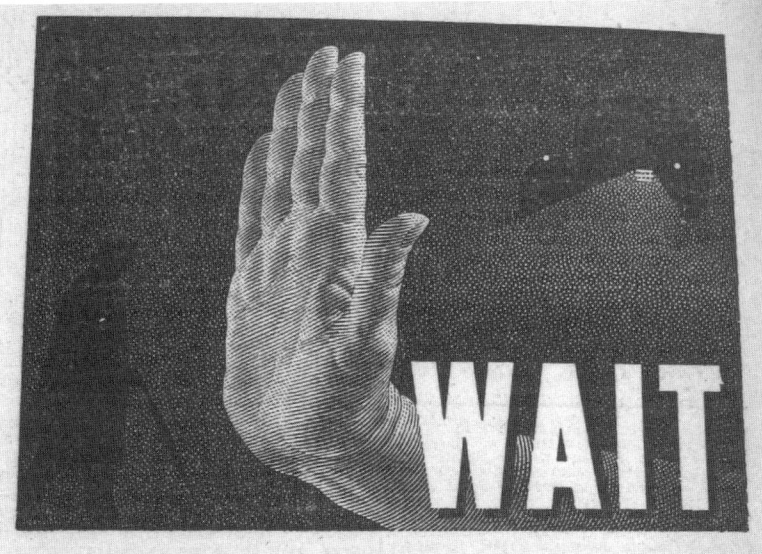

The blackout posed a great danger to both drivers and pedestrians. (BHG, 4.2.40)

An appeal to Brighton's householders was made by Councillor Dutton Briant (Chairman of the ARP Committee) in early July 1940 to make the town's blackout arrangements as perfect as possible:

> The present black-out arrangements are quite good, but with every day bringing the danger of raids closer, it is the duty of every citizen to make sure he is playing his part for the safety of himself and his neighbours.

Aliens

Just as in the First World War, the presence of aliens in the community was a problem which needed to be addressed. Directly war broke out, the Chief Constables of Brighton and Hove directed the attention of ALL enemy aliens (i.e. persons of German and Austrian nationality, including their British-born wives) over the age of 16 to the instruction that they had to report 'AT ONCE' to the police of the district in which they were residing, irrespective of the fact that they were already registered. Scores of aliens, each with a respirator slung over their shoulder, promptly reported at Brighton and Hove police headquarters. Changes affecting particulars of registration of all aliens had to be notified to the police within forty-eight hours. No enemy alien was allowed to travel a greater distance than five miles from their registered residence without a travel permit issued by the Chief Officer of Police with whom they were registered. The temporary absence of a friendly alien from their registered address was permitted for two weeks, not three months as previously allowed. The special attention of hotel proprietors and the providers of paid accommodation was drawn to Article 7 of the 1920 Aliens Order regarding the registration of all persons staying at their premises – every person had to sign a registration form.

By the end of September, tribunals to consider which Germans and Austrians in Britain should be interned on the grounds of national security and which could be exempted from the special restrictions of the Aliens Order had been set up by the Home Secretary. Most of the Germans and Austrians now here were refugees, and many of them were anxious to help the country. Those whose suspicious activities had been under observation had already been interned, but in order to supplement information already held by the authorities, it had been decided to review the case of every German and Austrian over the age of 16.

In early January it was estimated that there were nearly 1,000 friendly aliens in Brighton and Hove who had sought refuge in the twin boroughs. The great majority of them were expected to take advantage of a new postal message scheme to contact relations left behind in enemy or enemy-occupied territory initiated by the International Red Cross and being furthered through the cooperation of the Citizens' Advice Bureaux.

Later in the month, a well-attended social for Central European Refugees was held at Friends' Meeting House under the auspices of the Brighton and Hove Liberal Association. The guests included nationals from Austria, Germany, Poland and Czechoslovakia, among whom were doctors of law, philosophy and medicine as well as prominent businessmen, engineers, and other professional classes. One H. Stoner, a keen Liberal, said that however much we all deplored the wrongs that Nazi Germany was inflicting on weaker nations, it was not the real Germany and that in our indignation we must not forget the true Germany's contribution to culture.

In May 1940, action was still being taken against enemy aliens. After receiving secret Home Office instructions overnight, Brighton CID officers swooped on all enemy aliens in the town on the morning of Sunday 12 May. Tracing German and Austrian residents and visitors continued from 10am to 5pm, by which time nearly forty had been arrested. Plain-clothes policemen visited their homes or lodgings and ordered them to pack a bag and leave for internment. All the aliens taken into temporary custody quietly did so and accompanied the detectives outside to a Black Maria or waiting flying squad car. They were taken to an internment camp on the outskirts of the town, and kept under guard. The rounding up of these undesirables continued the next day, since some could not be traced on the Sunday. Nearly all of them, however, went to Brighton Police Station voluntarily and reported to the aliens officers. They were allowed time in which to pack a bag and were escorted to join the other aliens at the camp. Altogether between fifty and sixty enemy aliens from Brighton were temporarily interned. Among the detainees was the Rev. Willy Oelsner (1897–1983), a refugee from Nazi oppression and former Lutheran pastor in Germany, who was the very popular curate at St John's Church, Preston, Brighton, and priest-in-charge at Preston Old Church. He had joined the Church of England soon after escaping from his country a few months before war broke out and was ordained by the Bishop of Chichester, who appointed him as his personal chaplain, at Preston Old Church on 21 December. Despite his mother being German, Oelsner had been persecuted by the Nazis because his father was Jewish. When he left Germany with his wife, a German countess, they had only ten marks between them. In 1941–50 he was curate at St Andrews in Brighton and in 1950–71 at the Holy Trinity Church in Hove.

Among the cases brought against aliens was that of Herman Reiter, who said he had travelled from London to Brighton underneath a railway carriage. He pleaded guilty before the Brighton Bench in June 1940 of being an alien and entering a protected area without the written permission of the registration officer. He had been found hiding in a train which was in a siding at Brighton station and had told the police constable who interviewed him that he did not know he had to obtain the written permission of the Chief Constable before he could enter Brighton. Speaking in broken English, Reiter said he had nobody in London. He was working fourteen hours a day for which he was not paid. People were treating him very badly. 'When I ask for something better,' he said, 'people tell me to go back to China where I come from. I want to join the Army, but I am too young [he was 17], so I wanted to get away from London. I took a platform ticket at Victoria and travelled under the carriage of a train to Brighton. I come here and give myself up. Somebody saw me and took me to the Police Station.' Reiter, who had come to England in June 1939, was remanded in custody pending consultation with the Home Office. The outcome of his case was not recorded in the *Gazette*.

Sandbags and breeze blocks

The week following the declaration of war saw intense ARP protective activity, especially in the form of sandbag-laying. Prime locations were the Town Hall, which by Wednesday 6 September was fully protected, the seafront and the Fire Station. The appeal for volunteers (including women) met with a ready response, so that by the end of the week the finishing touches were being put to the protective works. All peacetime improvement works, such as those in North Street, on Madeira Drive and the subway to Marine Drive, and all housing and road maintenance closed down, with the men transferred to Air Raid Precautions work.

Numerous enquiries continued to be made for respirators, and these were directed to the Head Wardens of the various groups throughout the town.

By April 1940, a preferred alternative to sandbags had been found in breeze blocks. A picture in the *BHG* showed men at work at Devonian Court – one of the largest shelters in the town, capable of holding 1,400 people. At the end of June, another picture showed splinter-proof concrete blocks being built around a police box to replace the use of sandbags, which, the caption informs us, 'frequently burst through foul weather'.

BEFORE THE BOMBS 59

Brighton's Town Hall was strongly fortified against any aerial attack. (Chris Horlock collection)

Shelters (again)

Just days after hostilities commenced, fourteen public shelters with accommodation for 7,000 were available. The provision of additional accommodation for 3,000 was imminent. It was stressed more than once by the ARP authorities that the trenches and shelters were only for use by people caught out in the street and away from their homes at the time of a raid. People were not to leave their homes and run for safety to a shelter. Nor were they to avail themselves of protected premises such as Wardens' posts or the Central Fire Station (to which people rushed during the warning on 3 September, thereby hindering the brigade in getting the mobile patrols out).

On 20 October 1939, the staff shelter constructed at New England Street on the premises of Elders and Fyffes Ltd, the banana distributors, was held up by the *Evening Argus* – which described its facilities in some detail – as a model for all air raid shelters.

Towards the end of June 1940, it was reported that in order to provide additional air raid shelters in Brighton, the staffs of the electricity and waterworks undertakings and the Parks and Gardens Department were engaged in their construction. It was recognised that, in consequence, some playing grounds, bowling greens and the like might not now receive the same level of attention as they had, although members of the clubs using the grounds and greens could undertake essential maintenance work. The *Gazette* affirmed that:

> The provision of further area protection is urgent and the mobilisation of all the town's labour resources is necessary to enable the work to be done without delay.

In early July, the provision of additional street shelters was being rapidly pushed forward. Among the locations listed in the local press were Marshall's Row (off London Road) with capacity for 450, Norfolk Square, which could accommodate 400, and Montpelier Crescent near the Seven Dials, whose capacity was being increased from 250 to 350 persons. Further shelters were under construction, including on bus routes and at bus stops. It was again emphasised that the shelters were for the use of people caught in the streets when a raid alarm was sounded.

At this time, an underground air raid shelter was built at a cost of £1,500 in the grounds of the Royal Alexandra Hospital for Sick Children in Dyke Road. It provided accommodation for practically the whole staff, including the children. It was fully equipped and had room for forty-four cots, fifty-five walking cases and forty adults. A slope from the hospital enabled the cots to be wheeled straight down to the shelter, which measured approximately 70ft by 35ft.

A scheme, just authorised by the Government, to advise and assist Brighton householders to construct their own trenches was announced at a meeting of representatives of various organisations in the town at the Town Hall on 10 July 1940. The trenches were to be constructed by the householders themselves on the advice of architects and construction engineers. The Corporation had agreed with a number of the best known and most experienced among them for them to be attached temporarily to the Borough Surveyor's staff, and they would each be appointed to a certain section of the town. The Corporation would provide every possible assistance, including materials, as they become available. Councillor Dutton Briant stated that they were authorised to provide shelters for 17,500 and now this had been increased to 25,000. Already there was accommodation for over 20,000. This was well up on what was previously envisaged, because those evacuated to the town were leaving and many others had also gone. There was, in addition, accommodation for 12,000 schoolchildren. Groups of householders who wanted a shelter for their own houses would in the first instance be advised by the architects or construction engineers with regard to the construction of trenches. It was suggested that a group should comprise about six houses. The architect for the district would visit the houses, site the trench and tell the householders what should be done so that they could get on with the digging. The scheme was meant only to apply broadly to those people who were in insurable employment or with incomes up to £5 per week. Those above that limit were expected to provide for themselves, but so far as they could they would be given technical advice through the architects for the various areas. David Edwards (Borough Surveyor) explained that the town had been divided into sixteen districts, each of approximately 1,500 houses, to which an architect had been, or would be, appointed. In addition, there was the congested area of the old borough for which his department would be responsible. He had met the architects that morning, and already appointments had been made for nine of the sixteen districts, which were then specified.

A recent publication by the Ministry of Home Security gave advice on the protection of homes – even household furniture could be used to make houses secure from the effects of blast.

ARP highs and lows

The administration of the ARP service in Brighton did not operate without problems. At the end of December 1939, Mr H.B. Johnson tendered his resignation as a protest against the imposition of a 'means test' in respect of all full-time paid Wardens following a decision by the Town Council that unemployed or ex-servicemen should be trained and, if suitable, appointed to positions held by persons with adequate means of subsistence. Mr Johnson's resignation was accepted, but no successor was appointed. Finally, in April 1940, Mr Johnson wrote in offering to again place his services at the disposal of the town. The Emergency Committee, in view of the contemplated reduction in the number of paid members of the Wardens' Service and the need to maintain a still stronger volunteer service, welcomed his offer and reappointed him as Chief Warden. His earlier stance had, incidentally, been supported by the town's five Divisional Wardens (Messrs W. Mather, E.J. Reeves,

A.W.C. Wingfield, I.V. Darling, and R.D. Swann), who had undertaken to carry out Mr Johnson's last instruction, which was to carry on. The Wardens were making the efficiency of the organisation their first consideration. The voluntary part-time unpaid Wardens of Brighton's Group 22, Division 2, among others, had been up in arms about the means test and had unanimously condemned it in a resolution passed in January. In their opinion, greater thought should have been given to the treatment of those who had come forward voluntarily many months before the war.

One bright spot in the following month – January 1940 – was the success of 'ARP Sunday' on the 11th, when a united service for Civil Defence workers at the Dome was followed by an exercise for all ARP organisations in the borough. Regional Officers who watched the programme were so impressed that all districts were to be recommended to hold Civil Defence Sundays, with church services for Civil Defence workers in the morning, followed by full-scale exercises in the afternoon. A few minutes after the service the imaginary air bombardment of Brighton started. There were two raids, the first at 2.35, when ten 'incidents' occurred, with high explosive, incendiary and gas bombs. The Lewes Road viaduct was presumed to have been bombed while a train was crossing, and a German plane was brought down close to St Peter's Church. In the second raid, ten minutes later, there were again heavy casualties, and direct hits were made on three bridges on the main London railway line. In all there were fifty dead and nearly 600 casualties. So bad was the 'raid' that assistance had to be sought from Shoreham and Southwick,

Ready for anything! ARP Post 22, Brighton, 3 September 1939. (Author)

which sent ambulances, first-aid parties, and casualty services to the scene. There were, however, no staged incidents as on previous occasions, and every incident was left entirely to the imagination of the Wardens patrolling their sectors. Each bomb, or 'incident' was handed to the nearest Warden in a sealed envelope, and the test became an exercise of mobility and communications.

A blot on the record of Brighton's ARP personnel was recorded in early July, when 29-year-old warehouseman Albert Edward Meadows, of 48 Milner Road, a Warden, was summoned before the Borough Magistrates for 'defacing a glass panel of a goods shed, the property of the Southern Railway', on 30 May. Meadows admitted painting a swastika in creosote on a glass roof in the goods yard where it could be seen from the air. Above it was written the word 'Heil' and below it 'Rat'. Defendant pleaded guilty, adding: 'I realise it was a very foolish thing to do.' Meadows, a married man who had been a Warden for eighteen months, stated he had acted on the spur of the moment. It was, he admitted, a quite childish thing to do. He was fined £3 plus £2 for costs.

A Civil Defence exercise

In May and June 1940 respectively, a large-scale demonstration by the Civil Defence Services and one featuring an incendiary bomb in the Pavilion grounds were held. The former was watched by officials of the Brighton, Hove and Eastbourne ARP organisations and several hundred Brighton Air Raid Wardens. The incident was a major one in the demolition area of Carlton Street and Richmond Hill, which provided a realistic background for the 'complete demolition of a street of houses by two high explosive bombs'. It was supposed that fires had broken out, people had been injured, six had been killed and two had been trapped by debris. The medical representative of ARP Regional Headquarters at Tunbridge Wells warmly praised the Wardens and stated that he was delighted with everything he had seen, declaring 'I have been to 15 or 16 exercises during recent weeks and I have never come across such an efficient rendering of first aid by the Wardens.' In the June event held on the Royal Pavilion grounds, it was shown how an incendiary bomb could be put out. A picture in the *Gazette* depicted the demonstration.

The ATS

Women played their part in defence in numerous ways. The women's branch of the British Army during the war was the Auxiliary Territorial Service (ATS),

Recruitment poster for the Auxiliary Territorial Service. (Author)

formed on 9 September 1938, initially as a voluntary service. The first recruits were employed as cooks, clerks and storekeepers but the duties expanded over time to include work as orderlies, drivers, postal workers and ammunition inspectors. Members were based in 'depots' and the local one was the requisitioned Ocean Hotel in Saltdean, some four miles east of Brighton, which from December 1939 housed 500 girls anxious to 'do their bit'. (It later became the National Fire Service College, which played a vital part in the local and national war effort.) The *Gazette*, without naming the hotel, published an in-depth feature with several photographs on 10 February 1940 on the day-to-day life of these new recruits. A picture published in mid-March in the same paper showed them smartly parading in the grounds of the Royal Pavilion under the expert instruction of a guardsman. By June the service had acquired a recreation room in Kemp Town furnished and equipped by the Shilling Fund, a charity to benefit serving troops.

Local Defence Volunteers stand ready

The forerunner of the Home Guard was a force named the Local Defence Volunteers (LDV), created in response to an appeal broadcast on 14 May 1940 by the Secretary of State for War, Anthony Eden, calling for men between the ages of 17 and 65 to enrol for service in defence of their country. By July, nearly 1.5 million men had enrolled. Locally, the response was massive, with 1,500 men and boys volunteering in Brighton and many hundreds enrolling in Hove. The *Gazette* reported that local police stations had been in a state of siege since Anthony Eden's broadcast. Several men volunteered even before he had finished speaking and there was a steady stream in both Brighton and Hove until midnight. On the following morning, special arrangements were made to cope with the rush of volunteers and all day long men queued up, with 1,000 signing on in Brighton, over 700 in Hove and 180 in Portslade. A Brighton alderman and four councillors volunteered before midday, while a number of car-owning volunteers offered to organise mobile detachments of four and six men. Many office workers and shop assistants gave up part of their lunch hour to sign on and in the evening, when the homeward rush began, the queuing up restarted. One old soldier commented:

> A response like this just shows what eagerness to do something there is among the men who are too old to join the army or are in reserved occupations.

It soon became clear, however, that the town simply had too many defence volunteers. When more than 2,000 applications had been received for enrolment in the Brighton Company, Chief Constable Hutchinson told a *Gazette* reporter that this number was 'many in excess of requirements, and I'm afraid there will be a certain number of disappointments in selecting men. It is, however, a remarkable response and shows that there is behind it a wonderful amount of public spirit and a desire amounting to anxiety to serve the country.' Lieutenant Colonel Julian Fane, of 'Mountford', Peacock Lane, Brighton, was appointed commander of the company, with Sir Home Gordon, Bart., of the Union Club as staff officer, and Mr T. Harrington of 'Walintune', Roedean, as quartermaster.

When No. 5 Platoon, P Company, of the LDV was inspected on 1 July at Brighton goods yard, it was judged to be 'One of the most efficient sections yet inspected' by Mr G.W. Sheppard, the London Central Divisional Organiser for the LDV of the Southern Railway. The General Manager of that railway, Mr E.J. Missenden, was very pleased with the Brighton Section, the first to be formed. All ranks of railwaymen were represented – porters, drivers, firemen, clerical staff, shunters, guards, and signalmen, most of whom had varying hours of duty and all of whom were devoting their spare time to drills, shooting practice and valuable patrol work; 75 per cent of the volunteers were ex-servicemen, a fair number of whom wore medals.

Brighton College formed its own section, composed of all boys over 17. They were organised into an LDV section, which from 1942 was officially classified as 30th Platoon, 10th Sussex Home Guard. Throughout the war they paraded and drilled with other Brighton platoons. During the Battle of Britain, the college unit was given the job of guarding the pumping station at Balsdean Reservoir each night against saboteurs or German paratroops. Each cadet carried ten rounds of

A company of Local Defence Volunteers takes part in a Sunday morning parade on the sea front road. (Author)

A Section of the Southern Railway Home Guard marches down Queen's Road. (BHIB)

live ammunition. Those were the days of 'We shall fight in the fields and in the streets'. If the Germans landed, Churchill told the LDV, 'take one with you'.

Towards the end of June 1940, the *BHG* published a detailed feature on the LDV, whose members (now half-a-million strong) were making a demanding sacrifice to do their bit. One who was interviewed said:

> I have been out on duty into the small hours for three nights a week since I was enrolled early a month ago. I carry a rifle and wear the white L.D.V. arm-band. I have been measured for my uniform, and I shall be proud to wear it, if only to show that I am doing a little bit for my country. Some of us are in uniform already, but the rest of us have to wait our turn. The equipping of the B.E.F. must take first place.

As regards the administration of the LDV, Lord Leconfield, the Lord Lieutenant of Sussex, presiding at the meeting on 8 July 1940 of the Sussex Territorial Army Association in Brighton, told members that the volunteers in the county had been placed in the hands of the Association. This was 'a very large extension of its responsibilities'.

Eager cyclists

The Sussex centre of the National Cyclists' Union decided, at an emergency meeting in Brighton, to support energetically the NCU scheme for raising cycling patrols to help cope with German parachutists. It was felt that the speed and mobility of the average club cyclist made him or her an ideal person for patrolling the countryside. The centre approached Colonel Fane offering their services and he welcomed the idea, saying that cyclists would be invaluable also as dispatch riders if willing to ride over downland as well as on the roads. He would be putting a number in each district under his control. The hours required to be covered would be from dusk to dawn.

Enlistment

The very day after war was declared, a new recruitment office for the combined Forces – the Navy, Army and Air Force – was opened at the Oddfellows Hall, Queen's Road, (demolished in 1969, see Appendix 1) and saw a stream of recruits from early morning until closing time. Among many of those offering themselves were men exempt by reason of reserved occupations, and their applications were refused. The good quality of the applicants and their fine bearing was warmly commended by the authorities. Recruiting for the Royal Navy commenced a few days later. Recruiting by the Sussex Territorial Army Association had ceased and was being conducted by the Regular Army on its behalf.

The *SDN* noted that there had been another rush of volunteers at the Hall on 7 September, although applicants were fewer than during the earlier days of the week, since recruiting for the Royal Air Force had been suspended until the end of September, while that for the Army was restricted to men of certain trades: skilled tradesmen (mechanics) up to the age of 45 were being accepted and others between the ages of 21 and 38. The men particularly required were drivers with heavy goods licences, engineers, fitters, carpenters, bricklayers and others engaged in the building industry. An Army recruiting official stated that they had been working from 8.30am to 9.30pm every day since the offices had opened on Monday and commented: 'We are getting all we want and they are a nice lot of lads.' There was a queue all day of men anxious to join the Royal Navy or the Royal Marines. They were required for the 'duration of hostilities only', and had to be between the ages of 18 and 30. They were asked to report at the Hall between 9am and 11am each day.

Towards the end of October, voluntary enlistment opened (for men aged 20 to 35) for the Cavalry of the Line, the Royal Armoured Corps, the Royal Artillery, Royal Engineers (certain trades), and Infantry of the Line (the Buffs, or Royal East Kent Regiment, the Royal West Kent Regiment, and the Royal Sussex Regiment in the area). Those enlisting were not required to join their corps or regiment before 15 November 1939.

Billets and comforts

By the spring, recruitment had settled down and attention was being paid to the billeting of servicemen locally. Arrangements were in the hands of Sub Area Quartering Commandants, of whom there were forty, appointed by the War Office. Their headquarters were at 5 Springfield Road.

At the end of April, a Shilling Fund was launched by the *Brighton and Hove Gazette*, the *Sussex Daily News* and the *Evening Argus*, all of whose proceeds were intended to provide a little home comfort for the troops. Some of the men had been placed in less-than-comfortable accommodation, such as an empty requisitioned house lacking adequate furniture and facilities. The troops, for their part, made themselves useful by maintaining requisitioned properties and their gardens. Communal welfare was catered for by a rest and recreation room in Withdean, the first to be provided. Five more in Kemp Town followed suit.

By early June, the sum raised by the Fund exceeded £1,000.

On 27 May, the Brighton Services Club was opened at 26 Bedford Place by Lord Leconfield. The premises had been placed at the disposal of the Forces Welfare Committee by Charles Smith JP and three rooms had been given for the use of troops stationed in the Kemp Town district. These were being furnished by the Shilling Fund. J. Baxter Somerville, General Manager of the Theatre Royal, was so struck by the efforts being made locally for the welfare of the soldiers that he arranged a special matinee for troops stationed in the town. The management of the Norfolk Hotel organised a dinner, dance and cabaret in aid of the Fund and the wounded in local hospitals. Supporters enjoyed one of the best dinners the hotel could provide, a first-class West End cabaret and an evening's dancing in an up-to-date ballroom to the music of the Norfolk Hotel Orchestra directed by Joe Kaye, formerly of the Savoy and Ritz Hotels, London.

Max Miller, a Brighton resident, was often seen cycling in the town with a tin hat on the handlebars. (Chris Horlock collection)

Contributions to the Fund were made by a wide variety of supporters, including comedian Max Miller, the Brighton, Hove and District Bus Co. and London factory girls convalescing in Brighton, who contributed coppers amounting to five shillings.

Farms and allotments

It was recognised very early on that the productivity of farming and the adequate supply and distribution of food would be key to the nation's survival.

Only two days after war was declared, the Minister of Agriculture, Sir Reginald Dorman-Smith, announced in a broadcast that the Government proposed the extension of the £2 an acre ploughing subsidy to 31 December 1939 in the case of land that had been under grass for at least seven years. Also, with the exception of hops, all existing restrictions on production or acreage would be removed. It was the farmers' immediate task, he said, to plough up as much land as possible for the following year's harvest; at least 10 per cent of the present grassland should be ploughed up. There was no shortage of feedingstuffs for livestock, and he urged farmers not to take any hasty step such as reducing their flocks or herds. 'The contribution which those engaged in agriculture are being called upon to make,' he declared, 'has never before been of such tremendous importance,' adding that everybody with a reasonably-sized garden could, in the prevailing emergency, help (more perhaps than they realised) to feed themselves. 'Some,' he said, 'can be preparing the ground for vegetables in the spring, and others can keep a few poultry.'

On the following day, the *SDN* reported that a War Agricultural Executive Committee had been set up for East Sussex. In a letter addressed to every farmer in the county, it stressed that it was 'the national interest alone which

Haymaking in 1940. (Picture courtesy of Trevor Mitchell, www.trevormitchellartist.com)

must guide us all at this time.' The demand from farmers for land girls was strong, especially for milkers, tractor drivers/harvesters and fruit pickers; just over forty applicants trained to do such work were placed in early September by the temporary headquarters of the Land Army in East Sussex established at Cockhaise Farm, Lindfield. The number of volunteers received from Brighton was reportedly so large as to present real difficulties in the matter of immediate training. The *Evening Argus* reported in December that to date only 2,000 women landworkers out of 25,000 overall – not all of them trained – had been required.

Doris Williams of Falmer recalled that a civilian contractor was in charge of thirty to forty land girls who worked in the fields and Stanmer kitchen gardens. In the early years of the war, ATS girls were brought to Stanmer to pick ripening strawberries, blackcurrants and gooseberries.

Arrangements were made for the loan of soldiers to farmers for work on harvesting operations. These facilities were extended until 31 December 1939 to cover work on the potato and sugar beet harvests.

By November, the campaign for increased production from farmland was well under way and farmers had responded quickly to the appeal made by the Government. A substantial amount of the effort being made focused on lessening

Land Girls at Rottingdean. (Author)

dependence on purchased foodstuffs and maintaining production as far as possible of livestock and their products, particularly meat, milk and eggs.

A new source of labour was identified in mid-July 1940, when the Brighton Juvenile Employment Bureau encouraged young boys to take up agricultural work on Sussex farms; it was expected that sixty would be placed in the near future, according to Miss W. M. Everden, Juvenile Employment Officer for Brighton, who addressed the Brighton Rotary Club at its weekly luncheon at the Old Ship Hotel, on problems of juvenile employment in wartime. The instructional period would last three months and then they would receive the usual agricultural pay. The position of juvenile employment in Brighton had, said the speaker, been dislocated by the influx of evacuated children into the town. Since the outbreak of the war there had been a turnover of boy labour from the distributive to the light engineering trades, and as this was likely to continue it was not expected that there would be difficulty in finding employment for boys. The figure of girls unemployed, however, had risen very markedly.

Food and rationing

On the food front, no time was lost in making suitable administrative arrangements, with a Food Control Committee for Brighton being appointed just days after war was declared. Its offices were located at the Princes Hall at the Aquarium and its purpose was to control the retail supply of food to the public. Some reassurance was given by R.W.S. Morrison, the Minister for Food, in a statement on 8 September 1939 that, although food rationing would come, we had plentiful supplies at present, and he did not think it would be necessary for the Government to begin rationing for three or four weeks. He emphasised that rationing did not imply any scarcity of food. He did, however, want the public to remember that, owing to the difficulties of transport at the beginning, they might find a shortage of bacon and butter. Towards the end of November, it was reported, on the authority of the Ministry of Food, that rationing was still in doubt and that there would be adequate supplies of good fare for the festive season, with most things to be had at moderate prices. Home-bred turkeys were in good supply and prices, so far, were reasonable and were likely to remain so. As for fruit, the home crop had been an exceptionally good one, with English apples expected to be plentiful over the Christmas period. With the exception of a few luxury lines of hothouse fruit, fresh fruit was being imported freely. Inexpensive recipes for bananas were published by the *Evening Argus*.

That paper, in its issue of 14 November 1939, reiterated the 'Dig for Victory' slogan first heard (in relation to this war) in a radio broadcast on 3 October, when Minister of Agriculture Sir Reginald Dorman-Smith had declared: 'Let "Dig for Victory" be the motto of every one with a garden and of every able-bodied man and woman capable of digging an allotment in their spare time.' The *Argus* drew attention to the intensive effort being made by the Ministry (primarily by posters) to revive interest in allotments and induce men everywhere to join in the production of food. Whereas in the previous conflict, many applicants for allotments had been disappointed due to the non-availability of land, this time there was plenty of it to meet the strong demand from multitudes of town workers.

Digging for victory was a major WWII survival initiative. (Author)

Schools also did their bit. The history of Varndean School for Boys tells us:

> some 120 boys, with members of staff, volunteered to work the ground immediately south of Big Field. It was staked out into 80 plots with two boys responsible for digging and planting each plot. The work involved in double-spit digging to bury the coarse turf was backbreaking, and frustrated initially by an acute shortage of tools and then by the very harsh winter of 1939–40. But by the summer of 1940, tomatoes and cabbages were being picked and the worst was over. It was all formalised into the School Allotments Association which proved one of the most successful of all the societies. By 1945, it had produced over ten tons of vegetables and had a membership of 140.

In the summer of 1940, a number of boys cycled out daily to Horsted Keynes for fruit-picking.

At Brighton College, part of the Home Ground was dug up to grow vegetables, and at least one boy kept rabbits there. Some pupils were drafted off school for entire days to pick sugar beet or plant potatoes at Ovingdean Farm. Digging for victory did have its bonuses. Besides access to off-ration food and the chance to smoke, senior boys could join the Ministry of Agriculture scheme to train tractor drivers. The college was sent a Fordson in June 1941 and, by the end of term, twenty-six had passed the test and went off to help harvest in various parts of England.

On the livestock side, in November 1939 a Small Pig Keepers' Council, based in London, had been formed to assist the allotment holder, cottager and other householders to keep a pig or two and advise those who wanted to form Pig Clubs. The pig was a great converter of waste into human food, being able, by consuming waste from garden and allotment, food shop and dwelling house, to provide the population with valuable pork, ham and bacon.

Rationing, long anticipated, began in Britain on 8 January 1940 (although petrol had been controlled since September 1939 and the distribution of coal, gas and electricity had been regulated by the Fuel and Lighting Order which came into effect on 7 January). Sugar was rationed to 12oz and butter, bacon and ham to 4oz. Other meat soon followed. Unlike all rationed foodstuffs, the allowances were measured in shillings and pence instead of pounds and ounces. The ration was one shilling and ten pence (1/10*d*) at first, but after some fluctuations it went down to 1/2*d* on 7 July 1941 where it remained for the rest of the war. Cooking fats were rationed in July 1940 as was tea (2oz), while preserves and cheese were added to the list of rationed goods in March and May 1941. The Ministry of Food's authority was delegated to nineteen Divisional Food Officers who supervised and coordinated the work between Local Committees and Food Offices, and also acted as a link between the regional Food Offices and the Ministry in Whitehall. Then there were 1,500 local Food Control Committees appointed by the local authorities. Each committee, appointed annually, consisted of representatives both of the consumer and the retailer. Under those committees were about 1,300 Local Food Offices, and these did all the detailed work of licensing food dealers, enforcing orders and distributing the ration books.

Prosecutions for infringement of the food regulations occasionally occupied the attention of Brighton Borough Bench, as in the case of Frederick Charles Davis of 25 Gloucester Road, who pleaded not guilty to selling meat without a coupon on 18 May 1940. Davis's son, Philip, had not helped his case by his attitude to the inspector, saying in the shop that it was 'a pity he had not got something better to do'. The magistrates imposed a fine of 40*s* with 21*s* advocate's fee. Davis Snr retorted: 'This is what I have got for seven sons serving with the Army!' The Brighton Equitable Co-operative Society Ltd pleaded guilty at Brighton Borough Bench on 19 June to having supplied bacon for household consumption without detaching the appropriate coupon on 25 May and was fined 20*s* and 21*s* advocate's fee. In other cases, Cuthbert Harold Major, trading as G.W. Harrison of 102 London Road, admitted having sold cooked bacon at 2*s* 6*d* instead of 2*s* 6*d* per lb and was fined 40*s* plus 21*s* advocate's fee. Sydney Joseph Bryant, of the Saltdean Café, Longridge Avenue, Saltdean, pleaded guilty to selling cooked ham at 3*s* 6*d* instead of 3*s* per lb and a tin of canned salmon at 1*s* 1*d* instead of 1*s* on 1 June. He said he did not know home cooked ham was controlled, or that the price of salmon had been reduced; fines of £2 in each case, with 21*s* advocate's fee, were imposed. John Short, of the Midget Café, Rottingdean, was fined 2*s* 6*d*. with 10*s* 6*d* advocate's fee for selling condensed milk at 9½*d* per tin instead of 9¼*d*.

Sport and entertainment

Much-needed distraction from the war was provided by entertainment, sport and leisure activities. On the day before war was declared, Brighton and Hove Albion drew 3-3 with Bristol City (although this result was disappointing inasmuch as the Albion had scored all their goals within the first twenty-two minutes of the match…). Just four days later (6 September), however, the English Football League and the Scottish Football Association held separate meetings and both decided that all contracts between clubs and their professionals should be suspended. Thus all organised football remained in abeyance. On the 4th, the Brighton Autumn Croquet Tournament, an important annual Croquet Association event which would have continued over two weeks, was cancelled on account of the war, although golf was unaffected by the national emergency, since most players were not of military age (18-41). The clubs could carry on. All horse racing was cancelled, but greyhound racing was allowed to continue. Plans for the ice hockey season were reported in mid-October, Brighton being 'probably the first provincial town to start ice hockey this season' (*Evening Argus*). A new Sussex Ice Hockey League was formed and its four teams would play each other over a period of twelve weeks. A dearth of goalminders was noted.

The hours permitted for dancing and other forms of leisure activity were initially controlled, although an extension to 11.45pm was granted by the magistrates to the Hotel Metropole in early October for a series of dinner dances, on the basis of the proportion of patrons from outside being low. The Mayor (Councillor J. Talbot Nanson) said that the magistrates 'feel it is in the national interest that people's spirits should be maintained and legitimate entertainment should be encouraged'. A similar application on behalf of the Grand Hotel was granted. However, due to objections from the Chief Constable quoting the Public Entertainments Restriction Order of 14 September, an extension till 11.45pm at the Aquarium

A packed programme of ice hockey action was advertised in mid-February 1940. (BHH, 17.2.40)

Restaurant on 27 October for a dance for the Southern Railway Orphanage was refused, since payment from the public was involved. The Chairman of the Bench (Mr W.T. Curtis-Willson MBE) nevertheless had misgivings, asserting that 'the people should not be debarred from having reasonable enjoyment in the hours of black-out'.

Brighton's theatres remained alive and well. Writing in the *Evening Argus* on 27 September, 'Barbara' (Betty Rundell) reported the convinced view of Miss Phyllis Neilson Terry (visiting Brighton to appear in Emlyn Williams' comedy success *The Corn Is Green*) that 'the value of the theatre as an outlet for the emotions of the public, as a medium of relief from the pressure and uncertainty of everyday life, had never been greater than to-day when the dreadful catastrophe of war threatened the morale of the people'.

In February 1940, *Gas Light* (written by Patrick Hamilton and starring Sarah Churchill, daughter of Winston) was enjoyed at the Theatre Royal. Two of the plays put on there attracted mild controversy in April and June 1940 respectively: *The Bare Idea*, a farcical comedy by Gordon Sherry about nudity, attracted glowing reviews in the local press despite the sensitive (to some) theme. Audiences 'responded in great zest to the wit of the dialogue and the robust burlesque of much of the action' (*Gazette*, 13 April). For its part, *Desire Under The Elms*, the much-banned play by Eugene O'Neill, centred around the cruder passions of simple country folk of nineteenth-century New England. The *Gazette*'s reviewer, however, felt that the author had 'acquitted himself brilliantly' in his tremendous task and the play would 'no doubt be remembered as one of the outstanding dramatic masterpieces of the period'. Also shown in June at the theatre was *Billeted*, the successful comedy written by F. Tennyson Jesse and H.M. Harwood (1874–1959). The former was one of the first women to serve as a war correspondent, covering the First World War in Europe for the *Daily Mail*. The authors' play had opened in London at the Royalty Theatre on 21 August 1917.

The West Pier was another popular venue and the plays shown there included, at the end of March, Terence Rattigan's famous light comedy, *French Without Tears* and, in the last week in May, the enjoyable *A Murder Has Been Arranged* by Emlyn Williams, styled as a ghost story in three acts.

On the day war was declared, all cinemas were immediately closed as a safety precaution. But most were back in business within a week as the authorities realised, like Mayor Talbot Nanson, that the nation needed entertainment to keep up its spirits. In Brighton, entertainment venues reopened on 9 September up to 10pm, subject to the police being satisfied that audiences were not exposed to exceptional risk in the event of an air raid.

Cinemagoers were spoiled for choice in 1940. In March, memorable films such as *The Hound of the Baskervilles*, *The Stars Look Down*, *Sherlock Holmes* and *Destry Rides Again* were screened locally and the already legendary *Gone With The Wind* was shown at the Astoria in June. War themes were equally popular: *Nurse Edith Cavell*, starring Anna Neagle, was shown at the Odeon in early

Poster advertising a drama by Sussex playwright Patrick Hamilton and starring Sarah Churchill, Winston's daughter. (BHG, 10.2.40)

January, followed in February by *Professor Mamlock*, the international sensation described as the 'best anti-Nazi film yet made'. It was a 1938 Soviet drama production, one of the earliest films to deal directly with the persecution of Jews in Nazi Germany. In March came *Pack Up Your Troubles*, a new British film about the Army of the day, while in early May, Brightonians enjoyed *For Freedom* at the Regent, starring Will Fyffe. This was a propaganda drama combining dramatised scenes with real newsreel footage and told the story of father and son newsreel reporters going in separate directions when Hitler's invasion of Czechoslovakia brought the threat of war ever closer.

Also relating to Czechoslovakia was a film featuring the aggressive incursion of the Nazis into that country shown on 19 May at the Co-operative Hall, Hanover Place, to a meeting of members of the Brighton Co-operative Party. The film dealt with the building up of the Czech nation, its agriculture and industries and its tackling of social problems until the country was overrun by Germany. Its closing stages showed the plight of the Czech refugees after the invasion, and illustrated how the menfolk of the country were rallying to fight against Nazi oppression and tyranny.

Brighton's Sports Stadium in West Street had opened on 29 June 1934 as a large covered swimming pool but in the following year was converted to an ice rink, which became immensely popular. It was open for regular skating sessions daily and Brighton League ice hockey matches were held every Sunday

Poster advertising For Freedom, *a British drama film focusing on the Battle of the River Plate and blending fiction and documentary. It was made largely for propaganda purposes.* (*BHG*, 4.5.40)

at 12 noon. In early February 1940 it played host to a Grand Ice Gala, fresh from Belfast and Falkirk and featuring the first Appearance of 'Ice Follies' stars with Lise Koenig, the 15-year-old Viennese star, and the celebrated comedian 'Wondrous'. The next fixture after the Gala was a match between the Demons and the Furies. On 23 March, the Stadium held its Easter Ice Carnival, starring the world's two greatest amateur ice skaters, the British and European Champion, Cecilia Colledge, dubbed the 'Queen of the Ice', and the runner-up in these two championships, Freddie Tomlins.

Many a show was enjoyed at the Hippodrome in Middle Street, which had started life as an ice rink in 1897 but was by now Brighton's principal variety theatre. Performers there included Brighton's own Max Miller and other top names. In February, the musical, *Me And My Girl* (in its third year at the Victoria Palace, London), starring Len Clifford and Bertram Dench, was rated 'an astounding success' locally. At the end of June, the venue hosted *Old Soldiers*

Cecilia Colledge, the celebrated ice skater, in 1938. (Author)

Never Die, a farcical revue, starring comedian and film actor Ernie Lotinga (alias Jimmy Josser) and Jack Frost; it was a 'two-hour, non-stop laughter production' (*Gazette* critic).

Between March and July 1940, the extraordinary story of the Imperial Theatre (later the Essoldo) in North Street played out. Its scheduled opening in April was proclaimed in mid-March by the *Gazette*, which highlighted the fact that the newly-built theatre, with seating for 1,800, would be opened by no less a personage than Jack Buchanan, the managing director of the proprietary company, Southern Counties Theatres Ltd. The paper remarked that 'Brighton will find itself in proud possession of what is certainly the most modern and comfortable, and will probably be accepted as the most beautiful, theatre in Britain today.' The actor would also be appearing in the first show to be presented, namely *Top Hat and Tails*. The Imperial opened its doors to the public on the evening of 9 April, when the show was enthusiastically received by the very large audience. Crowds outside witnessed the grand opening, by the Mayor and Mayoress, of the venue, which 'so far as smartness and modernity of appointments are concerned [...] sets a new standard for the provinces' (*Gazette*). The show attracted glowing reviews, with praise for both the performers and the music. Then on 6 July this splendid theatre closed, with losses of £1,850. The *Gazette* reporter lamented the

Opening night at the Imperial Theatre, where there appears to be little sign of austerity. (Chris Horlock collection)

closure, dwelling on the wartime aspect, stating 'the war effort has claimed the attention of so many people that entertainment has had to take a back seat. Thus Brighton, which was once called the most theatred town in the country, makes one more sacrifice to the common end.' On 28 January 1941, the Imperial was taken over by the Official Receiver and reopened on 1 December of that year. Yet it closed again on 8 June 1942, only to reopen on 3 August (Bank Holiday Monday) under new management, showing films on Sundays. In the following year, it was acquired by Gaywood Cinemas Ltd and film performances were increasingly included. A chequered wartime history indeed.

Without doubt, the two leading dance halls were Sherry's in West Street and the Regent Dance Hall in Queen's Road. An advert for the former venue in mid-January 1940 announced continuous dancing till 11.30pm on Saturdays, making 'this dance hall an ever-increasingly popular rendezvous. Two famous bands, playing the latest numbers, a floor that is unsurpassed in Brighton, perfect organisation for your enjoyment, these are features at Sherrys. Dancing takes place daily, with an afternoon and evening session, and varied programmes are provided.' In early March, the venue held what it called the 'First South of England Jitterbug Rally', which was a great success. The *Gazette* reported 'An American idea of a crazy dance has invaded our shores once more, and folks, young and old, fling each other into the air with the greatest enthusiasm. The ladies are taking it up locally.' The Regent was a mecca for dancers and hosted celebrated bands and orchestras. On 8 March 1940, Eddie Carroll's famous orchestra under Eddie himself, a noted swing composer, was specially engaged for the Annual Ball of Brighton and Hove Entertainment Managers' Association, attended by 'all the world and his wife' (*Gazette*). Despite the drop in attendance from the previous year, due inevitably to wartime conditions, there were still 1,200 present. The proceeds of the evening went towards the purchase of a light field ambulance to be presented to HM Forces.

Our fishermen and vessels at Dunkirk and St Valéry

'Operation Dynamo' was the code name for the evacuation of Allied soldiers from the beaches and harbour of Dunkirk in northern France between 26 May and 4 June 1940. Many Belgian, British, and French troops had been cut off and surrounded by German troops during the six-week long Battle of France and a fleet of over 800 boats was hastily assembled to rescue them. The first day saw only 7,669 Allied soldiers evacuated but by the end of the eighth day, 338,226 of them had been taken off the beaches. As well as the larger vessels which took part in the operation, there were the 'little ships', a flotilla of hundreds of fishing boats, pleasure craft, yachts, merchant marine boats and lifeboats sent out by Britain to save the men. Brighton gallantly played its part in the drama.

One pleasure steamer which had operated from Brighton and other South Coast resorts between the wars and which bore the town's name was P&A Campbell's *Brighton Belle* (built in 1900 as PS *Lady Evelyn*), although her last season in Brighton had been that of 1935. In the following year, she was transferred from the south coast to the company's services in the Bristol Channel. Requisitioned as a minesweeper in October 1939, she sank on 28 May 1940 while engaged in withdrawing 800 troops from Dunkirk, having collided with submerged wreckage just off the North Sand Head. Mercifully, all the soldiers and crew survived.

A sister paddle steamer in the Campbell fleet was also lost. The *Brighton Queen* (built in 1905 as the PS *Gwalia*) was stationed on the South Coast from 1933 and also taken over by the Admiralty for service as an auxiliary minesweeper, although her career – in the 7th Minesweeping Flotilla under Temp. Lieutenant A. Stubbs RNR – would be brief. On 1 June 1940, some four miles out from the beaches on her second trip and carrying about 700 French and Moroccan troops, she took a direct hit aft of the paddlebox with a 500 lb bomb and sank within seven minutes. The minesweeper *Saltash* picked up about 400 survivors and reported that, 'The French troops behaved steadily and intelligently though nearly half of them were killed by the explosion.'

Apart from the steamers, twenty-eight of Brighton's fishing and pleasure boats, in some cases manned by Royal Navy personnel, went over to France, both to

Dunkirk proper and to the 'other Dunkirk' – the attempt to evacuate troops from the small coastal port of Saint-Valéry-en-Caux, 109 miles east of Dunkirk as the crow flies.

Two of the four *Skylark* yachts, *Skylark* No. 3 (SM 391, known affectionately as 'the big Skylark') and *Skylark* No. 4 (SM 281), both owned by F.P. Collins, were lost. Reporting on their service, the *Herald* dated 15 June 1940, noted: 'Captain Collins and his men took three *Skylarks* from Brighton beach to Dover and handed them over to the Admiralty, who found them of enormous service in conveying troops from the beaches of Dunkirk to larger vessels waiting to bring them back to England.' Mourning their loss, the *Gazette* commented: 'The beach at Brighton seems empty without them, particularly to those who know anything of the *Skylarks*, and the generations of the Collins family who have sailed them.'

Skylark No. 4, *seen here in happier days, was lost at Dunkirk. She had been so badly damaged by shellfire or bomb splinters that she had to be sunk by the Navy.* (Alan Hayes collection)

The other twenty-six vessels which participated in operations off France were:

Vessel name	Reg.	Skipper	Owner
Anzac	SM 34	J. Brooks	G. Morgan
Boy's Joy	SM 232	D. Martin	Danny Martin
Challenger	SM 24	C. Watts	J. Gillam
Cornsac	SM 313	A. Bishop	George Rolf
Dorothy Helena	SM 7	W. Sinden	G. Andrew
Estella	SM 387	T.C.P. Hefferan	W. Humphrey
Fair Irene	SM 11	Nelson Sayers	Bob Leach & Sons
Favourite	SM 225	T. Allen	B. Allen
Flower of the Fleet	SM 146	J. Andrew	J. Andrew
Four Winds	SM 53	F.C. Jupp	William C. Woolgar
Loreen	SM 258	Naval Rating	H. McDonald
Marie J. Leach	SM 309	A. Carter	Harry Leach
Marie Joyce	SM 279	H. Leach	Frank Leach
May Queen	SM 270	Joseph Leach	Frank Leach
Mizpah	SM 296	M. Rothwell	James Ovett
Our Doris	SM 74	J. Edwards	G. Mitchell
Our Johnny	SM 377	E. Gillam	E. Gillam
Our Kathleen	SM 236	Naval Rating	J. Mitchell
Perseverance	SM 257	E.J. Pierce	J. Andrew
Pop Gun	SM 10	G. Watts	Bob Leach & Sons
Princess Mary	SM 129	F. Virgo	H. Jordan
Royal Rose	SM 265	G.W. Grinyer	J.W. Nye
Seaflower	SM 56	J. Howell	J. Howell
Skylark 1	SM 2	W. Stephenson	W. Knight & L. Manzi
Skylark 2	SM 5	A. Divine	Frederick P. Collins
Sportsman	SM 97	H. Marchant	Hazelgrove Bros.

A feature in *The Argus* (issue of 2 June 2000), focusing on the experiences of some of Brighton's fishermen and boat owners at Dunkirk, referred to the involvement of sixteen vessels as participants in the operation, namely *Skylark* 1, 2, 3 and 4, *May Queen*, *Fair Irene*, *Pop Gun*, *Marie J. Leach*, *Favourite*, *Challenger*, *Dorothy*

Helena, Our Doris, Marie Joyce, Royal Rose, Seaflower and *Our Johnny*. Two of the boats, *Pop Gun* and *Challenger*, were skippered by brothers George and Charlie Watts respectively. George survived unscathed but suffered severe shock and died four months later in hospital at the age of 45. Charlie (d. 1973) stated: 'He wasn't hit at all, but I am sure the evacuation killed him.' George's son, also George, ran a fishmonger's shop in St James's Street for many years after the war. He was positive that his father's experiences at Dunkirk, including the terror of constant air attacks, brought on his premature death.

For his part, Charlie, who served on board the four-ton trawler *Challenger*, recalled the terrifying scenes on the beaches, where he narrowly escaped death:

> I lay down in the bottom of the boat. I remember my face was a few inches away from a big tin of hard tack and a duffle coat hanging on a peg. There was a tremendous explosion and shrapnel hissed all round me. The coat was torn to shreds and the tin was hit by a lump as big as my fist. It was a very near thing.

Brighton boats were also present at the unsuccessful evacuation from the beaches of the small coastal port of Saint-Valéry-en-Caux (and Veules-les-Roses). The focus on Dunkirk overshadows any thought for the thousands of brave British

Challenger, built in 1938/9 by Cantell's in Newhaven for James Gillam, somehow survived the evacuation operations at Dunkirk. (Alan Hayes collection)

troops stranded elsewhere in France and vastly outnumbered by the German war machine. One group left behind was largely made up of General Victor Fortune's 51st Highland Division, fighting as an integral part of the French 9th Army. Hoping for an orderly evacuation, Fortune led his troops, with a fair number of French soldiers, to Saint-Valéry, alerting the Navy to his plight at 4am on 10 June. With Hitler desperate to avoid another Dunkirk, however, the General was unaware how aggressively his men were being pursued by the 5th and 7th Panzer Divisions. By 11 June, troops were organised into a horseshoe shape from Veules-les-Roses across to the far side of Saint-Valéry, but there were gaps. Both towns were in valleys between steep cliffs and, worryingly, there was no sign of the Navy. The troops were forced back by superior fire power and numbers and there was nowhere to escape. Despite a fierce defence, the 7th Panzers soon held clifftop ground overlooking each harbour, making an evacuation highly dangerous. Thick fog, meanwhile, kept 209 ships of the Royal Navy far out into the Channel and Fortune was unable to contact their would-be rescuers.

Those soldiers who were able to reach the beaches, strewn with the bodies of their comrades, had to pick their way close in to the rocks to avoid attracting machine gun fire from the clifftop. At Veules-les-Roses, after tying whatever they had together to make a rope, some soldiers fell down 300ft-high cliffs in their attempt to flee the advancing Panzers when their makeshift ropes frayed. And still General Fortune was unable to contact the Navy.

With the odds against them impossible, the French army surrendered at 8am on the foggy morning of 12 June 1940. For his part, General Fortune, realising there would be no rescue by sea and that further sacrifice on the part of his exhausted men, surrounded and vastly outnumbered, would be pointless (they had been fighting almost continuously since 27 May at Abbeville), made the difficult decision to surrender, a surrender accepted on that same day by General Erwin Rommel at Saint-Valéry. A few soldiers to the west of the town managed to escape and a few made it on foot to Le Havre and were evacuated. Others made their way through to Spain and Gibraltar before finally sailing home. For most, however, escape was impossible. They were quickly marched into Germany and Poland to spend the rest of the war in captivity.

Charlie Watts, recording his experiences in 1965 aged 62, remembered the operation vividly:

> No one told us anything about where we were going but we all thought it was another Dunkirk. We were towed across to Le Havre in strings of ten by two tugs. We anchored there for a day and then we sailed to the beaches

at Saint-Valéry. But it was nothing like Dunkirk. The Germans had taken the high cliffs and were expecting us. Twice we tried to go in and twice we failed. The fire was murderous. Then the naval officer in charge saw that the Germans were down on the beaches and we were told to scatter. As the small boats strove to get out of range, German planes came in to finish them off. They were saved by sudden, heavy fog. 'We were like sitting ducks,' he recalled, 'and there was nothing we could do. That fog was the nicest thing I ever saw.'

Tom Markwick (d. 1988) of Oriental Place thought the Saint-Valéry operation was a disaster:

There's no other word for it. When we approached Saint-Valéry we saw the beaches were practically overrun. Some Frenchmen rowed out in a dinghy under very heavy fire and were picked up. Five planes bombed us and I wore a cabbage strainer for a tin hat. Several boats were hit and one was sunk just a few feet away from us. I think it was an Eastbourne craft. One plane made several determined runs and strafed us with machine gun fire. We had a Lewis gun on the bows and the young naval rating held his fire until the last possible minute. Then he banged away and hit it.

The splendid contribution made by Brighton's fishermen off both locations in France was acknowledged at the Quarterly Meeting of the Sussex Sea Fisheries Committee held in Brighton Town Hall on 11 July 1940. The Chief Fishery Officer (H.M. Boniface) said fishing had been good until early May, after which almost the entire fishing fleet and many of the personnel placed themselves at the disposal of the Admiralty. On 29 May, vessels capable of crossing the Channel were requisitioned. He stated that many fishermen from Brighton, as well as Rye, Newhaven and Eastbourne, also responded to the second call for operations off France and all had received the thanks of the Commander in Chief at Portsmouth for their services.

On 27 November 1940, at the Royal Pavilion, Rear Admiral T.P.H. Beamish, CB, MP, acknowledged the important contribution of the skippers and owners of the Brighton and Hove boats which played so gallant a part in the epic of Dunkirk and the evacuation of Saint-Valéry, saying:

Gentlemen and Seamen and Citizens of these two great seaside towns, we salute your craft, for your noble national work at sea in defence of the freedom of this country.

The occasion, presided over by the Mayor of Brighton (Councillor J. Talbot Nanson), accompanied by the Mayoress (Mrs D. Scott Prime), was the presentation of commemorative plaques to each of the boats. Others present included the Bishop of Chichester, Captain Sir Cooper Rawson MP, Lady Rawson JP, the Vicar of Brighton (Canon G.H. Warde) and the Town Clerk (J.G. Drew). A great many of the townspeople attended, overflowing from the Music Room into the North Drawing Room and corridor. The plaques, some of which are on display today in Brighton's Fishing Museum, were of bronze and bore the inscription 'B.E.F. 1940' and the name of the craft concerned, surmounted by a crown and surrounded by a wreath of oak leaves. Admiral Beamish, addressing the skippers and owners, declared they would be 'shining memorials to be handed down to future generations to inspire them with your spirit – the spirit of freedom'. He mentioned the loss of the two *Skylarks* at Dunkirk and the fact that Skipper A. Divine and his engineer had been dangerously wounded but had fortunately recovered. Five owners had actually taken part in the operations and more than 100 of the crews volunteered for duty. Paying tribute to them, he stated:

> With the courage of the RAF, the grit and resolution of the Army, the ever-present help of the Royal Navy and the incomparable skill of our seafaring islanders, represented by the sailors of Brighton and Hove as far as we are concerned, we as a nation snatched success from the very jaws of disaster.

Not until thirty-four years later, however, did the fishermen receive their medals, prompting *The Evening Argus* to describe them as 'forgotten' (issue dated 30 April 1974) and recording that they had been 'discovered' by the Mayor of Dunkirk, Claude Prouvoyeur, during a visit to Brighton. On the evening of 29 April, Brighton's Mayor and Mayoress, Councillor and Mrs Danny Sheldon, together with Horace Leach, handed over the medals and diplomas to the worthy recipients.

Not all the boats of Brighton had been pressed into service. Two comparatively large vessels, the *Elizabeth* and the *Belinda* (obtained by George Andrew as new in 1911 and during the Great War respectively), had stood unused for the previous four years and were ordered to be broken up, a task undertaken by ARP demolition squads. This was a hard blow for the 75-year-old Brighton fisherman, who had been at sea for sixty years. The reason the boats had stood unused for so long was that the younger generation would not go in for big fishing, preferring the smaller boats, where there was a larger share-out.

The officials and medal recipients pose in front of George Howell's Lady of the Lake, *built around 1959. Dunkirk's Mayor is on the far left of the bottom row.* (Alan Hayes collection)

The sad end of the Elizabeth *and* Belinda. (Alan Hayes collection)

Pleasure boats, too, were deemed to be obstructions. The motley collection of rowing and motor craft was removed to the lake at Queen's Park towards the end of June, much to the displeasure, the *Gazette* noted, of the resident swans.

Impeded access everywhere

Both in town and in the suburbs, citizens were now subjected to much restriction of movement. An insight into the limitations widely imposed is provided in a letter in the author's possession dated 8 June 1940, written by one Bessie Cuthbertson, who had moved with her husband, Duncan, and their three children to the sparsely populated Downs Estate in Woodingdean in 1925. In the letter, and in many others she wrote during the war, she described the family's daily life to her son, McLennan (nicknamed Douglas), who was on active service. The following are slightly edited extracts:

> Everywhere round here is being guarded and barricaded – have to show identity card to get on beach – slipway [at Rottingdean] is blocked, except for narrow path with barbed wire – machine guns in sandbag nests everywhere.

Bessie's 16-year-old daughter, Mabel (known as Babs), wrote to Douglas on the same day:

> On Thursday at 10 to 2 the air raid sirens went and we heard aeroplanes flying around in the West, many lorries and cars and motorcycles dashed up and down the roads. The air raid Wardens and soldiers with guns and such like were all sent out. All the searchlights went on. We could hear gunfire out at sea. At about 10 to 3, the all clear came on but in the middle changed to the warning again and we heard more planes faintly and a quarter of an hour later the all clear went.
>
> Along the Ditchling road, the Lewes Road and the Dyke Road there are barricades across them. No cars, motorcycles, bicycles whatsoever are allowed on the lower road from the Palace Pier to Blackrock. At each end and on the roads leading from the top road to the bottom are large iron stakes dug in the road so that pedestrians can just squeeze through. All the steps leading from the top road to the lower road have sentries posted there. Also all along there are sandbags and lookout posts with big guns in each. Both piers at Brighton are mined so that they can be blown up at any time, for they are such a landmark. They were used for landing the Holland and Belgium

refugees. Most of the signposts have been taken down. At Rottingdean you can't get on the beach unless you have your identity card or a sentry questions you. All day long we can hear the guns from France, which slightly shake the house. At present we can hear the soldiers being trained to use machine guns up in the hills somewhere.

In a letter to her Aunt Molly dated 28 October 1940, Babs reported further observations:

Several German planes have crashed into the sea just off here. Along the coast there is barbed wire and landmines. A dog was blown to bits walking on one also three people and a soldier. Out to sea a half mile from the land there are hundreds of large boats all in a line. Another landmine went off and smashed the Palace Pier clock.

CHAPTER 3

Death from the Skies
15 July 1940 – December 1942

The first casualties

Not until Monday 15 July 1940 did Brighton suffer any attack from the air, although neighbouring Hove had had some bombs harmlessly dropped on it towards the end of the previous month. By the end of the year, however, no fewer than ninety-three lives would be lost in Brighton in enemy raids – eighty-six of them occurring in the fateful month of September.

July began with an inspection by King George VI of the anti-invasion defences in the town. His visit was followed the next day by one from Winston Churchill, recently appointed Prime Minister, also making a tour of inspection and taking lunch at the Royal Albion Hotel.

Very early on the morning of the 15th, with no warning from sirens, bombs dropped by a Dornier Do 17 caused the deaths of 67-year-old retired nurse Mrs Ettie Hargreaves of 13 Prince's Terrace (believed to be the first civilian in Brighton to be killed in the war), 35-year-old Henry May of 64 Manor Hill, the father of six children all under 12 years of age, and 43-year-old Francis Sawyer of 11 Manor Road. George Wood (52) of 9 Maresfield Road, died in the RSCH two days after the raid. The bombs landed in Whitehawk Road, Bristol Gardens, Bennett Road, Henley Road, Prince's Terrace and Rugby Place.

George Allen, an ex-naval man, told the press: 'I heard a plane droning up pretty high. It flew round and round for quite a quarter of an hour. I stood on the street to watch, but I dived for shelter when I saw the bombs dropping.' Another resident said: 'I watched the plane flying high overhead for ten minutes. Directly it released its bombs it turned out to sea at great speed. Apparently it flew inland along the coast and bombed another town.' That other town was neighbouring Hove, where Albert Charles (46), a member of the Home Guard who had been on night duty and who lived at 37 The Gardens, Southwick, was killed in New Church Road. The bombs – jettisoned, according to a witness – fell in both that thoroughfare and the Pembroke area of the town.

After the first raid on 15 July 1940 — Whitehawk Road, Brighton. (BHUF (Brighton & Hove Under Fire))

In Brighton, the police, specials, ARP services and the AFS promptly attended the scenes of destruction – indeed, it took less than five minutes for ambulances, casualty and rescue services to join various teams. Nearly every pane on many streets was blown out, and numerous shops and a public house, the Clyde Arms, were wrecked. Repairs to many properties were carried out swiftly and efficiently by a large number of building firms.

There were some lucky escapes: a bus conductor was shaving when a piece of shrapnel missed his face by inches and embedded itself in the wall. Another house was hit by a bomb, but the two occupants, a woman and her daughter, escaped unhurt. One man had moved from a seafront flat with his wife and 5-month-old son to live with his parents. A bomb fell in the back garden outside the bedroom where the couple and the baby were sleeping. The child's father recalled: 'I was flung out of the bed by the explosion, which was terrific. I found both my wife and the baby were safe. A draught screen had been blown over on top of the cot and it saved the baby's life. Our bedroom was wrecked and the ceiling collapsed on top of the cot and our beds.' A Corporation clerk stated: 'I was fast asleep in my bedroom when the explosion woke me up and I found everything in the room was wrecked. The bed was covered with glass and plaster, but I was unscratched.'

Many others also had stories of lucky escapes to tell. One householder told a reporter that a bomb fell within 1ft of his bed, while in another area an old lady of 83 insisted on returning to her home after a bomb had set light to the chair in which she had been resting.

Within half an hour the stricken residents had recovered from the shock, and cheerfully exchanged experiences with their neighbours. Hundreds of families spent the morning clearing up the glass. Many others in the badly damaged houses were taken to shelter in the homes of friends, while demolition squads cleared the wreckage. The book *Brighton and Sussex at War* mentions the experience of a Mrs Agnes M. Hill, of Princes Terrace, who was trying to clear away soon after bombs had shattered her home. A pile of letters showered through the front entrance onto the floor and the postman shouted: 'Here you are, Ma. I see they ain't even left a door for me to knock on.' Mrs Hill opened her first envelope and read: 'Birthday greetings. Many happy returns of the day!' Her home was bombed again twice.

August visit

Not until nearly six weeks later – on Sunday 25 August – did the enemy return, although by some miracle there were mercifully no fatalities on this occasion. However, the incendiary bombs showered on the central district by the lone aircraft did cause numerous blazes. The properties affected included the Intermediate School in York Place, whose roof and top floor were severely damaged, Eede and Butt's timber yard in Trafalgar Lane and the wine store of Tamplin's Brewery behind Richmond Place. Firemen were promptly on the scene of every outbreak, swiftly subduing the flames and preventing the fires from spreading. Other missiles which fell in streets, public gardens and a pleasure park burnt themselves out without causing any damage. The German pilot circled the town several times before making his attack, which he facilitated by using a flare to light his target. Not content with bombing, he also resorted to machine-gunning firemen and rescue parties. Happily, there were no casualties from bullets or fires, although one man was injured by a falling roof.

A community hall was opened up for those residents evacuated from their homes who were unable to find accommodation with friends in the town and there volunteers and public assistance workers quickly made them as comfortable as they could. A number of people were given breakfast not long after the raid and

DEATH FROM THE SKIES   95

Damage to the Intermediate School in York Place, 25 August 1940. (BHIB)

those staying on were served at lunch and teatime. Many slept on the premises that night and were fed during Friday. Breakfast was again served on Saturday morning to the reduced number of evacuees still present.

The vicar of the parish stayed at the hall for one night, and church workers laboured to feed and provide sleeping accommodation for the evacuees. The older people slept on stretchers, while camp-beds and cots were provided for the children. As if it was just another day, working men went off to work at 5am after their breakfast. Four local relieving officers worked in shifts to supervise the temporary hostel and women volunteers did cleaning and washing-up. A lively concert was arranged by the relief workers to cheer up the unfortunate occupants of the premises. A black-bonneted little woman of 79, affectionately known to all of her neighbours as 'Grannie', had been offered a bed with friends but had refused to go, telling a reporter that she was in fact grateful for the ordeal of her homelessness. 'It has proved to me just how much kindness and goodness there is in the world.' The *Gazette* dated 31 August remarked:

> The spirit of the workers and of those they served, was the same, a cheerful spirit of optimism, of willingness to do their bit either by helping others, or by making the best of a difficult position—the spirit in fact that will win the war.

Black September

The lull in August and the fortnight which followed would be shattered in September, a month during which, as mentioned, no fewer than eighty-six victims of air raids died – 92 per cent of the total figure of ninety-three fatalities recorded for the whole of 1940 in Brighton.

A great many of those who died perished in the attack by a lone raider – possibly a Dornier Do 17 – on Saturday, 14 September. Prominent in people's memories of that day is the direct hit sustained by the Odeon cinema in St George's Road, Kemp Town, which caused the immediate deaths of two adults, a teenager and a child, namely Emily Barton (62) (also recorded as Barton-Tales) of 137 Whitehawk Crescent, Johanna Marchant (55) of 4 Manor Hill, Frank Stuttaford (15) of Portland Place and little Pamela Sturgess (6) of 2 Rifle Butt Road. Other victims recorded as dying subsequently – predominantly on the day of the actual bombing – at the nearby Royal Sussex County Hospital but who in some cases may well have been dead at the scene, were two children (Sydney Borrow (11) of 113 Maresfield Road and Mary Sharp (11) of 24 Manor Way), five teenagers (Stanley Baldwin (14) of 93 Twineham Road, Freda Harris (14) of 26 Freshfield Street, Ivor Davies (14) of 108 Hervey Road, Nellie Loftus (15) of 42 Manor Hill and Alfred Chapman (18) of 36 Hervey Road), along with two adults (Lilian Rosenzweig (46) of 34 Camelford Street and Ronald Walker (40) of 5 West Hill Street). Edith Mason (68) of 15a Eaton Place died at the hospital on 18 November. The total deaths attributable to the cinema bomb were therefore

The interior of the Odeon cinema in St George's Road, Kemp Town, showing the bomb damage after the air raid of 14 September 1940. (Royal Pavilion & Museums, Brighton & Hove)

three children, six teenagers and five adults. Bearing in mind that some 300 patrons were estimated to have been in the building, the fact that the number of dead and injured was not higher was something of a miracle.

In his book *The Tree Climbers*, local historian David J. Knowles (1933–2011) recalls his mother telling him and his elder sister, Jill, that they could not go to the pictures that day because she (their mother) was going to visit a friend who had just been discharged from hospital, following an operation, to convalesce at home. This friend lived in a street not far from the 'little Odeon' (to distinguish it at the time from the 'big Odeon' in the town itself). Aged 7 at the time, he and Jill, who was four years older, were naturally disappointed, but there would be other Saturdays. Before long, the children heard a terrible explosion in the distance. Frantic with worry, they were later immensely relieved when their mother returned, dishevelled and emotional but otherwise fine. David recalled:

> She had been helping a couple of boys, who had slight injuries, up to the hospital. Immediately after the bombing she had left off from her friend's flat

to get home as quickly as possible, but, on being told by a passer-by that the Odeon had been hit, she decided to head in that direction and see if there was anything she could do; there were other people hurrying to get there as well. When she arrived there she found that the cinema had received a direct hit. To her horror, she saw that bodies were laid out on the ground just outside it – these, heartbreakingly, included some dead children. There were many people there helping, including doctors, nurses, ambulance men, air raid wardens and members of the general public – and what had been chaotic pandemonium, was now, slowly, coming under efficient control. An air raid warden asked my mother and another lady to escort one child, bleeding from high up on his leg, but still able to walk, and another slightly older boy, with cuts – who although dazed was also still able to walk – to the Sussex County Hospital no more than 100 yards away. They arrived there to find this place also coming grimly and efficiently under control, and there seemed to be injured and shocked people everywhere. It was from the hospital that she had managed to get to a phone to let us know she was alright. After delivering the two boys to the hospital she had returned to the scene of devastation at the Odeon – helping where she could, and all the time fiercely trying not to break down and cry for the dead and wounded, at the same time as offering countless prayers of thanks that we hadn't gone to the cinema that afternoon. An hour later, on leaving this scene of devastation, where rescue work was still going on – and would do for quite some time – she had then walked back home in something of a daze, hardly believing all that had happened in the course of nearly two hours of nightmare! She arrived home to one very grateful family, now all fussing around her. She sipped from a strong and soothing drink, and then the tears came – readily and deeply!

The book *Brighton and Sussex at War* recounts the fortuitous change of plan of two happy-go-lucky local children:

Charlie and Johnny were two Whitehawk brothers aged 9 and 12. They left home to go to the Odeon Cinema, Kemp Town, the Saturday afternoon it was bombed with a loss of 59 [*sic*] lives. For nearly five hours they were missing while their distraught parents waited for news. It was evening when Charlie and Johnny walked cheerfully in and said: 'We went to the Odeon but it was bombed, so we came out and went to another!'

Tragic as the cinema figures were, they were far outweighed by the statistic of thirty-eight other fatalities resulting from the raid. Here are the names, ages and addresses of those victims:

ALLWRIGHT, Robert William (14) of 18 Somerset Street

BAILEY, George (10) of 18 Upper Bedford Street

BALL, Frederick (57) of 4 Clarendon Terrace

BLACKWELL, Jane (67) of 10 Sussex Square

BRASHILL, Lillian Mary (22) of 33 Hodshrove Road

BROWN, Edward Clark (10) of 28 Somerset Street

BURKINSHAW, Charles (69) of 31 Upper Rock Gardens

BURKINSHAW, Charlotte (69) of 31 Upper Rock Gardens

CHAPMAN, Iris Lilian (14) of 30 Upper Bedford Street

CLANCY, Josephine Trissie (36) of 8a Kemp Town Place

CORDIER, Joan Mary (16) of 66 Queen's Park Rise

DUPLOCK, Monica Mary Ann (9) of 49 Whitehawk Avenue

DURAN, Julia (73) of 49 Oxford Road, Kilburn

EVERETT, Monica (9) of 30 Upper Rock Gardens

EVERETT, Susannah Mary (34) of 30 Upper Rock Gardens

INMAN, Nora (52) of 153 Holbein House, Holbein Place, London

JONES, David Thomas (31) of 30 Upper Rock Gardens

JONES, Leonard Henry (59) of 24 Sussex Square

LEECH, Louisa Kate Maud (60) of 4 Chichester Place

MACDONALD, Joseph Hilton Salvage (38) of 2 Hereford Street

MARTIN, Harry (18) of 19 Upper Bedford Street

MASKELL, Charles Hackney (67) of 7 Rock Grove

MEPHAM, Arthur (30) of 11 Peel Road

MITCHELL, Bertha Matilda (38) of 36 Upper Bedford Street

RENNIE, Elizabeth Ann (67) of 3 St George's Terrace

RICHARDSON, Alice (30) of 34 Hereford Street

RICHARDSON, George Noel (11) of 34 Hereford Street

ROGERS, Violet (17) of 13 Blaker Street

RUSH, Alan James (52) of 8 Kemp Town Place

RUSH, Margaret Lilian (17) of 8 Kemp Town Place

RUSH, Yvonne (11 mths) of 8 Kemp Town Place

SWAIN, Herbert (43) of 12a Cannon Place

THOMAS, Joyce Alma (17) of 17 Pankhurst Avenue

VARNEY, Lena (29) of 31 Upper Rock Gardens

WARNETT, Ellen Mary (41) of 69 Whitehawk Road

WOOD, Mary Marjorie (25) of 22 St George's Terrace

WOOD, Ronald (11 mths) of 22 St George's Terrace

WRIGHT, Maria (70) of 4 Hereford Street

[Total 38 + 14 cinema = 52]

Hereford Street, Kemp Town, suffered greatly from bombing. (BSAW (Brighton and Sussex at War))

The addresses shown are the places of residence, or work, of the victims, but on that fateful day many were elsewhere, such as at the homes of neighbours, local friends or relatives.

The death of Violet Rogers was recalled by her 80-year-old sister, Marion, in a feature published in *The Argus* on 21 January 2013:

> That day my sister had a bad cold and my mother told her not to go to work because she was ill. Violet said she had to go because the owner of the shop was out for the day and they had a row. Mum wasn't happy but she went anyway. She worked in a grocery shop opposite the Odeon cinema. That was the day it was bombed – and she was killed. She was so pretty and I still miss her. I can remember that day as if it was yesterday.

Later that year Marion herself and the rest of her family were bombed out of their home near Western Road. She said:

> Luckily we all escaped but the rescue crews thought they had found a body in the back garden. It was only when they got it out of the rubble that they realised it was actually a teddy.

Hereford Street, where there were ten fatalities (including the death of one person on the corner of that street), was the worst hit, followed by Upper Bedford Street and Upper Rock Gardens, where the bombing killed seven individuals in each case. Unluckily, two ladies from London were among the dead in the latter street, one being killed there, at No. 30, and the other dying on the next day in hospital from injuries sustained at the same residence. The most tragic location from a

Salvation Army girls did their bit dispensing hot drinks to Civil Defence workers engaged on clearing bomb damage in Lower Rock Gardens. (BSAW)

family perspective was no doubt 8 Kemp Town Place. Here Alan James (52), an ARP ambulance driver, was killed outright and here his two daughters – Margaret Lilian (17) and baby Yvonne (11 months) – were so badly injured that they died on the day of the air attack in the nearby RSCH. The same fate befell Josephine Trissie Clancy (36), who lived at 8a.

A graphic account of the aftermath of the raid was published in the *Gazette* on 21 September:

> I have walked for hours backwards and forwards through streets of shattered homes in Brighton. I am appalled by the loss of life, shocked at the utter destruction caused by the wanton bombing last Saturday afternoon when a solitary Nazi raider loosed 20 bombs on streets lined with proud little homes of working-class folk. This is the saddest story I have ever had to write.
>
> People, some of them children, sitting in the sixpenny seats of a Brighton cinema on Saturday afternoon, were the victims of the lone German raider who dropped bombs on the town, one of which scored a direct hit on the cinema. The bomb crashed on the roof and debris fell among the stalls.
>
> Many houses and shops were wrecked or badly damaged during the raid. It was a hit-and-run bombing attack on a civilian population. The other bombs wrecked houses, damaged churches and chapels, smashed public-houses, while windows were blown out over a wide area.
>
> The bombs fell far short of any possible military objective. The victims were mostly working-class families living in the most thickly populated area of the town.
>
> I feel sure the death roll would have been heavier still, but for the fact that many people had gone to another district to do their weekly shopping. Four air raid wardens and two ARP messengers, one a doctor's son, were among those killed.
>
> Some of the bombs fell within a stone's throw of a hospital.

There were lucky escapes and equally unlucky injuries and deaths. In one house a girl was found trapped on her back under a door which had saved her from being crushed to death. Through a gap in the wreckage, rescue workers passed her a steel helmet and a glass of water and an hour later released her unhurt. Two budgerigars survived in a house where a young couple was killed. A girl riding her bicycle along a street and a boy at a street corner were killed. A blind and paralysed woman was rescued from one of the damaged houses by ambulance men – she was unhurt. Two bombs fell close to the Roman Catholic church of St John the Baptist; four of the stained glass windows and windows of the adjoining presbytery were smashed. On Sunday morning, Mass was said for those who were killed in the vicinity.

The reporter joined the public in their heartfelt appreciation of the rescue services:

> People in the bombed area were warm in their praise for the work done by the ARP and casualty services. Within a few minutes of the explosions rescue work was in progress, and people were dug from the wreckage of their homes.
>
> A rescue party, hearing a woman's cries for help, found her trapped but unscratched among some debris. In the wreckage of the same house two others lost their lives.
>
> I saw where a fragment of one bomb hit business premises over half a mile away. A high proportion of the injuries were from flying glass.
>
> Women made jugs of tea for the Civil Defence men and women as they tackled their work. The whole of the ARP organisation worked without a hitch, and soldiers and police helped to probe the debris for further victims.
>
> By the light of dimmed torches the rescue parties continued their work until midnight. They started afresh at dawn, and more bodies were found as they cleared away the wreckage of collapsed houses.
>
> A Church Army officer pushed a tea barrow through one bombed street and kept the ARP workers supplied with hot drinks and buns. Salvation Army lassies served tea and biscuits to the rescue workers in other parts of the district.
>
> […]
>
> The spirit of the people was one of magnificent courage. Many of the homeless found refuge for the night with friends elsewhere in the town. I was there when they went back to the wreckage of their homes in the morning to try to salvage whatever they could of their cherished possessions. They went away with carts, lorries, barrows and even perambulators piled high with what they had been able to save from the debris. Some had lost mothers and fathers, sisters and brothers, as well as their homes, but they had not lost heart.

Even while the alert was still operating, the Mayor of Brighton (Councillor J. Talbot Nanson, JP) toured the affected area. Soon after the raid, the Bishop of Lewes (the Right Rev. Hugh M. Hordern) visited the stricken localities and helped the distressed people by encouraging and sympathetic words. On Sunday morning, Sir Auckland Geddes, the Regional Commissioner, toured the bombed areas of Brighton and saw for himself the wrecked cinema, the destroyed homes, streets piled with broken glass and debris and roads which had been blocked with collapsed houses.

Small flags fluttered pluckily outside many of the wrecked homes. Others less badly damaged bore chalked messages such as 'Back in ten minutes' and 'There's a good time coming'. A black doll found in the cinema was later returned to its owner, one of the injured children detained at the Royal Sussex County Hospital.

Mr Oscar Deutsch, Managing Director of Odeon Theatres Ltd., made a generous and spontaneous offer to the staff of the bombed cinema, to spend a week in the country as his guests to give them an opportunity of recovering fully from their alarming experience. A fund – the Mayor of Brighton's Air Raid Victims' Fund – was instituted at the suggestion of Councillor Guy Wallington and launched by Councillor Talbot Nanson to relieve the distress resulting from the raid. Within a week, contributions amounted to over £1,245, which included £10 10*s* from the Mayor himself. With the Mayoress (Mrs D. Scott Prime), he visited the Royal Sussex County Hospital and talked with those who were injured in the raid, telling them that they had nothing to worry about, that they must feel easy and comfortable and get fit as soon as possible. They would be given every possible help and support.

Yet just four days after this horrendous raid, on Wednesday 18 September, the enemy was back. Again it was a lone raider which unleashed death and devastation and again the affected area was to the east of the town. White Street, parallel to Upper Rock Gardens, took the full force of the attack. Of the death toll of twelve, eleven persons (including two 9-month-old babies) lived at Nos 2 and 4-6, all of which were almost completely destroyed. Damage was also sustained by a house (No. 5) in Blaker Street, behind White Street, and its elderly occupant, Julia Wickens aged 72, was killed.

Five members of one family, the Tuckers, perished at 6 White Street: Edward Ernest (55), his wife Maude Charlotte Mary (52), their son, Albert Edward (27), and, visiting from Harlesden, Middlesex, their daughter and granddaughter, Joan Constance Perry (22) and Rita Joan Perry (9 months). Another 9-month-old baby died at No. 2: Eileen Mary O'Connell lost her life under the rubble in the arms of her mother, Eileen Florence O'Connell (20). Also killed in the property was the other occupant present, Jane Maria Norris (70). Elizabeth Coatman (78) and her husband, Henry Joel Coatman, of 5 White Street both died, although in Henry's case not until 8 October in Brighton Municipal Hospital. Agnes Florence Mary Freeman (60) from No. 4 also died in hospital from injuries but in her case two days later at the RSCH.

Hard on the heels of this latest atrocity came the bombing raid on Lewes Road to the north of the town. Also hit on that Friday (20 September) were Caledonian

Devastation in White Street (1) (BHIB)

Devastation in White Street (2) (BHIB)

Damage in Caledonian Road. (BHIB)

Road and other streets in the vicinity. The death toll was seventeen, with another sixteen being treated in hospital.

A solitary German plane flew in from the sea and hovered over the densely-populated district. Two heavy calibre bombs were dropped. One scored a direct hit on a group of houses, and the other crashed through a public house, the Lewes

Road Inn. For hour after hour the rescue parties tore away at the debris for the victims. Finally they heard a faint call for help from Ernest Sully, the landlord, who appeared to be trapped between the walls of two bars. By the time he was reached, however, he had died. His wife, Rosina, was also dead. Yet the couple's pet white terrier was found, scared, but unhurt, among the wreckage.

The rescue men located the barmaid, Betty Marchant, trapped by an iron girder and wooden beams and unable to move. A military demolition squad lent valuable assistance in extricating her. For three hours the rescuers toiled unceasingly to free her, and a doctor stood by to give her injections of morphine but Betty refused everything except a sip of water, talking cheerfully to the men as they laboured among the wreckage. Once she was freed, many willing hands helped the stretcher bearers clamber down with her over the high mound of rubble and wreckage. As she was carefully placed in the waiting ambulance she was still talking. 'I am quite all right,' she assured bystanders, bravely making no mention of her injuries.

A few minutes later, a soldier volunteered to crawl down into the debris which filled the inn's cellars. As he laboriously fought his way through, he heard a faint

The remains of the Lewes Road Inn, in which two people died. A third victim subsequently died in hospital and a fourth, a passing window cleaner, was also killed. (Southern Publishing, copy owned by Peter Groves)

call for help. More rescue workers were called in and gradually, inch by inch, they burrowed through the wreckage to where they could hear the distress call. The woman, Violet Pullen, was trapped somewhere in the cellar, where she had been flung through the floor by the force of the explosion. 'I'm alright but I cannot see a thing; it is pitch dark and I cannot move,' she called out. A young curate went down into the wrecked cellar, working his way among girders and fallen timber, until he could speak to her and give her encouragement. Another hour passed and she was still trapped. 'I cannot breathe very well. I can smell gas,' she called out. Civil Defence personnel then got to work with an air compressor to feed fresh air to the trapped woman. Sadly, late that night, Violet died during the rescue operations. Aged 36, she had lived at 9 St Mary Magdalene Street. Another fatal casualty in that vicinity was a window cleaner, 56-year-old John Watson of 115 Bear Road, who was killed as he passed the inn and the bomb fell a few feet away from him.

The inn was eventually rebuilt and became the Franklin Arms. Recently taken over, it has been given back its original name, the Lewes Road Inn. Shadowy figures (the victims revisiting the premises?) have been seen by staff.

The following died at their home addresses:

GLYDE, Emily (57), at 21 Caledonian Road, wife of Horace William Granger Glyde.
HOOK, Ann Teresa (1 month), at 42 Dudley Road, daughter of Mrs Edith May Kathleen Agnes Hook.
HOOK, Edith May Kathleen Agnes (26), at 42 Dudley Road, mother of Ann Teresa Hook.
MORLEY, Arthur (62), at 22 Caledonian Road. husband of Mabel Frances Morley.
MORLEY, Mabel Frances (60), at 22 Caledonian Road, wife of Arthur Morley.
SAYERS, Eliza Lydia (88), at 17 Caledonian Road, widow.
SINDEN, Jane (87), at 17 Caledonian Road, widow.
George WELLS (65), married to Esther, at 72 Franklin Road.

The following perished at addresses other than their own:

BOYLING, Arthur George (35), husband of Alice Irene Boyling, at 159b Lewes Road, lived at 23 Hampstead Road.
DANNIGAN, Alma Madeline (26), wife of Thomas Dannigan, in St Leonard's Road, lived at 55 Southover Street.
RIDOUT, Freda Mary (25), in Upper Lewes Road, lived at 16 Bernard Road. Wife of Mr John E. Ridout.

The following died in the Municipal Hospital from their injuries:

WELLS, Sydney George (68), injured at his home address (7 Dinapore Street), died in the hospital on 23 October 1940. Husband of the late Nellie Wells.
TOOTELL, Emma (77), of 20 Shaftesbury Road, badly injured in Lewes Road. Died in the hospital on the day of the bombing, 20 September 1940.

The house adjoining the Lewes Road Inn was demolished and damage was done over a wide area to shopfronts, roofs and windows, but first-aid parties were quickly at work, helped by willing troops. The Salvation Army did valuable work for Civil Defence workers by keeping them supplied with refreshments while they toiled to free the victims. Neighbours used up their own tea rations to take cups of hot tea to helpers. The WVS, whose headquarters were at 60 Grand Parade, Brighton, became a central receiving depot for gifts of clothing, and the Salvation Army cooperated closely with them. A depot for receiving gifts of furniture and bedding was set up by a Mr S. Avery, the Superintendent of the Brighton Baths and Markets.

As regards financial help, the Mayor of Brighton's Fund did not necessarily confine itself to the 'Odeon raid', but continued to operate to meet contingencies arising from any subsequent events. Local officers of the Assistance Board met many pressing claims for relief, and cash payments were made without any delay at an office set up in the bombed area.

The dust from the attack on Lewes Road and environs had barely settled when more bombs were dropped, this time in the nearby Albion Hill area on Tuesday 24 September.

That afternoon, with no siren warning, a Junkers Ju 88 was seen circling the area. Dropping lower, it released two heavy-calibre bombs, causing serious damage among the tightly packed terraced houses of Albion Hill, Cambridge Street, Ashton Street and Dinapore Street. Nearly thirty properties were demolished or had to be pulled down not long after the attack. Some children who had been playing in the streets were injured by glass and flying fragments, a number of them seriously. Streets for a quarter of a mile around were littered with broken glass. The second bomb fell in the rear garden of a house in Dinapore Street, wrecking the backs of many houses in that street and Cambridge Street. A direct hit was sustained by houses in the latter at the junction with Albion Hill, the projectile being an oil bomb – the first ever seen in Brighton. A youth who was flung across a basement room in the chair in which he was sitting, rushed into the street and rescued an elderly woman from a house opposite which had been struck by the bomb. He then went back into his own home to rescue his 65-year-old grandmother from the debris. Many properties were covered in oil but only small fires, which were quickly brought under control, broke out.

Mercifully, the attack resulted in just two fatalities – William Henry Chubb (52) of 174 Hollingdean Terrace at his butcher's shop at 136 Albion Hill (on the corner of Ashton Street and Albion Hill), and Nellie Vincent (57) of 13 Albion Hill. The bomb which destroyed William Chubb's shop also wrecked the newsagent's run by Nellie and her husband Leonard at No. 13 opposite; she was pulled out, badly injured, from the debris after several hours' digging by rescuers but did not survive. The death toll would have been much higher but for the fact that many of the houses were empty and the womenfolk were out shopping in the town. Many, of course, returned from their shopping to find their homes in ruins and their children injured.

Fate was kind to John Osborne, the licensee of the Sir John Falstaff public house next door to the butcher's shop, who was rescued from the ruins. Rescue work in the district went on until nearly midnight by the light of dimmed torches.

While rescue work was still in progress the Bishop of Lewes (the Right Rev. Hugh M. Hordern), without a steel helmet for protection, walked through the bombed streets while debris was still falling into the roadway, and spoke encouragingly to those who had had to leave their homes, or had seen their houses wrecked. Later he walked to the casualty station and went from ward to ward,

Albion Hill, 24 September 1940, where two people died. (BHUF)

talking kindly to those children who were not so severely injured. The Mayor and Mayoress, as in the previous week, also toured the district and spoke to the residents. Temporary accommodation was arranged for the homeless families at the Congress Hall and Connaught Hall in Lewes Road.

So ended the bombing in September 1940 – the worst month in Brighton for civilian dead and the month in which London's Blitz began.

One bright note was struck in that month. In a warm and generous response to Churchill's stirring tribute to the RAF's fighter pilots, the Spitfire Fund organised by the Sussex Motor Yacht Club raised £11,250 in contributions. With this money two Spitfires were purchased through the Ministry of Aircraft Production, named respectively *Southern Belle* and *SMYC*. The aircraft came into service in 1941 to aid the ever-growing might of Britain in the air.

Two October raids

In October 1940 there were two raids locally, the 'Scarborough Road' raid and the 'Egremont Place' raid, which occurred on Monday 14th and Saturday

Scarborough Road, Preston, 14 October 1940 (BHUF)

26th respectively. In both cases, three people were killed. A fourth Egremont Place victim died several weeks later.

Houses in and around Scarborough Road, in the Preston Park area, were severely damaged. Two occupants of No. 12 – a shared residence according to the CWG civilian death records – were killed, namely Lilian Bertha Faith (54) and Annie Sophia Wood (82), widow of William Robert Wood. Lilian actually died in Kingsley Road, parallel to, and west of, Scarborough Road; Annie died at her home address. A 10-year-old neighbour, Charles Henry Siddall, of No. 14 Scarborough Road, died at his home address. Rescue workers were soon on the scene. The attack may have been part of an attack on Hove, timed at 8.10pm, when four high explosive bombs, an oil bomb and a number of incendiary bombs were dropped.

Nearly a fortnight after the Scarborough Road raid, the enemy returned. In this instance, too, no air raid warning had been sounded. The low-flying single aircraft's main handiwork on the afternoon of Saturday 26 October was the destruction of an unoccupied house in Egremont Place, the partial destruction of No. 20 next door and the death of its three occupants: Arthur Thomas Betts (76), his daughter Mary Cecilia Betts (45) and his sister-in-law Mary Louise Payne (75). Although Arthur was rescued alive from his wrecked house, he died later that day at the Royal Sussex County Hospital from his injuries. The body of

The Egremont Place bomb accounted for the deaths of four victims – three on the day of the attack and one subsequently. (BHIB)

Mary Betts, his daughter, was found when the collapsed masonry was cleared. Mary Payne had been in the back room of the ground floor and had fallen into the basement scullery when the house collapsed. Although she was taken to hospital and discharged several weeks later, she died, at 3 East Drive, on 10 December.

The plane also dropped an oil bomb on playing fields near Sutherland Road, but caused no damage other than a large crater, and another bomb in a nearby garden, breaking windows and roof slates.

Winter bombs

There were just two further attacks in 1940: one in November and one in December. Neither resulted in any deaths.

In her wartime diary, published as *Brighton's War*, schoolteacher Helen Roust (1903–81) wrote on Friday 29 November: 'Sirens for the night at 5.30pm. Bombs showered on Brighton in the East Street and North Street areas.' The brunt of the attack, carried out at around 9.30pm by an unknown number of German aircraft dropping incendiary bombs and four high explosive bombs, was borne by East Street. Severe damage was caused to Lyon & Hall's music shop on the west side of the street, with several expensive pianos being destroyed. At the junction with North Street, Hannington's department store had all the corner windows blown out, some passers-by being injured by flying glass.

One of the incendiaries crashed through the roof of the Savoy cinema and fell into a corner of the auditorium. The staff coolly put out the fire out before any serious damage could be done. The audience (other than a few seated near where the bomb fell) were equally unfazed and just carried on watching the film. Fires in a number of shops in East Street were swiftly brought under control by ARP personnel.

The rear of two of the small houses in Black Lion Lane was damaged by another of the bombs. Here an elderly resident, lying in bed, had her bed tilted by the blast, which brought down the ceiling. Firemen cut through some roof beams to reach her but apart from being covered in dust and dirt she was none the worse for her ordeal.

Elsewhere, fires broke out in Cannon Place, at the eastern end of Western Road, in Clifton Road and in Victoria Road. At the junction between North Street, West Street and Queen's Road, the clock tower suffered some damage when part of the clock face was shattered; the hands and parts of the mechanism fell onto the pavement.

Nearly two weeks later, on Wednesday 11 December, Brighton had a lucky day. The same could not be said for Newhaven. Seven enemy aircraft visited the port on their way here and the single bomb that was dropped – on 9 Folly Fields, Lewes Road – killed no fewer than five members of the Tucknott family: parents Herbert

Partial destruction of Hannington's department store at the junction of North Street and East Street, 29 November 1940. (BHIB)

John and Florence, their two daughters Hazel (18) and Doris (5) and, subsequently in the RSCH, Brighton, Herbert William, aged 16. At 8.50pm, Brighton's sirens warned of the approach of the enemy raiders. They dropped four large (500 kg) bombs on commercial and residential properties in Upper North Street, Ship Sheet and Western Road. Yet by some miracle, none exploded. A number of people sustained minor injuries and were treated on the spot by ARP first-aid teams; two were taken to hospital but were discharged after a few days. A large number of people were evacuated by the police and Wardens from the town centre area, many being temporarily housed in local church and school halls, where the WVS quickly organised light refreshments. By the following evening, all the bombs had been made safe and the people returned to their homes.

Attacks in 1941

In 1941 there were just four bombing raids by the enemy, three in the spring and one in the early summer. Two fatalities resulted from the two attacks in March and

Preston Village, 8 March 1941. (BHUF)

none from the visitation in May, but the bombs dropped in April caused a heavy loss of life, especially in Norfolk Square.

Late on the moonlit night of Sunday 9 March, an estimated eleven high-explosive bombs, soon followed by up to 300 incendiary bombs, were dropped on Preston Village and area, killing in their homes 3-year-old Bernard David Colbourne of 229 Preston Road and John Alan Warren Stone (61) of 1 Lauriston Road. Bombs also fell in North Road, Home Road and Cumberland Road.

Fred and Madge Colbourne lived above their butcher's shop with their three children, Stella, Bill and Bernard. The building took a direct hit, plunging the sleeping family through two floors and burying them in debris in the basement. Stella (17), however, was asleep in the back bedroom and managed to get to the window and call for help. Bernard – who had been sleeping in the same bed as his 5-year-old brother, Bill – could be heard by rescuers crying under the debris but died during the two hours it took for them to reach the family. Fred suffered a fractured pelvis but Madge and Bill escaped with just cuts and bruises.

After the home of John and Mary Ada Stone was hit, she was pulled from the debris badly injured but John was killed. His body was recovered an hour later.

Damage to property included the fracture of a gas main, which caused a large fire in the middle of the main Preston Road, just north of the junction with Preston

Preston Village, 8 March 1941, another view. (BHUF)

Drove and almost opposite the bowling greens. Severe damage was caused to St John's Church, with a large crack appearing in almost the whole length of the door, part of a wall being demolished, another wall being cracked and stained glass windows being shattered. Another bomb scored a hit on a grocer's shop run by Frank Kirby. On the corner of Lauriston Road the unoccupied Holes and Davigdor Dairy suffered severe damage. Luckily, many of the numerous incendiary bombs which landed, although causing small fires on some roofs, fell in gardens and in open spaces.

In the attack by a single aircraft which followed just two days later, two houses were wrecked in Dawson Terrace, a steep hill off Sutherland Road, burying Ernest and Laura Burnet-Smith at No. 5. The steepness of the hill hampered the rescuers and it was an hour-and-a-half before the couple were released. Laura was seriously injured and taken to hospital but Ernest was found to be dead.

At the opposite end of Sutherland Road, the terrace joins Freshfield Road. Here two bombs fell, one near the junction with Queen's Park Terrace, which caused serious damage and some injuries, and the other on the road itself, creating a large crater. Another bomb fell on allotments north-east of Dawson Terrace, near

Baker's Bottom. Incendiaries were also dropped and caused one small house fire but otherwise landed harmlessly on open spaces.

Just under a month later, on the bright moonlit night of Wednesday 9 April 1941, a major raid took place resulting in the deaths of twenty-five townspeople, nine of them at two addresses in Norfolk Square. Unfortunately, the event attracted publicity for all the wrong reasons.

At around midnight, a number of enemy aircraft flew in very low from the Channel, thus eluding the radar defences, and deposited some twenty high-explosive bombs across the town, causing death and destruction in George Street Gardens, Edward Street, Grosvenor Street, St George's Terrace, Hereford Street (hit the previous September) and Norfolk Square.

In narrow George Street Gardens, near St James's Street, a bomb demolished No. 14, from which Susan Harris (52) was rescued but she was so severely injured that she died later that day in hospital. In the ruins were the bodies of her daughter, Ivy (18), and that of Albert Gander (62) who lived at 8 Windsor Street. The body of Annie Peacock (61) was recovered from No. 13 next door.

In nearby Edward Street, three members of the Paine family were killed at the Shamrock Inn (No. 101), which suffered a direct hit: licensee Charles Paine (66), his wife Margaret Louise (63) and their 7-year-old grandson, Ian Robert Patterson. The next-door resident at No. 100, ARP ambulance driver Cecil Reginald Shorter (51), also lost his life.

Off Edward Street, on the north side, stood Grosvenor Street. Here Eliza Parsons (54), a cook, was killed at her home, No. 49.

Grosvenor Street, on the north side of Edward Street, 9 April 1941. (BHUF)

In St George's Terrace, located east of Upper Bedford Street in Kemp Town, Susan (64) and Minnie Stops (45) were killed at No. 11. Lucy Eade (73) was rescued from this address and taken to hospital, where she died later the same day.

A family of four was killed in long-suffering Hereford Street: Frederick and Elizabeth Young, both aged 49, and their children, Alfred (17) and Doris (15). Young Doris died of her injuries later in the RSCH, the others perished in the family home, No. 13.

Contrasting with these scattered tragedies was the concentration of fatalities in Norfolk Square, off Western Road, in the western area of Brighton. Although there were a number of lucky escapes at this location, members of two families perished in two adjacent properties divided by Norfolk Place:

At No. 9:
CASSLER, Nathan (47), the husband of Millie Cassler, and their three children died, namely Brenda (11), Edith (16) and Natalie Monica (5). Neighbours who had gathered in front of the building hoping that the children might be found alive wept openly as the bodies were recovered and removed from the ruins.

Also at this address:

CALCRAFT, Rupert Harold (51), the son of John and Alice Calcraft of 1, Railway Terrace, Disley, Cheshire, and SMITHYES, Rosalie (53), who lived at No. 9d.

At No. 8:
Three children of Arthur and Violet WALLIS, namely Robert Arthur (12), Rose Evelyn Emily (11) and Audrey Winifred (3).

Arthur Wallis was at the time recovering in hospital from an operation and mercifully his wife, Violet, and another child of theirs, 6-year-old Jean, survived, but only after a dreadful ordeal. It was some 2½ days after the raid that a policeman reported hearing a faint cry – 'Save my baby, save my baby!' – coming from beneath the mountain of debris. It took rescuers two hours to reach mother and daughter. Little Audrey, who had been killed instantly, was clasped in her mother's arms. The bodies of the other two children were recovered not long afterwards.

The townspeople were outraged that rescue work had, evidently, been concluded early and there were angry letters to the local press, (with one serviceman writing: 'Well, Brighton, it is up to you to wipe the slur from your name.'). In parliament on 24 April, Brighton MP Sir Cooper Rawson asked Herbert Morrison, the Home Secretary, under what authority the Regional

Damage to Nos 8 and 9 Norfolk Square, with Norfolk Place in-between, 9 April 1941. (BHIB)

Commissioner had postponed from day to day, for a total period of fifty-six hours, the rescue work of women and children imprisoned under air raid debris in spite of protests from Wardens (two resigned) and hundreds of people being willing to carry on the work. Morrison replied that no such instructions had been issued by the commissioner. He understood that in view of the extreme improbability of any living persons remaining under the wreckage and of the imminent danger of collapse of the surrounding buildings, the rescue parties had been withdrawn on two nights. The decision whether to suspend or continue operations in such circumstances was always a difficult one and had to rest with the officers of the local authority concerned. There was not enough evidence before him, he said, to make a prima facie case against the judgment of local officers. The responsibility really was theirs and not his. It was, he pointed out, the case all over the country that repeatedly rescue parties worked on all through the night in order to get something cleared away, but there were circumstances in this case in which officers of the local authority on the spot took the view that there were no live persons left – that turned out to be wrong, but that was their view – and that there was an imminent danger of a crashing of the wall which would have killed the rescue party. They may have been right or wrong about it, he stated, but that was their judgment on the merits of the case at the time.

In Brighton, the Council was in turmoil, with accusations as to who the blame lay with flying back and forth. It later issued a press statement stating that a resolution had been passed, by a majority of forty-four to four, 'that, having considered the incident, members of the Council desire to express their most sincere sympathy with those who suffered on that occasion and desire further to express their fullest confidence in the [ARP] controller, the borough engineer and the members of the emergency committee and air raid precautions committee.' It went on to say that the Council were satisfied that the account of the matter given in a letter from the Master Builders' Association fairly and correctly represented what had taken place.

A little over five weeks after the devastating raid of 9 April came the last attack of 1941 by enemy aircraft. A trio of Me 109s crossed the coast near the Hove border at around 8pm. Flying low at around 250ft, they each released their 250kg bomb before people could seek any sort of shelter, although the sirens had sounded (too late) at 8.06pm. Nobody was killed, but nine people suffered slight injuries and fifty-five houses were damaged.

The first bomb fell in Hollingdean Road, in the north-east corner of the Corporation yard, where it struck a pile of steel girders. After ricocheting off them, it exploded near the dust destructor, throwing up fragments of metal for distances up to 300ft. The railway viaduct over London Road was hit by the second bomb, which landed on earth banking alongside its south parapet wall and destroyed a 42ft-length of the parapet and 40ft of retaining wall below the tracks. The railway suffered again from the third – and most destructive – bomb, which struck signals and the telegraph section of the Railway Engineers' Department close to the eastern platform at Brighton Station. The entire west wall, with a frontage of 72ft, was blown out and a small factory was destroyed. Two of the main railway lines were blocked by debris and the nearby signal box was damaged by fire.

John Holden of Rottingdean was living at 120 Richmond Road and was 4½ years old at the time. He was in Pope's Folly, the small road in Hollingdean behind Hollingdean Road. At the end of Pope's Folly there used to be a dump of old cars near the low railway bridge. John and his sister, Iris, and another friend were playing in the area and went up the railway embankment nearby. A German raider came into view flying very low – John could almost see the pilot. A bomb was dropped and two pieces of shrapnel headed straight for John's head but, just in time, his sister pushed him down to the ground, tearing his new coat. The children ran along the road, crossed over it and were taken in by a family. The children's mother, Edith, was at home, where her parents also lived, and was going to go and look for the children but, with glass flying everywhere, her father stopped her at the front door until the all-clear sounded.

Not content with bombing the town, the three aircraft started to machine gun it before departing across the Channel.

The sole casualty of the raid was a woman taken to hospital suffering from severe shock.

Summer, 1942

Brighton was now to enjoy a respite of over ten months from enemy bombs – and even then the first three attacks in the summer of 1942 did not result in any fatalities. October, however, would see the return of death and destruction on a significant scale.

At 3.35am on the moonlit night of 1/2 June 1942, an unidentified German bomber crossed the south coast at Bognor Regis at an estimated height of around 6,000ft. It was heading towards Lewes but suddenly turned southwards, flying as far as Rottingdean. There it turned again, this time westwards. When north of Brighton, it dropped a cluster of four 250kg bombs, three of which fell close

Marine Gate in 1938, still partly under construction. (Chris Horlock collection)

to each other north-west of Moulsecoomb Place. The fourth landed equally harmlessly on downland 90ft away.

Towards the end of that month, an attack took place in the Black Rock area of East Brighton which caused damage – and one death – in the large, relatively new, apartment complex called Marine Gate. Eight storeys high and comprising 105 flats, the block was built to a design by Maurice Bloom between 1937 and l939. The enemy may have surmised initially that the substantial structure was a military installation of some sort, but it was doubtless a casualty due to its close proximity to the gas holders. It was at around 9.45pm on Saturday 27 June 1942 that two Messerschmitt 109s flew in low from across the Channel, firing their cannons both at the flats and at the nearby gasometers. Within the works some damage was sustained by a storehouse and a couple of workshops. Luckily there were no injuries among the residents of the block, despite windows being broken and the frontage of the building being hit by over a hundred cannon shells. Some minor damage was suffered among properties in nearby Rifle Butt Road. The windows there and at the flats were all repaired the following day.

The Marine Gate flats, August 1942. (BHUF)

The Mawby triplets. (Topfoto)

Dubbed 'the most bombed building in Brighton', Marine Gate would be targeted on two further occasions, once in that summer of 1942 (29 August) and once in 1943 (25 May).

Sadly the August 1942 attack resulted in one poignant fatality, that of 20-year-old former child actress Claudette Gabriel Mawby, who had recently moved into Flat B7. Her body was found at the bottom of the lift shaft after a bomb exploded there. It was believed that she had been blown through the metal casing of the lift door. The porter, 20-year-old John Shanahan, was injured.

> Claudette Mawby was one of three delightful blonde sisters marketed by Hollywood as 'The Mawby Triplets'. In fact, Claudette and Claudine were twins and (Sylvia) Angella was just under a year older. The girls starred in several films in Hollywood and in England during the 1920s and 1930s. Occasionally they performed roles apart from one another, as when Angella appeared in the 1930 John Barrymore film *The Man from Blankley's*. In addition to performing in a number of British films following their return to England in 1932, they

performed on the British stage in several plays from 1936 until the outbreak of the war, which effectively ended their career as performers. Interviewed in 1995, Claudine, who in 1941 married a fighter pilot, William Walker, said 'I used to regret bitterly that we came back because, almost certainly, had we stayed out there [in America], Claudette would still be alive now.'

The sisters were remembered by Pamela Sydney Wilson in her autobiographical *Home was a Grand Hotel*:

> During the 'phoney war', before the very real war began, even more unusual and interesting people continued to visit the hotel (and probably more so because it was no longer so easy to go abroad for holidays). About this time I became friendly with the three Mawby sisters – triplets who came regularly to dances and Sunday lunches with their parents. I also went to have tea with them several times and we became quite friendly. They were all strikingly attractive blondes – about my age, and always wore exactly the same outfits in three different pastel shades.
>
> [...]
>
> The Mawbys were nice girls but very shy. Their mother was a pushy woman who not only kept a very strict eye on them, but also let it be known that they had all recently returned from Hollywood, where they had been in several films [...] They would always be sitting with their parents looking rather bored!
>
> At the time they were living in one of the six or so large houses at the far west end of Hove near the lagoon [10 Western Esplanade]. Each house had its own private beach and the girls' rooms had balconies overlooking the shingle – lovely in the summer. However, they found them a bit scary in the winter when there were south-westerly gales blowing into their rooms, especially when the heavy seas caused pebbles to be thrown up high enough to crash against the glass.

It was not until many years later that Pamela learned of the tragic death of Claudette via the building firm of F.T. Wilson and Sons with which her family had links. Jack Walters, the foreman, had had to help the emergency services to remove the body of Claudette, 'who had been standing near the lift door with her mother and her two sisters, waiting for the lift to come, and the bomb blast had sent her crashing down the lift shaft while leaving the others behind unharmed.'

October's grim toll

The enemy left Brighton in relative peace until 12 October 1942, but when the attack came it cruelly claimed nine lives. Thirty-three people were seriously injured and another sixty-seven sustained slight injuries. Over 251 houses were damaged.

It was shortly before 12.30pm that four Focke-Wulf 190A4s flew in from across the Channel at a height of about 150 feet, each carrying a 500kg bomb. Although the air raid sirens sounded the alarm at 12.27 pm, the bombs had already started to fall, from a height of approximately 200 feet, with machine gun and cannon fire raking the busy town centre area.

The first bomb scored a direct hit on Buckingham Close, a three-storey block of flats, near the Seven Dials. It was located on the south corner of the junction of Buckingham Place and Bath Street. Six of the flats were reduced to rubble, which buried a number of the occupants. An elderly couple, Mercy Florence Shepherd (72) and Francis Joseph Shepherd (70) from Flat 24 were killed, as was Lydia Boardman Shuker Townend (76) from Flat 26, who died later that day at

Buckingham Close, 12 October 1942. (BHUF)

the RSCH. The rear of the block, which was completely demolished, backed onto Compton Avenue, where two people – William Ford (37) and Maria Williamson (73) – lost their lives in their home, No. 31A. The blast damage even extended to a number of residences in the Hove area of Seven Dials.

Writing to her son, Douglas, on 28 October, Bessie Cuthbertson of Woodingdean reported:

> There have been several nasty 'incidents' lately. The other morning, Dick [another son] was just going out of the school gate and he looked up and saw two bombs falling then four more. The guns roared but before the sirens screamed, the planes were halfway back to France. Dick said he just stood paralysed – fortunately, the nearest to him fell at Seven Dials. He said he'd never seen so much blood and glass. Everyone in the street seemed to be cut – glass everywhere.

Howard Place links Buckingham Place and Chatham Place and the properties in it face the wall at the top of the chalk cliff towering over the railway lines just outside Brighton Station. It was in the 20-foot wide roadway of that street that the second bomb fell, at a point 250 feet from the junction with Buckingham Place. Cutting a wide groove in the road, it detonated on the wall, a thirty foot length of which was hurled onto the tracks below. Five locomotives, six coaches and six wagons were damaged.

Concerning gunfire damage to the rolling stock, noted railway photographer R.C. Riley (1921-2006), who was stationed at Brighton during the war, contributed this memory to the book *Rail Centres – BRIGHTON*, published in 1981:

> Class S15 4-6-0 No. 836 was on the turntable at the time and got two or three cannon shells in the boiler side ahead of the firebox. It was hastily removed from the turntable and the fire thrown out. Four other engines suffered superficial damage from machine gun bullets, including the firepump engine No. 2255, which was specially cared for by one of the women cleaners at the shed. These engines were patched up on shed, but No. 836 went into the works, where it was repaired and returned to traffic within a fortnight.

Slight damage was caused to the rear of 15 houses in Buckingham Place, while seven casualties were treated for slight cuts but did not require hospital treatment.

However, this bomb did cause a tragic death in the nearby area. St Anne's Home for Invalid and Crippled Children, at 49 Buckingham Place, opposite All Saints Church, was overseen by a Catholic order of nuns founded in 1872, the Poor

Servants of the Mother of God. There were forty-one children accommodated in the home at that time, evacuees from Streatham whose children's home had been hit during the raids on London. Twenty-one of them were playing in the garden of the Brighton home when the bomb struck, instantly killing two-year-old Anthony Leadbeater, described as 'a lovely little boy' by seventeen-year-old Maureen Cunningham, who was in the garden looking after the children. In fact, several of the women who looked after the children suffered serious injuries. Many of the other youngsters were injured, five seriously, including Vivian Mayling and Marcia Hoyzer, as were those inside (two needed hospital treatment). Unaffected children were rapidly transferred to a local convent. Another nineteen in the neighbourhood were also hurt.

The building itself was considerably damaged. Inside, debris, broken glass and ruined furniture was everywhere, although a statue of the Virgin Mary stood undamaged in one of the dormitories.

Local historian Peter Groves has provided interesting information concerning the subsequent history of the Home:

Following the war, in 1948 the children's home moved to Lansdowne Road [...] Many years were to pass before a most unlikely 'Good Samaritan'

St Anne's Home for Invalid and Crippled Children, 12 October 1942. (BSAW)

purchased the property. It was in 1994 that eccentric Brighton WBO boxer, Chris Eubank, purchased St Anne's House, which he called Buckingham Palace. He knocked down the interior whilst keeping the grade II listed façade intact, and built 69 flats. The building was leased to the charity Sanctuary Housing Association with the lowest rents in the country. While he was widely applauded for his philanthropic action in 1994, some years later he was harshly criticised when he sold the building to a property investment company.

All Saints Church near the Seven Dials was seriously affected by the blast. Shrapnel hit its roof and the bomb blast blew out three beautiful stained-glass windows. The damage to the building, which had been in decline before the war, accelerated its demise. The church was finally demolished and in 1957 the low-rise block of flats Buckingham Lodge was constructed on the site. The old flint wall which once surrounded the church is still in place, but now surrounds the flats.

The third bomb caused the death of an elderly woman, a great number of injuries and serious damage to property. It fell in Elder Place, just west of London Road and parallel with it, made up of closely-built, terraced two-storey houses. It struck a rear garden wall, demolishing a brick-built (mercifully unoccupied) surface shelter and four houses. Seventy-year-old Florence Augusta Shorrocks was rescued from her home, No. 16, but was badly injured and died in the Municipal Hospital eleven days later. Many houses in the street sustained heavy damage and were rendered uninhabitable. Dozens of others suffered damage to their windows, roofs and ceilings. A great many residents were evacuated and sheltered at the Salvation Army's Congress Hall in Park Crescent. The interior of a local school was wrecked and its roof was damaged. Luckily the last of the young pupils had left the premises before the attack began. Two teachers were injured, however, albeit not seriously. In London Road at least ten shop premises had their windows broken and roofs damaged. The church, which can be seen in the background of a photo of bomb damage in Elder Place, has been traditionally described as St Bartholomew's but was in fact St Saviour's Mission, demolished in the early 1990s and replaced by a small block of flats.

The fourth bomb to land that day hit 64-67 Rose Hill Terrace on the east side of London Road, near Preston Circus. It fell just east of the junction with Kingsbury Road and destroyed all the houses, causing severe damage to two others opposite. Edith Orme at 63 Rose Hill Terrace was killed and seventeen people – all of whom needed hospital treatment – were seriously injured (six men, ten women

Elder Place, 12 October 1942. (BHUF)

and a child). The figures for those classed as slightly injured were thirty-seven (twelve men, twenty-one women and four children). However, many rescues were effected and there were a number of lucky escapes.

A reporter for the *Brighton & Hove Gazette* toured the area and wrote:

> Owing to the widespread character of the damage, considerable strain was imposed on the resources of the civil defence and the police. The challenge was well met and great efforts were made to deal with the wounded. Soldiers were brought in to help remove the debris in a search for elderly victims.

Over fifty houses and other properties were either demolished or severely damaged in this raid. Hundreds of others sustained damage of some sort. It would in some cases be almost three years before they were repaired, while others were pulled down and left as open spaces for many more years.

The last victim of the raid on 12 October – killed by cannon fire and not by a bomb – was 55-year-old John Dudeney of 6 New Cottages, Ovingdean. Members of the Royal Observer Corps on Rottingdean's miniature golf course had heard

Rose Hill Terrace, 12 October 1942. (BHIB)

Brighton being attacked and saw the German planes heading straight for them. The pilots, however, were distracted by people in the nearby grounds of St Dunstan's, the home for blind ex-servicemen at Ovingdean and strafed them with cannon and machine gun fire from an altitude of not much more than 100 feet. Having dispatched the harmless farm worker (the shell may have ricocheted off a plough) as he loaded sugar beet tops in a field adjacent to Greenways, the road leading inland to the village from the coast, the raiders fled for France at wave top height, immune from coastal defence fire.

Raid on Rottingdean

The last incident of note in 1942 involving attacking aircraft was the assault on Rottingdean carried out on Friday 18 December, in rainy, misty weather.

A Dornier Do 217 bomber flying in low from a south-easterly direction was sighted prior to the launch of its raid at 11.52am. Sirens and pips were sounded and local defence guns opened fire. Don Williams, then a schoolboy living in Saltdean, remembers the event vividly:

At the Rottingdean village school it was my job to open up the shelters under the playground and switch on the lights when the sound of the 'pips' (the warning that air raid sirens would soon begin) came over the loudspeaker. After hurrying all the pupils to safety, I was on the steps with the headmaster, Mr Dutton, when the bomber flew over Rottingdean. We saw the bombs leaving the plane and he virtually threw me down the steps.

Mum, who worked at W.R. Dean's butcher shop on the High Street, had just gone into Filkins' dairy near the crossroads and as the bombs fell she flattened herself to the floor. If she hadn't gone in just then, there was a strong chance she could have been killed.

The first of the four 500kg bombs it dropped landed directly on the roof of the six-storey high St Margaret's flats at the southern end of the high street. It hit the roof and exploded in the water tank, ending up down the lift shaft (bits of the tank were later found far up the High Street). The parapet on the top of the building was rendered unsafe. Relatively superficial damage was sustained by shops and other businesses on the ground floor in the main High Street, with some losing their ceilings and others losing their windows.

Thankfully, most of the residents were out at the time, although some injuries were inflicted, with two women being taken to the RSCH and other occupants, including two children, being treated by the ARP First Aid Party at the scene.

At nearby St Aubyns School in the High Street, Headmaster Arthur Lang recorded that the school was 'wearing the scars of war, with every window on the east and south sides of the main school building boarded up'. The roof of the Gymnasium was practically 'taken off', Mr Webber's classroom and the one next to it were wrecked, and the window of the (Art) Studio blown in. The windows of the Cottage were broken and some in Beacon View, while ceilings had come down in both buildings. The Cricket Pavilion doors and windows had been blasted in and there was a gap in the 'blackened and uprooted' hedge opposite the vicarage, halfway up Steyning Road (an allusion to the effect of the second bomb). The school was hit by large pieces of concrete from the flats (the roof of Finch dormitory was holed, the concrete landing on a bed) and the flagstaff from the top of the flats was found on the roof of the school; its heavy metal fitting, weighing 20 pounds, passed through both the window of the room behind the Headmaster's drawing-room and the interior wall, ending up in the passage outside. Further damage was noted in his record.

Left: *Wrecked stairway, St Margaret's flats, Rottingdean, 18 December 1942.* (BSAW)

Below: *Safety demolition work on part of St Margaret's flats, Rottingdean.* (Chris Horlock collection)

The façade of the wing on the south side frontage was destroyed but later restored.

More importantly, there was a fatality in the vicinity: War Reserve Policeman Harold Stone, who had been a policeman in London but had transferred to the Brighton Force after the London Blitz, had recently moved down to neighbouring Saltdean. When the bomb fell, he was on point duty at the High Street/coast road crossroads and trying to get people to safety and clear the street. Struck by pieces of flying debris and taking the full impact of the blast, he was seriously injured. Despite being rushed to hospital, he died later that day. His funeral took place at Brighton Crematorium on Wednesday 23 December 1942; among those present was the Mayor of Brighton, Councillor Bernard Dutton Briant. Harold left a wife and two children, a son and daughter.

War Reserve Policeman Harold Stone, killed while on point duty at Rottingdean crossroads, 18 December 1942. (Author)

Lang recorded that the other bombs all fell on the Outer Field of the school and richocheted from there, one passing through the goal post and demolishing the vicarage in Steyning Road, from which the vicar, William O. White and his wife, Florence, were absent at the time. They were shopping in Brighton town centre when news of the bombing reached them. The maid, Grace Newman, was in the building but was soon rescued from the debris. The vicar's pet dog, a Sealyham terrier named Robert, was eventually brought out from beneath a heavy beam and went on to make a full recovery.

The third and fourth bombs also fell on the Outer Field. One ricocheted over one of the houses in Steyning Road and into a nearby garden where, fortunately, it failed to explode and was duly dealt with by a Bomb Disposal Squad. The other, after hitting the ground three times, demolished the garden wall of Tudor Close, all the greenhouses and some of the annexe. The local gardener suffered cuts to his head and face caused by flying glass from a shattered greenhouse.

Three people were seriously injured in this raid, one being a Mrs Adams, former housekeeper to Robert C.V. Lang (Headmaster from 1919 to 1940 and

Rottingdean vicarage, Steyning Road, Rottingdean, 18 December 1942. (BHUF)

brother of Arthur Lang) at Corner House in Steyning Road for nearly twenty years. The property had all its windows broken and every ceiling brought down in the explosion.

Its attack over, the Dornier flew over Ovingdean and Kemp Town where it opened fire with its machine guns. Mercifully, there were no reports of injuries or serious damage in those areas. Later that day, the wreckage of a Dornier Do 217 – possibly the machine hit by a pursuing New Zealand fighter pilot – was found in the sea and there was a report by German sources that a Dornier Do 217 from II/KG40 [Fighter Squadron 40] had failed to return from a sortie over south-east England on 18 December.

CHAPTER 4

Life Goes On
July 1940 – December 1942

Duel over Brighton

Aircraft-related incidents in the second half of 1940 included a duel over Brighton and a crash landing on farmland north of the eastern suburb of Saltdean. In its account of the former incident, which took place on 18 September, the *Gazette* graphically described the battle between a Spitfire and a German bomber, which was forced to ditch in the sea following damage received. 'The scrap lasted for only a minute or so', reported the paper, 'but it was a great fight, and people who had not taken shelter were thrilled by the way the little Spitfire tackled the huge

The Harvey's Cross crash plane on fundraising display (6d per view) in the car showrooms of Messrs Rootes' in Maidstone, 1940. (Author)

Nazi bomber, and there were cheers as smoke was seen coming from the Dornier's tail.' Research has revealed that the machine was in fact a Junkers Ju 88. In the second incident, which took place on 25 October 1940, an ME 109 crashed on land near Harvey's Cross. The 19-year-old Austrian pilot, Karl Raisinger, escaped unscathed. His machine, virtually intact, was later transported to Maidstone, where it was put on display, with all proceeds from viewing it being assigned to the *Kentish Gazette*'s campaign to fund the purchase of a Spitfire.

ARP/Civil Defence Services

The ARP added a string to its bow at the end of June 1940 with the creation of a new unit, the Demolition Squad. Members of Civil Defence forces reporting for duty at the sound of the air raid siren would, at the next sounding, be accompanied by the new squad whose purpose was not to demolish but to rescue people from buildings which had been demolished by bombs and other means. It had come into existence with the authority of the Corporation. The squad met at Patcham Place and was equipped with demolition necessities, first-aid kit and lorries.

After a year of war, Brighton's ARP/Civil Defence Services were described by Councillor Bernard Dutton Briant, Chairman of Brighton Emergency Committee, as 'second to none in the country'. Looking back, he told the *Gazette*:

> 12 months ago we were all putting up sandbag protections and digging trenches. Everybody was helping their neighbours and showing a fine spirit of unity. Today, and this is the important point, that spirit is even more intensified. This has been proved by the way in which people have gone to the assistance of their neighbours immediately help has been needed. The unity between the public and the Civil Defence Services is most gratifying, and makes the work so much easier for everyone.

He went on to pay glowing tribute to the personnel of the services, who had to be constantly available for duty, and although they might have been on duty for many hours at night they had to be at their ordinary job the next day. Volunteers were still welcome to be trained as reserves, although the response was poor: at the end of October, a special campaign was launched to secure an additional 300 Street Wardens, women as well as men (even though Wardens already numbered over 1,500) and 250 Shelter Wardens to look after Brighton's 142 shelters, making a total of 550. (The shelter work mainly involved seeing that people were comfortable and that there was no overcrowding. Women were particularly wanted for this work and would be posted to assist at shelters nearest to their homes.) Wardens were wanted in all districts in the borough, with the exception of Hollingdean, Moulsecoomb, Rottingdean, Ovingdean and Saltdean, which were satisfactorily staffed. Take-up was, however, poor. The *Gazette* explained why in a feature. The Forces had, of course, taken many men away, the Home Guard accounted for a number (undisclosed) of those remaining, 700 were serving in the AFS while the pressures of business and a day-to-day job in the case of many others made the prospect of additional hours decidedly unappealing. They were not keen to join the ranks of some Street Wardens who were doing three nights each week or those in some areas so poorly staffed that they were being called upon to put in as many as four. Nevertheless, this did not clear everybody: 'Those who can offer some small service should do so. Even one night a week will be acceptable.'

An additional pressure on Warden numbers resulted not only from a 'means test' applied earlier in the year but also from the compulsory dismissal of 98 paid Wardens on the instruction from the Home Office which the regional authorities were now enforcing, an instruction which had insisted back in April that Brighton

Wardens and (presumably) a civilian administrator in the shelter beneath the Bedford Garage, St James's Street. (Royal Pavilion & Museums, Brighton & Hove)

and many other towns should be allowed only two paid Wardens per post. The Council had not carried out that instruction for reasons of its own but now the regional authorities insisted that it was to be obeyed – unless the people of Brighton met the cost of £3,000 a year. The Wardens as a body threatened to strike, but fortunately this did not happen. H. B. Johnson, the Chief Warden, was gratified to record that all but four of the 98 whose services had had to be dispensed with were still serving their country, either in the Army, as full-time Wardens in London or, to their very great credit, as voluntary unpaid Wardens in Brighton.

Firewatching

The Fire Watcher scheme was introduced in January 1941 following the destruction caused by the bombing of the City of London in late December 1940. All buildings in certain areas had to have a 24-hour watch kept. In the event of fire these Fire Watchers could call on the rescue services and ensure they could access the building to deal with incidents. At Varndean Boys' School, watching was carried out diligently by senior boys. From 1941, two members of staff and four boys were on duty at the school every night, including Christmas. The staff usually slept in the office and the boys in the Hall, on chairs or even on the tops of the grand pianos. Each person stood watch for a couple of hours although it was not unknown for someone to fall asleep on duty in the Headmaster's study and forget to wake his successor (who, given the circumstances, was unlikely to complain). Duty finished at 7am and there was a mad rush to get home to wash and clean up in time for Assembly at 9.05 sharp. The school history records that

> in the early days, firewatching was voluntary but later it was paid, which made it popular. Usually groups of friends were on together which made for much humour and comradeship. How effective it all was was never tested since no bomb of any kind ever fell on the School.

It is noted that, unlike the Grammar School, Varndean was lucky enough not to have anti-aircraft guns installed in the grounds although it would seem to have been an ideal position.

The history of Brighton College remarks that it was not until January 1941 – seven months after the bombing of Brighton began – that firewatching and fire-fighting procedures were put in place on the premises.

Membership of the splendidly titled Brighton College Fire Guard, which provided night-time cover in term time and holidays, was popular with senior boys. As Tony Worth (1941–45 pupil) recalls: 'to carry a fire bucket was almost a passport to walk anywhere'. In case the college received a direct hit, a second entrance to the Front Quad was created to improve access for fire engines and ambulances. During the Easter holiday of 1941 a roadway was thus prepared across the Headmaster's garden and a gateway knocked through the front wall.

Shelter shortcomings

Shelters – an important area of responsibility of the ARP – were occasionally a source of controversy and dissatisfaction, both as regards their provision and their condition.

Following an address by Professor J. B. S. Haldane at a meeting of the Brighton ARP Coordinating Committee on 6 October 1940 at the Labour Hall on the subject of air raid shelters, a resolution was unanimously adopted declaring that in the light of recent events the measures taken for the protection of the people were inadequate and that a representative deputation should be sent to the Regional Commissioner. A month later, the following resolution was carried unanimously by the General Council of the Brighton and Hove Trades Council and Labour Party:

> This delegate meeting, representing 42 working-class organisations, demands that an adequate number of public air raid shelters be built forthwith throughout the town, particularly in the more densely populated districts. Further, that this resolution be forwarded to the ARP Controller and to the Government.

In mid-December 1940, the *Gazette*'s editorial, 'A Brighton and Hove Notebook', commented:

> Now in the middle of the most ghastly war that has ever harassed humanity, we are still dithering about what is the best type to provide, still haggling over the cost and wasting money in work which in some cases is of more than doubtful utility.

There were complaints that the Kemp Town railway tunnel, potentially the finest air raid shelter in Brighton, was still out of bounds – two years after its use had been thought of (it would, however, be made available as a shelter in due course).

In early October, the *Gazette* relayed the experiences of some public shelter users. It had learned that 'some shelters are now becoming rather smelly, and

Girl pupils of Moulscoombe School head for their shelter. (Royal Pavilion & Museums, Brighton & Hove)

there are also complaints of the litter left behind by the people who make use of them'. In fairness, it made the point that it was probably never contemplated that air raid shelters would be in use hours on end – sometimes for whole nights – in places like Brighton. Had this been anticipated they would no doubt have been differently constructed and provided with different sanitary accommodation and some form of heating. Some school trenches came in for criticism on 3 December by Brighton Education Committee. Of the sites visited, two had been bad – that at Moulsecoombe [*sic*] Girls' School and the other at Whitehawk annexe. The two Moulsecoombe trenches had been wet ever since they had been built, and it was only in particularly fine weather that they were dry.

Gas mask test failure

Wardens were also responsible for the distribution of gas masks. Disappointingly, an initial test to ascertain the public's use of the equipment was something of a failure. The exercise on 7 October 1940 was an even greater failure. The loudspeaker sounded the rattles shortly before 12.30pm but the people in the

The result of the gas mask test in Brighton on 7 October 1940 was disappointing. (BHG, 12.10.40)

streets ignored them. It was evident from this drill that only a handful of people carried their respirators about with them and few people heard the rattles. Police officers and Civil Defence workers quickly had their masks on but there was a complete lack of response from the general public, until policemen tactfully reminded pedestrians that they should put their respirators on. A few did as they were advised but the majority could not do so because they were not even carrying their masks.

The Home Guard

On 20 July 1940, the *Gazette* referred to Winston Churchill's new name for the Local Defence Volunteers – the Home Guard. The piece sought to dispel some misconceptions about its members' role, commenting:

> Many [...] people seem to think that we are an indoor army, or our services are only to be called upon when the country is in difficulties. Happily, we have hundreds who do not embrace that idea, for only the other evening I visited a post nearby, and whatever misgivings I might have had about that guard turning up in full force were soon dispelled – the guard had doubled itself. That, I assure you, is no small achievement, for one has to remember that these volunteers go on duty, some from nine to midnight, some from

then to dawn, while many prefer from nine to dawn next morning, and since this is done twice and three times during the week, you will appreciate that their task is no light one.

A week later, 'V.C.' wrote, in the same paper:

This week has been one of great importance for the L.D.V., and perhaps the most conspicuous happening was the statement in the House of Commons that we should be known in future as the 'Home Guard'.

There were now, he commented, '1,300,000 [...] old warriors of the past and young warriors of the future' in the organisation nationally. Credit was given, in respect of the formation of the original Brighton Company, to First World War veteran Tom Harrington, the first adjutant appointed. Eventually the Company here became so strong that it was turned into a Battalion. Having done his task, Adjutant Harrington sought other activities and joined the Observer Corps 'somewhere in Britain'. Prior to the outbreak of the war he had been in retirement, having worked for many years in banking and had been the well-known manager of one of the local banks.

The paper noted that there had occasionally been reports of a lack of cooperation between the police, the Home Guard and the ARP and of incidents which had caused irritation. However, bearing in mind the sheer total numbers of members of the three services, such occurrences were extremely rare. A member commented:

I find the police ready to work with us and we are eager to reciprocate. Indeed, seldom a day or night passes without some tangible evidence of our cooperation. Of our contact with the ARP, I find them all excellent fellows and helpful in the extreme.

Owen Mason, who had been carpenter and Estate Foreman on the Earl of Chichester's estate at Stanmer prior to being called up for coastal protection war duties, joined the Home Guard at the time this had become compulsory. Combining service in the unit with his daytime duties was difficult, as his daughter Doris Williams (d. 2002) described in her book on his life:

In spite of the nature of his work, he was required to report to the headquarters of a party of Brighton Home Guard based in a house in Sussex Square. [...] Failure to do so could result in a month's imprisonment or a £10 fine, or both. Despite doing his best to explain the nature of his work and difficult hours

Orderly Home Guards in 1940. (East Sussex Record Office/The Keep)

worked, there was no exemption. When the pattern of tide work permitted, Owen climbed into his Home Guard uniform and travelled from his home in Hollingbury to Sussex Square ready to perform his duty. Standing in the hall at Headquarters with a stick under his arm, saluting smartly any Captain Mainwaring who passed in or out of the building. Owen, on more than one occasion nodded off, fortunately for him not observed. Court martial would surely have followed. I think he was forced to walk home sometimes when he missed the last bus. The service finished at 9.30pm or so. But what did that matter to some retired first world war old buffer. Wartime military rules had been carried out. If some poor civvie collapsed in the gutter from sheer exhaustion on the way home, what matter!

Local impressions of the force were recorded in a feature published in *The Argus* on 5 February 2016. Mrs Denise Bennett, then 87 years of age, remembered the Home Guard patrolling around Brighton:

At one stage, if the Germans had come over, they would have walked right through. We wouldn't have survived. We realised a lot of the Home Guard in the countryside only had pitchforks. A lot of them were very efficient but there were other units very similar to *Dad's Army*. Mind you, they did some very good work, too. When the bombs dropped, they helped along with everyone else. And they were very strict about carrying ID around with you. If you didn't have your ID or your gas mask with you, you got into trouble. [...] Some of them were very officious and enjoyed acting up to the role.

She remembered the Home Guard men meeting on Varndean fields in Brighton for training and also in the copse where Dorothy Stringer School is now. Other training areas in Brighton included sites in Circus Street and at Preston Circus Fire Station. The force, as it expanded, needed separate headquarters. Clerks at the Army Hall in Gloucester Road were kept busy signing up new members. Meanwhile, Brighton Station was also signing up members for the Southern Railway, needed to guard important railway installations on the line. 'I think everybody wanted to do their bit. It didn't matter what age you were.'

Alan Dart, then 79 and living in Hove, was a young boy during the war. After being bombed out of his home in London, his family moved to Brighton in 1940. He recalled the time he occasionally spent with the Home Guard as a big adventure. His father was in the Home Guard as well as serving with a detachment of the Royal Electrical and Mechanical Engineers. Alan sometimes rode in the van – painted sky blue with big chrome letters on it – which was used by a Home Guard unit at Moore's Garage in Russell Square, Brighton. 'It was quite exciting riding around in it. We were only kids but they let us hang around with them. It seems strange now, really.'

He recalled a shooting range near St Wulfran's Church in Ovingdean and how he and his friends used to sneak ammunition from it to make fireworks. He also remembers seeing early units dressed in denim outfits, equipped with only wooden rifles before getting the proper kit; 'I used to laugh but that's all they had.'

Food production

Food and the productivity of food production and farming were seldom out of the papers in 1939–42. Economy was the order of the day. Odd snacks during the day and eating more than one needed at mealtimes were decidedly unhelpful indulgences in wartime. The nation's money had to be saved and the cargo space needed for munitions had to be freed. 'Remember that this is not only a war in the air and on land and sea, but a war in the kitchen as well' (*Gazette*, 10 August 1940).

The 'Pavilion Pigs' were still on display in July 1942. (Royal Pavilion & Museums, Brighton & Hove (Herald collection))

At the end of August 1940, at the annual exhibition of the Patcham Horticultural and Allotment Holders' Society held at the Mackie Hall, Councillor Bernard Dutton Briant asked for gifts for certain poor persons in temporary distress in the town, and was extremely gratified with the result. Among the products on display were jams made with very little sugar and cakes made without any eggs and without any sugar at all. A month later, Brighton's Food Production Exhibition, showcasing the wealth of edible produce grown in the town's allotments, was opened by John Morgan MP, an authority on agriculture, who was well known for his broadcast talks. The produce was remarkable evidence of the response of Brighton's 3,000 allotment holders to the 'Dig for Victory' campaign. A luncheon preceded the opening of the exhibition, at which A.H. Thomas (Chairman of the Brighton Horticultural Committee) presided, supported by the Mayor (Councillor J. Talbot Nanson JP).

The recycling of kitchen waste to feed pigs was a scheme adopted by the Corporation in mid-December 1940. It purchased 300 of the animals for the piggeries at Warren Farm, Woodingdean, and placed 100 swill bins in various parts of Brighton to encourage the practice. At first only two sections of the town – the Whitehawk area and the district bounded by Viaduct Road, Ditchling Road and Stanford Avenue – were tried out as an experiment for such collection. Posters and handbills featuring 'Percival the Porker' were circulated to remind housewives of the scheme. Councillor H.B. Hartnell (Chairman of the Brighton sub-committee dealing with agricultural matters) made a special appeal to Brighton shops wishing to dispose of food scraps. Bellman's store in London Road got the ball rolling by promising all its waste food and vegetables.

In another scheme, the Corporation arranged, in mid-September 1940, to bring under cultivation 1,000 acres of downland, much of it previously covered in gorse. To make the ground suitable after being covered for countless years with grass and gorse, a gyro-tiller was used. Further cultivation of such areas to assist the great national effort was planned as a follow-up measure (by the end of November, a total of 1,250 acres had been ploughed). Shortly afterwards, when the Report of the Sites and Works Sub-committee was submitted to the Education Committee, reference was made to the decision to plough up, as a first instalment, 21 acres of the Varndean playing fields and to a proposal to have seven acres of wheat and 14 acres of potatoes grown on the land.

Members of Brighton Corporation and the East Sussex War Agricultural Executive Committee view the downland cultivation work carried out and the gyro-tiller. (BHG, 14.9.40)

On 13 January 1941, a visit was paid to Brighton by Earl Winterton, MP for Horsham, to share his wide agricultural knowledge and see what was being done here. Accompanied by the Mayor and relevant officials, the visitor saw no fewer than 1,500 acres of land in the Brighton area under cultivation. The tour of inspection also included some of the 5,600 allotments, 1,800 wartime plots and 200 smallholdings, a number of which stocked cows, pigs and goats. At Saltdean, where there were 400 acres under the plough, he noted that nearly every little strip of land between the properties had been tilled. One of the outstanding features of this tour was the acreage of gorse which must have been cleared. This difficult task had to be undertaken from Saltdean to Woodingdean and from just south of Coldean to Sweet Hill. Progress near Coldean had been such that the tips of the wheat could be seen coming through a stretch of land covering more than 60 acres. Winterton's tour ended at the Corporation Nurseries, where flowers were now replaced by vegetables. Lines of greenhouses housed French beans (ready for picking), while in others thousands of lettuces stood where once there had been geraniums. Commenting on Brighton's great effort, the earl expressed his admiration to the *Gazette* for the 'energy and cooperation […] applied to an important task', referring to the frequency with which he had supported in the House of Commons such a step as Brighton had taken. He concluded by saying: 'What Brighton has achieved should be known to all England!'

By early March 1941, thanks to the enterprise of the Brighton Sub-committee of the East Sussex War Agricultural Executive Committee, 560 extra acres of ploughland were growing food within the Corporation boundaries, where the farms and smallholdings covered about eight square miles.

On the labour front, senior boys from Varndean School – continuing the good work noted earlier – undertook general agricultural work elsewhere in the county (*Gazette*, 31 August). For a time, a party of them travelled every day to the outskirts of Ashdown Forest, near Horsted Keynes, where their tasks included harvesting, hoeing and fruit picking. The school history records that in 1941,

> an Agricultural Service Camp was established in a field near the church at Horsted Keynes and throughout the summer holidays parties from the School went out and lived under canvas for up to a fortnight at a time. The days were spent fruit picking on nearby farms, for a modest piece-rate payment. The administration and catering were looked after by members of the staff. The camp was a great success and was repeated again the following year. Fruit picking was popular because the harder one worked the more one earned and this bred a good deal of competition. Plums and apples were the most popular fruits because their size made picking easier; conversely,

blackcurrants were detested because of the difficulty of picking effectively although the crafty soon worked out a technique of running their hands through the bushes, stripping leaves as well as fruit. The pay-out back at Varndean in the first weeks of the Autumn Term was eagerly awaited.

In 1942, the camp was shifted to Court Meadow, Mayfield, near the village school and Brighton College joined in, thus renewing a pre-war association through the Sussex Boys' Camps. The camp was on a more substantial scale with five marquees, ten bell-tents and a caravan. Instead of fruit picking, boys went out in small parties under a senior boy to do mixed farming [...] a slight misnomer since it seemed at the time to consist largely of hoeing, with occasional haymaking. It was hard work and lacked the more obvious rewards of fruit picking. The pattern was repeated in 1943.

In 1944, the opening day of the camp coincided with the opening of the German VI 'Doodlebug' offensive, so the announcement early in August that the camp

Over 70 Varndean School pupils helping on the land near Horsted Keynes. The inset picture shows the group leaving by coach at 5pm after a day's work starting at 7am. (BHG 31.8.40)

would have to close down did not come as a surprise, although a small party did carry on through August and the early part of September, living in a hostel in Mayfield, shared with boys from the rest of Sussex.

At the end of November 1940, a Brighton woman and three men were presented by the Mayor with the Ministry of Agriculture's certificates 'for cultivating a plot of land to the best advantage and so making a valuable contribution to the Nation's effort to grow more food in time of war'. The presentations took place at York Place Hall and the recipients were Mrs R. Harris of Queen's Park Road, Mr G. Gander of Stanmer Park Road, Mr W.J. Amy of Hampden Road and Mr A.P. Newcombe of Tillstone Street.

On 25 January 1941, the Sussex Area of Federated Allotment and Horticultural Societies held their annual conference at the Royal Pavilion. One of the points made by R. Howells, the Allotments Manager for Brighton, was that without the support of the local societies, he could not have got 6,000 people digging for victory in Brighton.

At this time, a demonstration plot of land stood in the Pavilion grounds as a model and guide for would-be allotment holders to grow the most suitable crops in wartime. In its issue of 19 July 1941, the *Evening Argus* featured a picture of winter greens being planted in the flowerbeds bordering the Pavilion lawns. A photo in the 6 September issue of the *Gazette* depicted a fine crop of runner beans being picked from the 'educational allotment' in the grounds. The paper's caption reported that the plot was 'now at its best'. Round the corner, in the Old Steine, the kitchen garden in front of Brighton's Education Offices was constantly admired, especially by bus passengers who had a grandstand view from the upper deck. The caretakers responsible for the venture were a Mr and Mrs D. Crowley. The picture in the *Gazette* showed an outsize marrow growing on the sandbags. Also in the Steine (at No. 11) stood the residence of Police Surgeon Dr H.J. Pulling, whose large garden was depicted replete with vegetables in September 1941. The police themselves dug for victory: at the end of August 1941, their produce (over 350 entries) was exhibited at the Annual Show of the Brighton Borough Police Horticultural Society held at St Peter's Memorial Hall. The standard of the crops, especially root crops, significantly exceeded that attained in 1940. Captain Hutchinson revealed at the event that no less an area than seven acres of land was being tilled by various members of the Force. Pupils of Brighton, Hove and Sussex Grammar School took an active part in digging for victory, sacrificing part of their playing fields for allotments, while Arthur Moreland, of 20 College Road, who had once earned the title in London of 'the Marrow King', concentrated on growing his produce 'in the air'. His garden measured only about 5 x 10yd, yet contained as much produce as many a far larger allotment. Runner beans were to be seen growing all round the garden to a height, in places, of nearly 20ft. Mingled with the runner beans were some fine marrows – one football-sized specimen was growing up a tree.

Yet despite all these splendid efforts, the *Gazette* dated 13 December 1941 carried the headline: 'DIG FOR VICTORY CAMPAIGN A FAILURE AT BRIGHTON'. How could this be? The verdict was based on a report from the Parks Committee, which it had received from the Acting Allotments Manager, stating that a Ministry of Agriculture representative had drawn attention to the less than satisfactory results achieved from the cultivation of private gardens and open spaces, due, it was felt, to the lack of the necessary 'drive' in propaganda. This was, it declared, a matter of importance and urgency and the representative looked forward to hearing what steps the Corporation intended taking to remedy the position. In response, the Town Clerk proposed certain administrative changes involving transfers of functions between the Brighton Horticultural Committee, the Parks Committee and the Allotments Sub-committee. The *Gazette* columnist regretted the unexpected and unfortunate assessment but felt that if the complaints proved to be justified, 'energetic measures will be taken to put matters right'.

Communal feeding

As regards food distribution, mass catering played an important role. An urgent appeal was made at the end of November 1940 at a meeting held at the Royal Pavilion for more financial support to enable the Southover Street and Whitehawk canteens (which incorporated the North Moulsecoomb Kitchens) to remain open. The Mayor and a number of officials attended. It was acknowledged that rationing necessitated a curtailment of meals, but no one was refused a dinner. The difficulty was overcome by reducing the free tickets given through social workers – where previously given daily, these were now given three times a week. Much sympathy and financial help had been given by the Justices and municipal authorities. The Moulsecoomb kitchen had proved a great success and a similar one was now open at 4 Manor Close, Whitehawk. Describing the work of the canteens, Alderman Wilfred Aldrich JP mentioned that, at one of them, fifty to sixty men, mostly elderly, sat down each day to a dinner. One hundred dinners were taken away daily to be eaten at home, and on average about 100 schoolchildren had a meat and pudding dinner. 'What would happen to those people,' he asked, 'if the canteens were not carried on?' They were in fact closed, but thankfully only on a temporary basis; in early December 1941, at the same time as a mobile canteen offering a two-course meal for 7*d* made a successful visit to Whitehawk, both the

Southover Street canteen and that at North Moulsecoomb were reopened for the benefit of local old people and deserving schoolchildren. From January 1942, a further establishment carried on the good work at Whitehawk.

For the convenience of the public (rather than charity), the Council started, in April 1941, to consider a scheme of mass catering – or 'communal feeding', to use the term current at the time. Centres located in different quarters of the town were planned. At three of them, meals were to be supplied for consumption on and off the premises and at the fourth (East Moulsecoomb) for consumption off the premises only. About 1,000 people were to be catered for in this way. In the following month, the Council conducted an experiment in 'Blitz' feeding at Brighton Boys' Club. Here, 100 diners (who included the Mayor and Town Clerk) had a meal costing 7¼*d* in a test to show what could be done under 'Blitz' conditions, and on the assumption that water, gas and electricity services had broken down. All the cooking was done on coal or coke fires, and trench fires, with burning twigs and scraps of wood being used for cooking the custard which accompanied the baked gooseberry turnovers, and also for brewing the cups of tea at the end of the meal. The chief course consisted of stewed steak and carrots with potatoes and greens, all piping hot and brought varying distances up to four miles to the feeding centre in insulated containers originally used on the tricycles of the 'Stop-me-and-buy-one' ice-cream men in peacetime. The object of the exercise was to ensure that within six hours, one-third of the population of Brighton could be served with a hot meal. The *Gazette* dated 17 July 1941 reported that 'these emergency feeding centres are to be called Brighton Civic Restaurants'. The Mayor thought the meal excellent, and felt that the town was as well served and as well prepared as any other town or city in the country. Councillor A.J. Lux, Chairman of the Council's Communal Feeding Committee, recorded that 58 per cent of the lunch was the produce of Brighton, 38 per cent was the produce of Sussex, and only 4 per cent was imported from overseas.

The Committee designated the Boys' Club, St Wilfred's Hall in Elm Grove and Moulsecoomb Hall as the locations of the restaurants. Each had a maximum capacity of 300 meals, for which tickets were issued daily, and all the cooking was done in the Corn Exchange kitchens, whence the food was taken to the centres in containers.

Concurrently with these developments came an appeal from the Mayor for funding the provision of a mobile food unit for use in emergencies and designed to carry hot food to people compelled to evacuate to outlying districts. Such canteens were absolutely essential in a blitz. The cost of the first unit of what was hoped to be a fleet was £300–£400.

The Civic Restaurant in St James's Street was officially opened on 8 September 1942. The Mayor (Alderman M.W. Huggett) and the Mayoress are shown being served at the counter. (Evening Argus, 9.9.42)

Holding the menu card outside Brighton's first Civic Restaurant at the Boys' Club, Edward Street, on 23 June 1941 is the Mayor (Alderman J. Talbot Nanson), one of the diners. (BHG, 28.6.41)

The first restaurant (in the gymnasium of the Boys' Club) was opened on Monday 23 June 1941 and served 104 diners in the first hour. The other centres followed suit on subsequent Mondays. The *Gazette*'s reporter enjoyed his meal at the Club, where he paid 8*d* for two courses and 1*d* for a cup of tea. Children's dinners cost 5*d*. The restaurant at St Wilfred's, which opened a week later, was staffed by members of the WVS and the church. Here the lunch cost 9*d* but the charge for children's half-helpings was still 5*d*. The food was supplied to the centre in containers from the Dome.

All was apparently going well until strong criticism of the feeding centres was expressed at the Town Council's meeting on 25 September 1941. The Committee responsible reported that the 'British Restaurants' were being run at a loss, that Council members had said that people did not get value for money, that food was wasted, and that the restaurants were run on cheeseparing lines. It was thought that one of the reasons for the failure to make them pay was that the restaurants were not in a central position. The Council's criticism was indignantly rebutted in a letter to the *BHG* from one Elizabeth Deville of Wellington Road, who was running a canteen for workers. She thought the claim of poor value was 'ludicrous beyond words', and drew attention to the rationing system enforced on all catering establishments. Indeed, from her visits to the Corn Exchange she had the impression that the allowance per head was far too generous. In London, she had found only gratitude for what was being done to help rather than 'continual complaint and ignorant criticism'.

At a Council meeting in late November 1941, the proposal to use the Corn Exchange as a feeding centre was defeated, plus it was learned that the existing facilities (where the cost had now risen to 11*d*) were not being fully used. There did not seem to be any need for them and some felt the experiment should be ended. At least the ratepayers had not lost a penny, since central Government was subsidising the restaurants. They were indeed in the wrong positions but none were permitted in the centre of town. Also, there had been trade opposition from the very outset. It was reported in early October that in Hove, by contrast, the British Restaurant at the Town Hall had actually shown a profit of £65 on the first 4½ months' working, and the average number of diners for September had been 1,831 per week.

Shortly before Christmas 1941, the Communal Feeding Committee persuaded the Council to give the Civic/British Restaurants a fresh lease of life – despite the recent disclosure of a substantial operational loss – producing a report showing a material and progressive reduction in their shortfall and indicating proposed extensions and modifications of the business which should lead to still further improvement in the results. The Council seemed inclined to lend the scheme stronger support. The overall prospects were now as bright as they had ever been.

Defence Area

Brighton suffered a severe blow as a bathing resort when, on 3 July 1940, every beach between it and Selsey Bill was closed to the public under emergency legislation. Three days later, the *Gazette* reported, with photographs, the last-minute rush to the sea by hundreds of bathers before the total ban against civilians came into force. The Chairman of the Brighton Emergency Committee, Councillor B. Dutton Briant, hoped the public recognised that the steps taken were for their protection and that everything being done was in their own interests. Soon, however, there was a partial relaxation of the ban. On 27 July, the *Gazette* reported, with reference to Brighton and Hove, 'the restoration of their promenades and a long stretch of their beaches', adding:

> It was unfortunate that the first day of renewed enjoyment of these amenities should have been dull, cold and wet. Had it been fine there would have been a rush to indulge in bathing once more.

Although the closure of hotels remained in place, Brighton was lucky as regards the 'defence area' or 'defence zone' status imposed on the whole of Sussex and other selected counties. The relevant Order had been made in June by Sir John Anderson, Minister of Home Security, initially declaring the strip of country along the coast from the Wash to Rye, and extending about twenty miles inland, to be a defence area. On the 13th of that month, he had issued an appeal to the public to refrain from making unnecessary journeys to the zone. Any persons entering it were liable to be questioned by the police or military as to the reasons for doing so or for being there. If they were unable to produce satisfactory evidence that they were engaged in business or had similar good reasons, they were required to leave. This applied to all holidaymakers and all persons visiting for pleasure. There was relief in Brighton, which came to be included in the area, when its Emergency Committee stated, on 5 July 1940, that no order had been issued prohibiting visitors coming to the town. The Ministry of Home Security had empowered Regional Commissioners to issue instructions on certain matters but, apart from the order closing the beach, no restrictions had yet been placed on the entry of visitors into the town. No permits were therefore needed.

Sadly, the situation changed in the following spring, when the coastal area from Brighton to Littlehampton inclusive was banned to pleasure trippers with effect from

LIFE GOES ON 155

Close checks were kept on anyone wishing to enter the Defence Zone. (BHG, 7.6.41)

25 March 1941. The banned belt extended inland as far as the northern boundaries of Chanctonbury and Chailey Rural districts, and included Arundel, Burgess Hill, Ditchling Beacon, the Devil's Dyke, Chanctonbury Ring, Steyning, Hassocks, and Hurstpierpoint inland and Hove, Shoreham, Lancing, Worthing, Goring, Ferring and Rustington on the coast. The restrictions did not apply to persons ordinarily resident in the area, people wishing to enter it for business reasons, or persons either wishing to visit schoolchildren evacuated to the area or to see sick or injured relatives.

Visitors took full advantage of the opportunity of the last weekend to visit the resort before the clampdown:

> The amenities that Brighton can still offer her admirers were taken full advantage of. Cinemas and restaurants were busy, and 'regulars' at the hotels spent the week-end at their favourite residences, there being a distinct increase in business at those hotels that are still pluckily maintaining open house. Although the famous Front looked strangely forlorn in its wartime guise, with its shuttered hotel facades, empty ice cream parlours and vacant

stalls, promenaders took their usual after-dinner stroll while the town had a new attraction to offer – the opening day view of her War Weapons Week Exhibition at the Corn Exchange. (*Gazette*, 29 March 1941)

A new record was set at Easter the following month in Brighton and Hove: no visitors at all.

The first of many cases brought against persons entering, or attempting to enter, the area was heard on 7 May 1941. Ansell Jack Lewis, a London AFS man from Chingford, was ordered back to London on his arrival at Brighton Station but instead went to Hove, claiming to have caught the wrong train. From there he returned to Brighton, where he was again seen by police. He admitted 'I have been a fool to-day. I didn't know the ban was so strict.' For causing the police a lot of trouble, he was fined 20*s*. The case against him was not pressed further, due to his membership of the AFS since 1 September 1939 and his good work during the Blitz.

Fifteen cases were dealt with by Brighton Borough Bench on 17 June. A group of four had been turned back by police on the main London Road on 1 June but had returned by another way and gone to a dance. They were caught on the way back, the two men being fined £5 and £3 respectively and the two women £1 each. Summonses against eleven Londoners (not as a group) were recorded in the *Argus* dated 4 July. The defendants put forward a wide variety of pretexts for their arrival, including ignorance of the regulations, and were mainly fined 40*s* or 20*s*. A fine of 30*s* was imposed on Alfred Frederick Gadd from Horsham who tried to enter Brighton on 29 June in order to visit a 'very sick uncle', but enquiries revealed that the gentleman was actually in very good health. On the same day, a couple from the Isle of Wight were stopped at the Aquarium, having supposedly visited a relative's grave at Preston (as they did every year) but no mention of a cemetery visit was made to Superintendent Crouch, Deputy Chief Constable. They were fined 20*s* each.

In early October 1941, the ban was reviewed by the Regional Commissioner in the light of a report by Worthing Town Council's Finance Committee drawing attention to its great concern at the way it was being enforced in that borough; many cases of hardship were being reported, and public dissatisfaction was rife and accentuated by the formal manner in which replies to inquiries and requests for information, especially by relatives of residents, were dealt with by the police. A month later (on 7 November), the ban was temporarily lifted – to the relief of the overworked force and those hotels which were still open but poorly patronised. Christmas and New Year at least would be made more enjoyable. Yet journeys to Brighton were not to be made without a good reason (whatever that might be …).

At a meeting of the Brighton and Hove Entertainments Managers' Association held on 13 November 1941 at the Golden Cross (which once stood on the corner of Western Road and Marlborough Street) to discuss the staggering of closing hours and the curfew, the members expressed the opinion that they would much rather have had the curfew lifted than the ban on visitors lifted.

On the end date for the lifting of the ban (15 February 1942), a two-month extension was warmly welcomed by the townspeople and traders. However, come Wednesday 15 April 1942, Brighton, in common with the scores of other towns from the Thames to the Hamble, was again barred to visitors. This meant no more visitors for (a) holiday (b) pleasure, or (c) recreation; no more trippers or joy-riders; and no more 'new residents'. 'It was,' complained the *Herald*, 'Easter-to-November, 1941, all over again.' Easter 1942 had been quiet, but the previous Sunday had brought visitors down in their thousands, bent on the last weekend stroll on the 'prom', the last 'breath of the briny' before the axe descended. The downside was that the great influx of visitors created a noticeable shortage of food, spirits, tobacco and cigarettes, since no replenishment was allowed.

It was not long before a procession of court cases for infringements made the news. On 2 May, a determined 80-year-old visited twice on the same day! Charles Tait, from Edinburgh, got off the train at Preston Park after returning to London following his first attempt. He could not be sent home on the Saturday evening so had to be put up in the Town Hall overnight. In the following week, a group of five trying to 'break the ban' by also alighting at Preston Park would find it a costly exercise. Mrs Lucy Dorrell, accompanied by her daughter, Pamela, a section leader in the WAAF, was uncooperative when stopped at Brighton Station on 26 July. She clearly felt, as the wife of a VC Holder – Major George Thomas Dorrell of the Royal Artillery – that she possessed some special entitlement, asking Superintendent Crouch: 'What are you asking all these questions for? You are exceeding your duty. Here is my husband's address.' This did not stop mother and daughter being fined 40*s* each. A visiting Australian living in London, Norman Plunkett, said after his case in August that he thought the regulations 'a farce'.

In early August 1942, the Chairman of Brighton Bench, Mr B.N. Southall, declared

> we are getting so many cases now that the penalties will be made very much more severe […] Simply to fine these people 20 shillings seems rather playing with the wishes of the Government.

and warned that the penalty for the offences laid down by law was £100 and/or three months' imprisonment.

Curfew

The curfew dated back to early July 1940. On the 13th, the *Gazette* commented:

> BRIGHTON and Hove have surrendered still more of their peace time freedom this week. First came the 5pm curfew for beach and promenades. Next these were placed out of bounds for the whole 24 hours. Now the curfew extends over the entire district south of the great east to west traffic artery from half an hour after sunset to dawn. [...] One need not say what the effect on business generally must be. The tragedy of it is that all this has happened in the most glorious summer that has been enjoyed for twenty years when the two towns should have experienced a bumper season.

The order, introduced on 2 July, was soon modified to specify the clock time of 10pm rather than the variable (according to the season) basis of time after sunset. It was introduced to assist the entertainment houses and their patrons. It did not apply to townspeople. The Chief Constable of Brighton (Captain W.J. Hutchinson) told the *Gazette* that the modified measure – introduced on 21 July – applied to the Hippodrome, the Savoy (back entrance), Academy, Sherry's, the Odeon, and the Sports Stadium, all of which were allowed to continue their entertainments until 9.45pm so that people could get indoors in the curfew area by 10pm. The Military Commander, he said, wished to emphasise that people should hurry home after the entertainments were over, and it was also desirable that people should go to the boundary streets by the nearest possible route.

The area under curfew was the seaward side of a line formed by the A259 road, Bristol Gardens, Eastern Road, Chesham Road, St George's Road, Bristol Road, St James's Street, North Street and Western Road to the Hove boundary. It fell to the police to create an organisation for dealing with applications for permits to be out of doors in the area during the curfew period, and to local magistrates to deal with the inevitable infringements. On 31 July, for example, a Hove lady ARP Warden, Winifred Webb of Albany Villas, was stopped by Superintendent Crouch in Montpelier Road, south of Western Road, at 10.55pm. She was not on duty and had been to visit a friend. Unable to produce a permit (although she did show her National Registration Card), she was subsequently fined 5*s*.

The post-sunset/dawn curfew applying to the general public was irksome in the extreme. The *Gazette* commented on 24 August 1940:

> Nearly three weeks have elapsed since the Mayors of the two boroughs made representations on the subject and meanwhile we have reached the point at

Plenty of dances were held at the Dome in the summer of 1940. (BHG, 31.8.40)

which residents of the large and important area affected are confined to their homes at 8.30 each evening. This, be it remembered, in August when the rigours of the black-out make ventilation difficult. Even to stand on their doorsteps to get a breath of fresh air would render householders and visitors subject to the penalties of the law.

Gratifyingly, things changed on 31 August, when the curfew was modified by the Regional Commissioner to apply from the fixed – and later – time of 10.30. Hove, Worthing, Eastbourne and Hastings also benefited from the change. Entertainment venues were now able to start performances later (at 5.50pm and 8pm at the Hippodrome, and at 6.45pm at the Odeon in West Street) and other local businesses were given a boost: at the Norfolk Hotel, the weekly dance attracted something like the pre-curfew patronage. Maurice Bloom, the Managing

Director, hoped the concession would cause an extension of the season now people were allowed to get a little fresh air along the Front after dinner. The curfew now ended at 5.30am. Come December, there was a further favourable development on the 8th, when circulation in the area on the 24th to the 26th inclusive, and on the 31st, was to be allowed up until 1am. Entertainment venues and hotels were also allowed to stay open until 12.30 instead of 10 on those dates.

Two years later to the month, Brighton was faced with the least popular curfew ever – the bus curfew. The announcement in November of its planned imposition on 8 December was greeted with a storm of protest from all quarters of the twin towns, with the Regional Commissioner, Colonel F. Gordon Tucker, being urged to reconsider his decision. The rationale behind the move was the anticipated economies in rubber, petrol and fuel oil which could be achieved. Bus services after 9pm and on Sundays before 1pm were to be axed. Councillor F.G. Field pointed out at one meeting that the curfew would hit every section of the community – the workers, the entertainment industry and in fact everybody, since public transport was no longer an amenity but a necessity. Thousands of workers would never be able to get any entertainment with a 9 o'clock curfew.

In the event, the introduction of the measure was postponed until 17 December – and it was accompanied by a welcome concession on that date from the South-Eastern Regional Transport Commissioner following representations made to him by the Brighton Transport Advisory Committee, namely the later imposition (from 9pm to 9.30pm) of the evening curfew. Also, the Sunday morning curtailment of services was to be delayed until 3 January 1943.

The Army moves in

Another imposition, in terms of accommodation this time, was experienced in April 1942 in Stanmer village, north of Brighton, and, of course, in many other places at various times. Doris Williams recalls:

> I shall never forget that day in April 1942, when my father came into our cottage and informed us we were to be evacuated, with only six weeks to find new homes and jobs. Not only us, but everyone else as well, including farms in the parish where people, implements and livestock all had to move out. What an exodus for a small community, with many having lived in the village all their lives and in some cases, their parents before them. But after the initial shock, new homes and jobs were found and everyone moved elsewhere.

Stammer Park, Big House and village were already occupied by troops, English and Canadian, who were billeted in the House. Bren gun carriers and small army trucks lined the the village street. Tanks covered in camouflage netting were parked under trees in the park with Nissen huts used as workshops just about everywhere.

During 1941–42 we settled down to life with the army. Most of the villages welcomed the increase in the population into their otherwise uneventful lives. One or two were generous in inviting soldiers into their homes for social evenings. Walking up the village street on dark evenings, it was usual to hear the sound of music and singing coming from the village post office, the home of Albert and Sarah Hills. Peggy, their daughter, was playing the latest hits on the piano, with lusty voices joining in!

The park and village became an army camp, with no civilians allowed in who were not authorised to enter. Any with legitimate reasons for entry were issued with army passes examined by a sentry at the park gates before being allowed into the park. Two hundred members of the Pioneer Corps were drafted into Stanmer and billeted in Stanmer House. Half a dozen or so were given private billets in houses in Falmer. The Pioneer Corps consisted of men called up in time of war, but considered unfit for active service. The soldiers at Stanmer worked in the gardens or on other land designated for growing cabbages, corn and root crops. All this produce was sold, or possibly distributed to officers' messes.

Walking through the camp could be unsettling for civilians, especially at night. Buses from Brighton were usually crammed with soldiers returning from an evening at the pictures or sampling wartime beer in some of the numerous pubs in the town.

Doris and her family moved to Mill Street in nearby Falmer. She remembers that harvesting could be a hazardous business,

> especially when the army decided to go on manoeuvres using live ammunition on the Downs. Tanks and bren gun carriers fired shells and mortar bombs, which often landed on the corn setting it on fire and destroying half the crop. Another danger was unexploded bombs lying on the ground which were a hazard to soldiers, landgirls and civilians working on the land. Two accidents occurred at High Park and Balmer, when two tractors working in the fields were struck by shells – fortunately there were no casualties. Falmer too had its share of excitement on battle training days. The sounds of the conflict clearly heard, with the screaming of shells followed by subsequent explosions going on for most of the day.

Saving and fundraising

In January 1940, Lord Leconfield (Lord Lieutenant of Sussex from 1917 to 1949) appealed, in a letter to the *Gazette*, to the men and women of Sussex to save in every possible way and lend the money to the Government. The Chancellor of the Exchequer had, he wrote, recently described the work of the National Savings Committee as the fourth arm of the war. Six million pounds a day were being expended by the nation in its fight against Hitlerism. Without that money the Navy, Army and Air Force could not function.

The people of Brighton responded splendidly, as individuals and in savings groups, doubtless largely in response to the many posters and features in the local press urging readers to 'invest as much as you possibly can in National Savings Certificates, Defence Bonds and in the Post Office and Trustee Savings Banks'. At the Royal Pavilion on 19 February, C.D. Curtis (Hon. Assistant Commissioner for Brighton), speaking at the second of a series of three meetings in furtherance of the campaign, mentioned that there were between 400 and 500 voluntary workers connected with National Savings groups in Brighton. These, a promotional poster subsequently pointed out, could easily be formed wherever people came together for work or play. By the spring, great results were being achieved by the town. Towards the end of April, it was leading in the contest with Southend and Blackpool for the highest War Savings total. The total savings in the three seaside towns from 1 January to 27 April were approximately: Brighton, £695,142; Southend, £539,929; and Blackpool, £385,919. Brighton's total to the week ended 11 May was £1,264,418.

To keep up the momentum, Brighton Labour Party, in early June 1940, placed the whole of its organisation at the disposal of the Brighton War Savings Committee in an intensified drive to increase the volume of saving throughout the town (in the twenty areas in which it was proposed to divide the Borough) and was prepared to supply twenty members of the party to act as officials in charge of those areas who would direct the activities of the collectors. A fortnight later, the Mayor, Councillor J. Talbot Nanson, as President of the Committee, issued an earnest appeal in the *Gazette* in support of saving, part of which read as follows:

> Every man and woman must take part in this struggle and here is a way open to all. The State requires on loan the surplus earnings of the people. Collection from every householder in the town must be organised at once, and the Brighton National Savings Committee calls for the voluntary services of those who have an urge to do something tangible to assist the State.

Poster urging everyone to save in order to win the war. (BHG, 18.5.40)

An editorial in the paper a month later stressed:

> What is needed is a canvas of every street in the town with a view to the formation of groups whose members will save a weekly sixpence.

The town obviously did something right because by mid-March 1941 its savings amounted to £3.859 million. One group, Brighton Houseguards of No. 2 Division, formed a Savings Group at the end of February and collected just over £910 by the end of June. Its ultimate goal was to raise £2,500 – the cost of a naval launch. The Division was one of the largest in Brighton and covered an area from Preston Circus to Patcham in the north and from Hollingbury to Dyke Road in the west. Membership was not in any way confined to Houseguards, nor to the area covered by the Division. Already members had been enrolled from outlying districts and surrounding villages. Shortly after this splendid result was made known, it emerged that the Houseguards of Division 1 claimed to have gone one better. Their Savings Group figures amounted to over £1,500 for the 4½ months they had been collecting. The Group's aim was to save towards the purchase of as many Bren guns as possible – the cost of each gun being £50.

In a novel initiative, eight members of the Brighton and Hove War Savings Committee (and in February 1942, some boys from Brighton College, who collected £27) rode in a line along the main streets from Brighton to Hove and back on box-tricycles of the 'Stop-me-and-buy-one' type, but instead of wafers and cornets they carried books of 1s and 2s 6d. savings stamps. The picture on the front of their tricycles closely resembled Herr Schicklgruber, and the accompanying slogan read 'Buy one and stop him'. One rider had sold £1 worth of savings stamps before the convoy had even left the grounds of the Royal Pavilion.

Two local businesses, Bellman's store and Clark's Bread Company (based in Hove but with branches across the twin towns), achieved extraordinary results in 1942. Bellman's funded the purchase of a Bren gun carrier in August, having saved £1,500 in nine weeks to pay for it, and in September, after investing most of their bonus, earmarked the money for the provision of two fully-equipped ambulances. On 23 August, the ambulances were brought to the store so that the staff could see what their money was providing. The Mayor of Brighton (Alderman M.W. Huggett) attended and warmly congratulated the employees, whose continued savings support had received commendation locally and from regional and national headquarters. Clark's had, for their part, already bought a light military ambulance with their savings in late 1941. There were 200 in the

Above left: *A striking War Savings Campaign poster issued by the National Savings Committee praises a housewife who has started a Savings Group.* (*BHG*, 12.7.41)

Above right: *Another National Savings Committee poster promoting the running of a Street Savings Group.* (*BHH*, 30.5.42)

group and their summer savings drive had realised £300. Since March 1940, they had saved £3,000.

By mid-September 1941, Savings Groups in Brighton numbered 652 and the town had reached a savings total of £5.86 million since the national movement

Members of the Committee starting on their ride to Hove. (BHG, 30.8.41)

was started. By early January 1942, this figure had risen to £6.73 million, and by the latter half of November that year to £9.26 million.

On 9 May 1942, at its first meeting since February 1939, Brighton Savings Committee agreed on a complete reorganisation, with the formation of area sub-committees whose primary duty it was to look after the street groups. The meeting closed with an address by James Laver, the Treasury speaker on National Savings, who said that the street collections up and down the country were playing an enormous part in keeping up the nation's stability against debased currency and inflation. The war was now costing £84 million a week. Mercifully, the people of this country had lent their Government £4 billion for the prosecution of the conflict.

Mr A.H. Gorman, a well-known speaker on behalf of the National Savings Committee, started a campaign on 5 October 1942 with the object of establishing savings groups in every street in Brighton. The Committee's familiar cinema van would visit several vantage points in the town and the campaign was to continue until 14 November. The first fortnight was to be spent in Brighton, after which Hove would be canvassed. The report in the *Herald* added that, 'As a result of the success in Brighton of the recent "Tanks for attack" campaign, Brighton is to have ten tanks allocated to it. These the town will have the privilege of naming.'

Poster urging townspeople to spend less on themselves on things they don't need and lend more to their country. (BHH, 18.7.42)

Targeted saving

Alongside general saving to aid the war effort, lending towards specific objectives, such as initiatives to adopt a battleship (the *Kipling* and its replacement, 1941 and 1942), purchase aircraft (130 Whirlwind fighter aircraft, 1943) or support the armed forces ('Salute the Soldier', 1944) was encouraged in Brighton. Goals of this kind on a small scale (e.g. the purchase of ambulances) were achieved by businesses, most notably Bellman's, as we have already seen.

War Weapons Week poster promoting savings towards two Super-Destroyers (target later modified). (*BHG*, 8.3.41)

The Junkers Ju 88 aircraft *arrives at the Corn Exchange for the War Weapons Week Exhibition. The Mayor, Arthur Nicholls, is in attendance, flanked by two RAF airmen.* (Pen and Sword/Exclusivepix Media)

War Weapons Week in 1941, held from 29 March to 5 April (both dates inclusive), was a joint venture between Brighton and Hove, initially to purchase twenty bombers. This was subsequently changed to the 'adoption' of two large destroyers, or a million pounds.

A clever incentive to encourage passers-by to donate in the build-up to the event was the use, in Preston, of the nose cap of a Nazi bomb dropped in a recent raid on the town as a collecting box. A notice beside it read: 'Your Money Will Help to Hit Them Back.' It raised £13 4s. Approximately thirty selling centres in Brighton and Hove were opened (that at Bellman's proved to be the most successful, raising £12,208). Two special indicators, the work of the Brighton School of Art, were placed at Brighton's Clock Tower and Hove's Town Hall.

On 23 March, an exhibition was opened in the Corn Exchange as a tangible introduction to War Weapons Week and attracted over 30,000 visitors. Among the exhibits were a two-ton bomb (one of the largest dropped on the South Coast), the German flag captured from the *Altmark*, articles from the *Graf Spee*, models of British planes and various items relating to Civil Defence and the Dig For Victory campaign, and even a concrete shelter. In one display, munition girls could be seen gauging various parts needed in the manufacture of munitions. The displayed Me 109, which had been brought down locally, was sent to Weymouth for another War Weapons Week exhibition and was replaced by a Ju 88 bomber shot down at Poling, near Arundel, a short while previously. Such was the popularity of the exhibition that it remained open for a third week.

Local cinemas contributed to the occasion with a special film to be shown throughout Sussex advertising the Week and depicting Brighton in prosperity and under war conditions. The Mayor of Brighton provided the commentary. Brighton's tank parade, arranged in connection with the Week, provided an impressive sight for the public, who were allowed to inspect them at close quarters (the front cover of this book depicts two tanks on view at the south end of the Royal Pavilion grounds). A similar parade took place in Rottingdean, where the Mayors of the twin boroughs took the salute. In Saltdean, a series of entertainments during the week, including dances, a darts competition, an onion competition, and a cinema show at the Saltdean Club (at which over 250 6*d* War Savings stamps were sold) yielded approximately £8,000. Brighton schools collected nearly £4,000.

War Weapons Week had a magnificent send-off at the Dome with a fighting speech by the First Lord of the Admiralty, the Right Honourable A.V. Alexander,

A useful Nazi bomb at last! Its nose cone made an excellent collection box. (BHG, 15.3.41)

Commander A. B. Campbell (left) with the Mayor of Brighton and Councillor Humphrys at the novel Kipling fundraising campaign indicator on the Pavilion lawn. The lowest blocks represent the letters 'N' and 'G' of what will ultimately spell 'Kipling'. (BHH, 4.7.42)

who mentioned that he had 'recently recommended His Majesty with success to name a destroyer HMS *Brighton*.' The Week was an outstanding success, raising no less than £1,551,375 in investments in war securities – enough to buy three destroyers and with some money left over for the purchase of quite a number of shells and other useful smaller weapons. Sir Kingsley Wood, the Chancellor of the Exchequer, sent the following telegram to the Mayor of Brighton (Alderman Talbot Nanson) on 7 April: 'Please convey my congratulations to the people of Brighton on splendid response to War Weapons Week.' A similar telegram was received by the Mayor of Hove (Councillor A.H. Clarke).

In September 1941, plans were laid for the 1942 targeted savings. The Savings Committee announced, at their meeting on the 13th:

Brighton and Hove, already with three destroyers to their credit as a result of their joint War Weapons Week, are to contribute further to the strength of the Royal Navy in a new savings drive to be known as a Warship Week.

That Week was held from 7 to 14 February and aimed to raise £700,000 to enable the town to 'adopt' HMS *Kipling* (F 91), a K-class destroyer. (Hove planned to adopt submarine HMS *Unbeaten*). *Kipling* had been laid down on 20 October 1937, launched on 19 January 1939 and commissioned on 12 December 1939. On 11 October 1940, along with another six destroyers,

Savers needed to amass £700,000 in Warship Week if HMS Kipling *was to be 'adopted' by Brighton.* (*BHH*, 24.1.42)

she had escorted the battleship HMS *Renown* to bombard Cherbourg. On 17 December 1941, she was lightly damaged during the First Battle of Sirte, fought against the Italian Royal Navy south-east of Malta. Eleven days later, she sank the German submarine *U-75*.

The Week commenced with the official opening by the Mayor of an attractive Naval Exhibition at the Corn Exchange. In the afternoon an inaugural public meeting was held at the Dome, at which the chief speakers were Sir Patrick Hastings, KC and Mr George Hicks, MP. There followed during the Week processions and pageantry, a fair, a big naval ball at the Royal Pavilion and a variety of other entertainments and events, including a boxing gala and an auction at the Dome. A decorated trolley bus was used as a mobile selling centre on all the routes of the town and a 53ft replica of Nelson's Column – the spare time work of Brighton firemen – was erected at Preston Circus to mark the progress of the Week.

Lord Kindersley, President of the National Savings movement, stated in a goodwill message: 'I am certain that Brighton will give a complete answer to the nation's call.' And it did. The final triumphant figure was £761,791, exceeding by £61,791 the official objective of £700,000. A plaque commemorating the effort was to have had a place of honour on board HMS *Kipling*, with a similar plaque being presented to the town, but this was not to be, for sadly, three months after this wonderful achievement – on 11 May 1942 – *Kipling* was attacked by German aircraft north-west of Mersa Matruh in Egypt and sunk. Twenty-nine of her crew were killed and 221 men were rescued. (Regrettably, Hove's HMS *Unbeaten* was lost on 11 November 1942).

On the evening of 15 July 1942, Commander A. St Clair Ford, DSO RN, the commanding officer of the *Kipling*, gave the public the full story, illustrated by lantern slides, of the vessel's exploits and of her untimely end through bombing by Stukas (one destroyer took 600 survivors from the area, including those of the *Kipling*, back to Alexandria). The talk was given at the Royal Pavilion. In the morning, accompanied by the Mayor, Alderman K.W. Huggett, and the Mayoress, he had been cheered and enthusiastically welcomed by young Brighton savers at the Astoria cinema, where naval and other thrilling war films were shown. The party had then visited the central Savings Bureau at 36, Ship Street and the newly opened Savings Centre at 84, London Road, where the Commander had personally issued certificates and stamps and had a friendly, informal chat with all the helpers. He had been particularly interested in the *Kipling* exhibition at the centre, with its fascinating naval exhibits and its large, unsurpassed collection of authentic wartime photographs. The exhibition, which was free, displayed portrayals of gallant deeds, plus there were models, including a 16ft one of the aptly-named

Notice announcing a Warship Week Naval Ball to be held at the Royal Pavilion on 7 February 1942. (BHH 7.2.42)

Courageous, and smaller ones, some shown by Brighton College Nautical Club. In the windows, girls could be seen at work on machines.

Following the loss of the *Kipling*, at the end of May 1942 it was unhesitatingly resolved that the battleship had to be replaced. 'Brighton's army of Savings enthusiasts,' reported the *Herald*, 'is mobilising its full strength for a "hit back" campaign.' The town set itself the target of raising £700,000 in war savings by

Christopher Stone MC (who opened the event) with the Mayor, who is showing interest in a model plane at the Warship Week fair and entertainment at the Royal Pavilion on 10 February 1942. (BHH, 14.2.42)

the end of July for a new vessel. In an appeal letter published in the *Herald*, the Mayor, Martin W. Huggett, declared: 'If every Brightonian can save double the amount of his or her War Savings each week, the required figure will be reached.' The response was initially slow, however. When Commander A.B. Campbell of the BBC Brains Trust visited on 3 July to open the magnificent fortnight-long naval exhibition at the London Road Selling Centre and address an open-air meeting on the Pavilion Lawns, only £218,402 had been raised. The Commander, reproaching Brighton for only having 20 per cent of its population connected with savings groups, when elsewhere the percentage was as high as 60 or 80 per cent, urged the town to do better – to go all out, in fact, for the full £700,000 by the end of July. 'Give till it hurts,' urged the *Herald*, 'it will hurt Hitler most!'

The link between Brighton and the late-lamented *Kipling* was cemented on 22 October 1942 in the Council Chamber where, in the presence of robed aldermen and councillors, Admiral L.A.B. Donaldson, CB, CMG, handed to the Mayor the ship's badge. In turn, the Mayor presented to the Admiral the plaque commemorating Brighton's original raising of £760,000 for the *Kipling*'s 'adoption'.

By then, Brighton had managed to reach its second great target, raising £730,000 between June and August, mainly from small investors. Perhaps the smallest amount was 10*s* from Sheila Allen and eight other girls who organised a back-garden concert.

The ship's badge of HMS Kipling *being presented to the Mayor of Brighton (Alderman M.W. Huggett) by Admiral L.A.B. Donaldson on behalf of the Admiralty. (BHH, 24.10.42)*

There was no fanfare this time regarding the vessel selected for adoption nor, in fact, did details of the allocation of the funds saved in support of it appear in the local press, as far as has been ascertained by this author. Research has, however, revealed that the beneficiary of the campaign was HMS *Cockade* (R 34), a destroyer of the CO Class. That ship was ordered on 12 September 1942, laid down on 11 March 1943 and launched on 1 March 1944. As she was commissioned on 29 September 1945, she was regrettably too late to see service in the Second World War. She served in the post-war Royal Navy, initially sailing to the Far East and subsequently saw service in the Korean War. Paid off in 1958, she was sold for scrapping in 1964. Curiously, the shield marking the adoption of the vessel 'by the citizens of Brighton', refers to the time this took place as being 'during the war savings campaign 1943', yet in that year, as we shall see, the town's cause was 'Wings for Victory'.

The adoption causes of 1941 and 1942 doubtless overshadowed a great many smaller appeals yet, to Brighton's credit, these met with solid and consistent support. Dominant among these was 'Aid to Russia', the precursor of which was the 'Brighton Greets Yalta' event held at the Corn Exchange on 7 September 1941 whereby Brighton sent a message of goodwill to its counterpart resort in Russia, a resort as yet untouched by war. Leonard Knowles, Vice-President of the Brighton, Hove and District Trades Council, urged all present to assist their Russian brothers 'against the worst thing in the world'. Two months later, a ball at the Dome and Corn Exchange 'in aid of the Aid To Russia Fund', attracted an attendance of over a thousand dancers under the auspices of the Brighton, Hove and Preston Division of the British Red Cross. The special attractions included a pumpkin competition and a 'Hitler Darts' (puncture the Führer!) competition. The ball raised £235, which was sent to Mrs Winston Churchill for urgently needed medical and surgical supplies. On a smaller scale, three Whitehawk schoolchildren, Jean Rogers (9) and John Rogers (7) of Whitehawk Road and Jean Claxton (9) of Henley Road, had tea with the Mayor and Mayoress in the Mayor's Parlour on 3 December as a treat for having raised £5 3s through jumble sales for Mrs Churchill's Aid to Russia Fund.

On 8 December, a representative gathering of townspeople considered, on the invitation of the Mayor, how best the inhabitants could raise money for this very worthwhile cause. The Mayor of Hove declared his support for his Brighton counterpart. A committee for the cause was set up. Among the ideas put forward was the holding of an 'Aid to Russia Week', as had been done recently in several other towns, and this in fact materialised in the following January.

During that month there was intense activity associated with the cause. A packed programme was planned for Brighton and Hove's Week, extending from 17 January to 25 January. It was a period of meetings, concerts, receptions, dances, church services, organ recitals and numerous other events, including a public luncheon at popular prices and a boxing tournament (which alone raised

These young performers gave a successful 'Aid to Russia' concert at St Andrew's Hall, Moulsecoomb, on 6 May 1942 and realised £6 10s. for Mrs Churchill's fund. The concert was arranged by Hazel Peters, Vera Jeans and Leslie Stickland – all of them under 14 years of age – assisted by seven other children, including Barbara Peters (aged 6). (BHH, 9.5.42)

£500). All proceeds were sent to Mrs Churchill for medical supplies. A meeting at the Dome on the 17th, at which a collection was taken, inaugurated the Week. Here a speech was delivered by philosopher and broadcasting personality Prof. C.E.M. Joad and the Royal Pavilion Orchestra gave a recital of Russian music. On the following day, a Celebrity Concert was held at the Imperial Theatre and special collections were taken at churches of all the major denominations in Brighton and Hove. Each morning during the Week there was a special showing of Russian films at the Princes Cinema, North Street. On the Friday, a deeply moving service was held at St Bartholomew's at which the Bishop of Chichester (Dr G.K.A. Bell),

Announcement of a forthcoming Grand Celebrity Concert to be held on 18 January 1942 at the Imperial Theatre in support of the Aid to Russia Red Cross Fund. (BHH, 10.1.42)

the Bishop of Lewes (the Right Rev. H.M. Hordern) and a representative of the Russian Orthodox Church were present. That evening, a dance for the charity took place at the Regent and on the last day, 25 January, a great Anglo-Russian variety concert was held at the Theatre Royal. Many thousands of 6*d* badges were produced for supporters to wear with pride – and possibly exchange for handsome prizes in a competition.

Gratifyingly, the Week raised over £4,000. Mrs Churchill wrote to say she could 'see how splendidly everything was organised, and [I] send you my warmest congratulations'.

The Fund faded from view until May, when support for the Russian cause was reignited at an Aid to Russia demonstration held in the Dome under the auspices of the Brighton and Hove Labour Party, the Brighton, Hove and District Trades Council, and the

Announcement of two forthcoming productions at the Theatre Royal to benefit the Aid to Russia Fund, namely Valentine Katayev's comedy Squaring the Circle and the Anglo-Russian Revue of 1942. (BHH, 16.1.42)

Brighton and District Co-operative Party. Subscribers raised £170. Some days earlier, stirring Ministry of Information films of Russia's war effort were shown at the Regent Cinema.

An Anniversary Ball was held on 23 June at the Regent Dance Hall and another on 7 November at the Royal Pavilion. The latter was organised by the Russia To-Day Society and featured the RAF and Canadian Bands, with all profits allocated to the USSR Medical Fund. Speakers from the Society had lectured at the Dome on 4 October, where the Canadian Military Band had also played. A week later, another warm letter of thanks was received from Mrs Churchill, 'acknowledging a further donation of £275 to her Red Cross Aid to Russia Fund, which now totals nearly £2,135,000'. (*Herald*, 10 October.) Also in October (on the 13th), a cheque for £542 was handed over to Mr William Dobbie, MP for Rotherham, at a ball at the Regent Dance Hall for the Help to Russia Fund, an event organised by the Joint Executive Committee of the Brighton Labour Party, the Trades Council and the Co-operative Party which had helped in the summer. The money had been collected in various ways, but was mainly the result of the flag day held in Brighton some time previously. That flag day was, according to the chairman of the Joint Executive Committee, 'one of the most productive Brighton had known'.

The following is a record of the various causes not already discussed for which support was sought in Brighton during 1941 and 1942:

Air Raid relief	Queen's Nurses (including Flag Day)
ARP/Brighton Civil Defence Comforts Fund	RAF Fund
Brighton AFS	Red Cross (including Flag Day and Penny a Week Fund)
Canadian Comforts Fund	Silver Thimble Fund (for Hero's Bed at the RSCH)
Flag Day for Forces' Welfare	
Flag Day to Aid Blitz Victims	Soldiers', Sailors' and Airmen's Families Association
Hospital Pound Day Appeal	Spitfire Fund
Mayor's Air Raid Victims' Fund	St Dunstan's
Mayor's Winter Distress Fund	Tank Fund for Brighton and Hove
Mobile Food Unit	Winter Relief Fund
PoW Fund	

Salvage

Salvage is really saving in a different form and it played an important part during the war years towards the ultimate goal of victory.

There was something of a frenzy of salvage activity in Brighton in the summer of 1940. The tram lines (all twenty-two miles of them) were laboriously lifted in June to provide metal for the war effort. Many items of household waste were a valuable resource. The *Gazette* reporter visited Hove Corporation's depot in July and noted:

> Every scrap of paper, no matter if it is only the counterfoil of a cheque, a butcher's bill or a newspaper, is thrown to one side, and men with pitchforks and rakes drag it away for baling. Tins, jars, bottles, scraps of iron, steel and aluminium are picked out by the sorters.
>
> [...]
>
> Everything is sorted, stacked, and packed for despatch. All the metal is put on one side and sold direct to dealers who collect it several times a week. Apart from tins and metal and odds and ends from the dustbins, the dust wagons bring in old bicycles, motor wheels, iron bedsteads, broken prams, dilapidated toy motor-cars and tricycles. They, too, go to the scrap metal men. The paper goes on to the baling machines which keep working non-stop for 8½ hours a day.

The 'Pans into Planes' drive was a vital initiative, not only in Brighton and Hove but across both parts of Sussex. The County Headquarters of the WVS declared

Lifting Brighton's tram lines for metal salvage, an operation involving the labours of many workmen, June 1940. (BHG, 8.6.40)

it an urgent one at the end of July, adding 'we aim at assembling every scrap of aluminium still remaining in homes in the county by the end of this week.' In the ensuing months, following the introduction of the national salvage scheme compulsorily adopted by all local authorities, the Pavilion Gardens in Brighton were plundered for their metal fences and with them went two bronze cannons which had for so many years stood in the Old Steine Gardens. The guns, captured from the Russians in the Crimean War, had been cast in 1826. They were removed by a firm of local scrap merchants on behalf of the Ministry of Supply.

Eighty WVS canvassers in Brighton (and forty-three in Hove) were working in Brighton at this time, their job being to distribute the Government pamphlets on salvaging and to outline to every housewife the application of national instructions to local needs. Mrs Lancaster-Gaye was the centre leader for the Brighton WVS.

A rather original initiative for inducing residents to part with their scrap was 'Scrap Night', held on 6 September at the Dome in conjunction with the *Gazette*. The publicity poster proclaimed:

Everyone who brings a piece of scrap – anything from a safety pin to an iron bedstead – will get in at a reduced price. When you arrive you deposit your old iron, or what have you, in the foyer, and prizes will be given for the most original, most humorous and most useful (for the war effort).

Salvage was wanted regardless of the source. Furniture and household effects salvaged from property damaged in air raids, for example, were accommodated in a section of the covered car park opposite the Town Hall set aside for the purpose.

The local press then virtually fell silent on the subject of salvage until the following summer, when the focus shifted to the value of salvage of another kind – kitchen waste for feeding pigs (as described earlier in this chapter). The *Gazette* dated 26 July 1941 announced that a pig pen would be added to the allotment garden within the precincts of the Pavilion grounds.

Two days later, the Mayor of Brighton (Alderman J. Talbot Nanson) opened a salvage exhibition in the grounds which was intended to show people how their waste paper, metals, bones, rags, etc. could be converted to help the war effort. He appealed for all waste to be put on one side in heaps ready for when the collectors went round. 'Leave it to us to decide what we want and what we do not want', he said. 'It will all help to make munitions and assist in winning the war and I know the people of Brighton will do all they can to make this Sussex Salvage Week a success.'

In January 1942, paper was again a leading candidate for salvage, the target being 200 tons of waste paper in a special campaign conducted during the whole month.

Housewife power! The success of the salvage effort recognised. (BHG, 14.9.40)

Some of the children who took part in Brighton and Hove's successful salvage drive. (*BHH*, 21.2.42)

In May, we learn of women in a new role – that of 'salvage stewards'. The *Herald* of the 9th provided details:

> WARSHIP Weeks, Spitfire funds, waste paper drives, and similar spectacular efforts for the prosecution of the war, with the attendant parades and wide publicity, are the high lights [*sic*] of the stupendous amount of energy which is directed to our national aims. These great endeavours are, however, but a part – and by no means the largest part – of the work which is being carried on week in and week out by patriotic citizens who get little of the limelight.
>
> In Brighton the W.V.S. have for many months been giving the most valuable assistance to the Borough Surveyor in the Salvage Department. Under the energetic leadership of Mrs Lancaster-Gaye, these women have been acting as salvage stewards, giving advice to householders and business firms on the collection and disposal of unwanted material which is turned into vital munitions.
>
> Their unobtrusive but valuable work has now received official recognition, and they are to receive certificates of appointment which recognise them as 'salvage stewards'. A chief steward, Miss B.A. Rowsell, has been put in charge, and already some sixty women have agreed to make this task their warwork. [*sic*]

More stewards were needed. In fact, it was the aim of the WVS to have an officially appointed steward in every street of the borough.

In the following month, women were again involved in salvage work. Under a county-by-county drive by the Ministry of Works and Buildings for scrap metal, a team of nine, under a section leader, established headquarters at 13, Dyke Road, and from there they combed Brighton and Hove for vital war materials, the target of these 'locators' being 900 tons.

It was estimated at the end of July that Brighton's railings, shortly to be removed, would yield as much as 13,000 tons of very valuable iron. The *Herald* thought them ugly anyway and commented that few people would 'mourn the passing of the serried rows of mock spears'. Metals were still being sought in late October 1942, when the authorities of Brighton and Hove made a special drive for the collection of all unwanted articles of brass, bronze, copper, lead, pewter, white metal, zinc or aluminium, all of which were vital to the war effort.

Christmas was a good time for the surrender and collection of paper as salvage. All seasonal paper, urged the *Herald*, should be disposed of for recycling as soon as possible. It stated that 50 million books were estimated to be still loading the bookshelves in our homes.

The locator in the picture is Mrs Mearns. She has discovered a dump, and is estimating the weight. (BHH, 20.6.42)

Let this old but valuable salvage go with your Christmas decorations and greetings cards, and hasten the day of victory.

The response nationally during the year had already been good (due in part, no doubt, to fear of the potential fine, or indeed two-year prison sentence, imposed from 1942 on anyone guilty of throwing away paper). A total of 433,405 tons of scrap paper was salvaged – a massive increase from the 50,000 tons typically salvaged per year before the war.

*

We cannot close the chapter on the 1942 home front in Brighton without a respectful tribute to our Canadian cousins stationed in the town and in surrounding areas. Doris Williams of Falmer recalled, in her *Wartime Memories*:

Dad and Alf [a younger brother] cycled through the park [Stanmer Park] on their way to work on a day in September 1942. A day in wartime the same as any other, or so they thought. As they cycled along the road, a dreadful sight met their eyes. Lying on the grass were soldiers in a completely exhausted state; many with their uniforms covered in blood. They were survivors of the Dieppe Raid, who were among the troops sent from Stanmer, on that ill fated attack which should never have happened.

The unsuccessful raid, codenamed 'Operation Jubilee', had taken place on 19 August. In this Allied amphibious attack on the German-occupied French port, over 6,050 infantry – predominantly Canadian – supported by a regiment of tanks, were put ashore from a naval force operating under the protection of RAF fighters. Of the nearly 5,000-strong Canadian contingent, 3,367 were killed, wounded or taken prisoner – an exceptional casualty rate of 68%. Continuing, Doris wrote:

Many of the army units in the park were Canadians. These casualties were members of army units from Ontario in Canada. Alf, who was only fourteen at the time, was absolutely horrified as the bloody realities of war lay before him in those poor young Canadians stretched out on the grass. He has never forgotten the sight. Father too, was upset, but he had served in the trenches and was well acquainted with battlefields on the Somme in the First World War, and the dreadful slaughter during those battles.

Canadians, we salute you.

CHAPTER 5

More Deadly Visitations
January 1943 – February 1944

The year 1943 was a black one for Brighton. The first attack of the year, on 13 February, was relatively harmless, with a number of bombs falling on grassland close to Crescent Drive South in Woodingdean. Two ferocious raids carried out in March and May, however, rivalled the Odeon bombing of 1940 for death and destruction. In March the Municipal Clinic was bombed, resulting in many deaths, but the worst air attack occurred on 25 May, when the skies above the town were filled with enemy aircraft and their bombs. The railway viaduct across Preston Road was targeted and Marine Gate was hit by several bombs, a number of which passed through the building. The churches of St Mark, Kemp Town, and the Wesleyan Church in Preston Road were both badly damaged. In August, another church, St Cuthman's in Whitehawk, constructed only five years previously, suffered a direct hit and a Warden who was on duty there was killed. A couple of months later, in the last air attack of the year, a large bomb damaged the track of the Kemp Town Railway when it landed in the cutting behind Bonchurch Road, between Hartington Road and Elm Grove.

The Clinic tragedy

The Central School Clinic, listed as the New Clinic in the 1939 Register, in Sussex Street (today Morley Street) had only been built in 1938. It was located on the corner of Ivory Place and was opposite the fruit and vegetable market in Circus Street.

At 11.08am on Monday, 29 March 1943, eight Focke-Wulf 190s flew in very low from the Channel. The formation then divided, with four machines veering off westward to attack Hove (where they would drop bombs on Shirley Street and Nizells Avenue) and four flying low over Brighton, just as the sirens sounded. Here they raked the streets with cannon and machine gun fire before dropping their bombs.

One struck the edge of a house roof in William Street, bounced off and then entered the upper floor at the southern end of the fruit and vegetable market. It travelled its entire length and emerged at the northern end. Before it crossed

The Municipal Clinic, Maternity and Child Welfare Centre (as also named in reports) in Sussex Street, where three children were killed and three expectant mothers were injured, March, 1943. (BHUF)

the street, it killed Stanley Bowles (39) of Woodland Avenue, Hove, then struck the clinic and exploded.

The blast killed an 8-year-old boy, Ronald Fenson, and his 10-year-old sister, Rosemary, of 44 Cheltenham Place, which linked North Road and Gloucester Road. They had been playing by the entrance to the clinic while their mother was inside at the antenatal clinic. She was one of a few expectant mothers in the building. A third child victim was Jose Clara Sayers (6) of 3 Hollingdean Road.

A handful of children were also at the clinic for dental treatment. Beryl Tucknott remembers:

> School children had free dental treatment there. We hated going but they did look after our teeth, as I found out later in life when a dentist asked me what treatment I'd had during childhood. He said that I'd had excellent treatment! The worst part was the waiting room, where we waited for our name to be called over the crackling intercom!

The doctor who had been attending Mrs Fenson suffered minor injuries and immediately set about treating the injured, while the senior dentist, despite a badly cut hand, assisted with the rescue work. Rescuers were unable to reach the chief clerk, Robert Ticehurst (37), until the latter part of the afternoon. He was found dead, buried in the wreckage of his office. His assistant, Jean Carter (21), was dug out alive, although in considerable pain from back injuries.

Betty Field was one of the youngsters in the clinic at the time of the raid:

> I was in the school clinic when it was bombed. I think I might have been about ten. I'd had toothache all the weekend and my mother said to me, well when you get to school on Monday, tell Mr Cooper and he'll let you go and walk down to the clinic. So, I walked down to the school clinic, walked past the fruit and vegetable market that was there on the right, and went in to the clinic. It was mother and baby day. There were a lot of small children playing in the foyer. There were mothers that were pregnant there, but the dental bit was upstairs and just as I went in, the pips sounded. Now the pips were imminent danger. If they hadn't enough time to do a siren and someone saw a plane coming over, imminent danger. So, I got to the bottom of the steps and went up to the dental bit and a dental nurse ran down and got hold of my hand and said quickly, we've got to go in the shelter. Now the shelter was on the side of the clinic. It was like a surface shelter, all concrete and she pulled me in there with some other people and slammed the door shut and we heard this… it wasn't really a bang. It was a bit like thunder. It wasn't a bang, it was a sort of rumble. Then we heard a lot of noise and the next thing was the light went out in the shelter and there was someone knocking on the door saying, we're going to dig you out (we couldn't open the door. I think the rubble from the clinic had come to the door). Don't worry, we're going to dig you out. They dug us out of the shelter. The clinic had collapsed by the side of it.
>
> They opened the door and there was an ARP Warden there and he said to me, are you alright? I said, well I've still got toothache and they said he's going to walk you home. Now, would you hand a child over to a completely strange man? And we walked up the hill and through Queen's Park to my home and apparently, the bomb had bounced all through that fruit and vegetable market. So, it must have followed me along more or less.

A commemorative publication of Ditchling Road School (now Downs Junior School) records:

> The worst scare of the war happened on March 29th 1943. Bombs fell over the town and machine-gunning was heard before any warning was given.

There was no time for the children to reach the trenches in safety, so they went in batches, while the waiting children took their place lying on the floor. During that raid the school clinic suffered a direct hit.

In the booklet, two former pupils share their memories of that day:

> It was about March I think. It was just around the time when people got measles. It was my first day out after having measles and I was supposed to be having my diphtheria jab, but my mother said I shouldn't go because of infecting other children with measles. About the time I should have been in the clinic a bomb came down and hit the pavement outside the Astoria and bounced across the road and hit the clinic. We were in the market and as the plane shot up the middle of the market stalls we all dived into the potatoes to avoid the bullets. The plane went out up the Ditchling Road shooting tracer bullets. An attack of measles and the vegetables saved me. That was my luckiest escape during the war.
>
> (Valerie Slade)

> I happened to work in the market at the time. It was a lone German raider coming in from the sea and he dropped his bomb. It was a low flying aircraft and the bomb was released and apparently took the top off a chimney and was going along at a low trajectory from the plane. It bounced into what was then the playground of the Circus Street School, which had been made into an ARP depot. The bomb went through the loading bay across Circus Street and into the entrance of the school clinic at about 10.30am and the bomb exploded and did all the damage. The school clinic sustained a lot of damage, there was debris all over the street. I walked down Circus Street and stepped over everything and saw how much damage was caused, then we retreated to our offices and started making tea for people.
>
> (Ray Hedgecock)

Gloucester Place and Grosvenor Street

Another bomb demolished the northern half of the Baptist church in Gloucester Place; mercifully, none of the people inside was killed. Properties near the church, including a motor showroom (Redhill Motors), a cafe and small flats, were reduced to rubble. The damage to a large building divided into flats was so severe that it had to be demolished.

The ruin of the northern half of the Baptist church in Gloucester Place, 29 March 1943. (BHIB)

Resident Beryl Tucknott has written: 'I can remember watching the remaining structure being pulled down by hand, with huge ropes tied to the pits of the wall, by Air Raid Wardens and volunteers.' Sound location equipment was brought in by the rescue services, who were joined by locally-based Canadian soldiers. Two young girls were rescued with only slight injuries after being trapped for around six hours.

But there were deaths. Muriel Gwendoline Eade (27) lived at 21 Gloucester Place with her baby, and had just returned from visiting her mother in Grand Parade opposite. She was killed, but her husband, James – a Private in the Seaforth Highlanders of Canada at home on leave – was rescued from the debris of their home suffering from facial and head injuries. Their baby, 4-month-old James Arthur was rescued with his father from No. 21 but was seriously injured and died at Brighton's Municipal Hospital on 19 April 1943.

A bus travelling northward in Gloucester Place made an emergency stop just in time before the bomb exploded. The driver later claimed that he saw it falling. Several windows in the bus were broken and two passengers received minor cuts. The conductor fell and suffered a head wound. The area all around was strewn with wreckage and debris and covered with a layer of white and greyish dust.

Unlucky Grosvenor Street 29 March 1943 – hit for the second time (previously in April 1941). (BHUF)

Another bomb fell in Grosvenor Street, off Edward Street. This unlucky road had already been hit on 9 April 1941, when Elizabeth Parsons had been killed at her home, No. 49 (see Chapter 3). This time a direct hit was sustained by No. 8, where Harriet Elizabeth Southon (52), the owner-occupier, and widow Caroline Cotton (68), a visitor who lived at 35 Upper Park Place, lost their lives. In the garden, Harriet's son, 12-year-old James, was lucky. He was off school, feeling unwell, and at the time of the raid was lying in his Morrison shelter reading a book. As the bomb exploded his house was wrecked and the debris landed on the top of the shelter, trapping him inside. Struggling to get out, he made frantic cries for help. These were fortunately heard by the rescue services and he was soon pulled out. He was later sent to a nearby boys' club to which he belonged so he could recuperate.

Three other fatalities in Grosvenor Street were Rosetta Alice Hardwick (33) at No. 11, her home address, 13-month-old baby Ruby Emily Newman in the same house and Mary Elizabeth Richardson (63) at No. 13.

Rescue work in affected areas was carried on well into the night, with over a hundred soldiers attending the various incidents to ease the pressure on the overstretched Civil Defence and police.

Two more bombs were dropped by the raiders, who had made off towards Hove. There, one bomb hit a printing works (the Shirley Press) and the other crashed through a house into the basement. Olive Wood Stammer (1907–92) records in *Letters To My Brother, 1940–1946* that Davigdor Road, Shirley Street, Nizell's Avenue, Goldstone Villas, Sackville Road, and several other roads were damaged.

However, the raiders did not leave for home unscathed. One of the FW 190s, piloted by 21-year-old *Obergefreiter* (Leading Aircraftman) Joachim Koch, was shot down over the sea about half-a-mile south of the Palace Pier by one of two Spitfires from 610 Squadron based at Biggin Hill which happened to be in the area engaged on telephoto training. Koch's body was washed ashore at Ovingdean on Sunday, 25 April. He was buried in Bear Road cemetery. The Spitfire pilot concerned in this action, Flying Officer François Venesoen, also shot down another of the raiders, but its pilot was lifted from the sea by his own rescue service. (Venesoen, a Belgian, had already dispatched two FW 190s in the previous year but would lose his life in 1944 by drowning at sea after baling out from a faulty Spitfire.)

On their way back across the Channel, enemy aircraft in the group shot down a Typhoon Mk 1b from Number 1 Squadron flown by Canadian Flying Officer Cyril Bolster, who was killed.

Civilians who died in this raid and who have not already been mentioned were:

In Gloucester Place:
BETTESWORTH, Florence Emily (46) at No. 20.
MILLER-MACKAY, Hugh (68) at No. 21. Rescued seriously injured, he died at
 the Royal Sussex County hospital on 22 April 1943.
NEWGERITZ, Verena Mary Elizabeth (54) of 26 Park Road, Coldean
PARR, Eliza (81) at No. 21.
WHITE, Philip Rampton (26) of 297 Hangleton Road, Hove, at No. 20.

In Sussex Street:
McALLISTER, David (54), a firewatcher, at No. 31.

Out of the blue

Just under one month after the 'clinic raid' there occurred, on 25 May 1943, a raid so serious that it is considered by some to be the worst suffered by Brighton during the war. Yet in terms of fatalities, the figure (twenty-four) was less than half of that resulting from the 'Odeon raid' overall (fifty-two). Nonetheless, many townspeople did suffer injuries – fifty-eight seriously and a further sixty-nine slightly. In terms of damage inflicted, it was indeed the worst,

Photograph taken shortly after the damage was caused to a central pier in the London Road railway viaduct, 25 May 1943. (BHIB)

with 150 houses being rendered uninhabitable and over 500 residents being made homeless. One of the central piers in the 65ft-high London Road railway viaduct was demolished. There was also severe damage to railway workshops and rolling stock.

The severity of the raid inspired local historian David Rowland (who witnessed the event first-hand as an 8-year-old boy) to devote an entire book to it – *Out of the Blue*, published in 2003. It contains, *inter alia*, historically valuable recollections contributed by fourteen eye-witnesses of that fateful day when more than two dozen of Germany's best fighter-bombers, led by a brilliant pilot, Leopold Wenger, carried out this low-level raid, bombing and machine-gunning the Brighton streets.

The first warning of impending disaster on that warm and sunny Tuesday came at 12.20, when, simultaneously with the air raid siren, followed swiftly by pips, no fewer than twenty-five Focke-Wulf 190s, almost all carrying large bombs, converged on Brighton. The enemy attacked in two waves, with ten machines crossing the coast in line abreast at Rottingdean and another fifteen coming in from the Channel three abreast east of the Palace Pier.

David Knowles, in *The Tree Climbers*, remembers

one wave coming in from an Easterly direction and flying low near the cliffs between Rottingdean and Black Rock before making their attack on the Kemptown area, and the second slightly larger wave coming in from the sea close to the Palace Pier, and then for ten minutes or so, circling around the towns [of Brighton and Hove] bombing and machine gunning various places as they did so.

None of the machines was flying more than 50ft above the sea and they rose to 150–200ft to circle the town. One was shot down into the sea as it approached the coast – the first of three to be destroyed that day by the Bofors guns positioned all along the seafront.

The planes hit the Marine Gate flats several times and scored a direct hit on their main target, the nearby gasometers. That bomb seriously damaged St Mark's School nearby and killed three people, including two Brighton Borough police constables who were on duty close by, namely Frank William Barker (33) of 7 Manor Road (a police house), killed near the junction of Whitehawk Road and Roedean Road as a result of taking the full blast of the bomb which fell on the playground, and Brighton Borough Police Constable Kenneth Grinstead (31) of 234 Freshfield Road, who was seriously injured in Arundel Road and died later the same day in the Royal Sussex County Hospital. The third victim was Leslie Albert Ockenden (33) of 18 Coldean Lane, a member of the Home Guard. He also died at the hospital. It is unclear how his injuries were received but they are believed to have been sustained near Marine Gate (a soldier was reportedly blown off the top of the apartment block during the attack). The schoolchildren had mercifully left for their midday break twenty minutes before the bomb fell, although one of the teachers, Marion De Witt (66) of 123 Preston Road, was badly hurt when approaching the door of the chemist's on the west side of Arundel Road. She was rushed to hospital where she died later that day.

The official record of bombs landed on this day compiled by a Sergeant Hilton of RAF Brighton (the administrative staff of that service were accommodated in various Brighton hotels) records this bomb as No. 11 of the total twenty-two dropped in this raid, although David Rowland firmly believes it to have been the first and provides a rare picture from the cockpit of lead pilot Leopold Wenger's FW 190A-5 showing the gas holder target being approached from East Brighton Park. He records that the Austrian pilot 'went on to machine-gun the streets, causing panic among Brightonians who had not managed to reach shelter, before crossing the Channel and returning to base'. The *Staffelkapitän* (Squadron Leader) would be killed in action against Russian fighters near Vienna on 10 April 1945.

Damage to St Mark's School, Kemp Town, 25 May 1943. Part of the targeted gasometer can be seen on the right. (BHIB)

It was not, of course, possible to state with certainty the order in which the bombs were dropped (although see the report below), but there is little doubt that all of them were 500kg in weight, making this the heaviest weight of bombs dropped on the town at any time during the war.

As in previous raids, East Brighton bore the brunt of the attack, stretching the rescue services to the absolute limit. Luckily, a large number of Canadian troops were stationed in Brighton at this time. David Knowles recorded that a unit based in St Mary's Hall School in Eastern Road was soon mobilised and assisted in rescues in the vicinity. First-aid posts were set up and dealt with long queues of people with minor injuries. At the RSCH, the staff worked to capacity to treat the more serious cases brought in.

A freak death was that of Annie Avis of 17 Bennett Road. While she was sheltering in her Morrison shelter in her ground floor front room, the blast from a bomb which struck her house blew her, still inside the shelter, down her garden, past a garden on the next street and into the rear wall of a house, against which she was found dead.

The official report on the raid summarised below recorded numerically the bombs which fell during the fatal five minutes of the attack:

Bomb No	Bombing information (raid of 25 May 1943) recorded by Sergeant Hilton of RAF Brighton (partial and edited)
1	This scored a direct hit on apartment houses on the east side of Eaton Place at the junction with Eastern Road. One house was severely damaged with lesser damage to three others within a distance of 70ft from the point of explosion. Slight damage occurred to many other houses to a distance of 120ft.
2	This was yet another direct hit. The point of impact on apartment houses occurred on the west side of Chichester Place, near the junction with Chesham Road. Severe damage was caused to two three-storey apartment houses with a 33ft frontage. Blast damage was caused to other properties to a distance of 200ft.
3	A direct hit on an apartment-type house on the north side of Eastern Road and about 20ft west of St Mark's Street. Severe damage to two three-storey terraced properties with a 45ft frontage. Serious damage also caused to the third house west of point of impact. Blast damage was caused to all properties in a 100ft radius, including the eastern part of the Royal Sussex County Hospital.
4	The point of impact was on a two-storey terraced house in Bennett Road approximately 160ft from the junction with Bristol Gardens. Severe damage was caused to four terraced houses with a frontage of 78ft. Further damage was caused to four similar houses and blast damage to properties within 200ft of the point of impact. [This bomb caused the death of Annie Avis recorded above].
5	The point of impact for this bomb was in the sunken grounds of St Mark's School in Arundel Road. This bomb ricocheted before exploding, causing a crater where the playground met the pavement of Arundel Road. This crater measured 24ft in diameter and was 5ft deep. Thirty-five coiled low-tension distributor mains underground electricity cables were severed in the crater. This affected nothing of any importance but the electricity supply was cut off in the immediate vicinity. Medium damage was caused to children's water closets at the school. Damage was also caused to a single-storey lean-to garage and minor damage to three two-storey terraced dwelling houses for a distance of 103ft. Window and roof damage was caused to properties to a distance of 250ft. A brick-built air raid shelter in the school playground some 25ft from the crater was undamaged.

Bomb No	Bombing information (raid of 25 May 1943) recorded by Sergeant Hilton of RAF Brighton (partial and edited)
6	This bomb fell on the extended pavement of the Clyde Arms Hotel on the west side of Prince's Terrace at the junction with Bristol Gardens. It ricocheted, bouncing to an angle of 40°, struck a glancing blow to a large block of flats about 18ft from the roof parapet and was then slightly deflected but continued rising. Its flight took it above the roofs of houses and business properties and it then fell into the sea, exploding approximately 1,800ft from the Clyde public house. [This bomb is officially 'unclassified' but was almost certainly one of 500 kg.]
7	This bomb scored a direct hit on terraced three-storey flats in Park Crescent Terrace at the junction with Park Crescent Road. Damage was caused to the flats with a 38ft frontage. The adjoining flats suffered severe damage. The surrounding properties, mainly made up of two-storey dwellings, houses and shops after a distance of 150ft were deemed to have 'C' damage. Glass and tile damage was recorded to a distance of some 200ft from the point of impact.

Flats in Park Crescent took a hit from Bomb No. 7. (BHIB)

Bomb No	Bombing information (raid of 25 May 1943) recorded by Sergeant Hilton of RAF Brighton (partial and edited)
8	Another direct hit, this time on a block of three two-storey shops in Down Terrace on the south side, near the junction with Queen's Park Rise. Class 'A' damage was recorded to the shops that had a 44ft frontage. Other shops within this block also suffered severe damage. Two terraced houses on the opposite side of the road were badly damaged. Slight damage was caused to properties 200ft from the point of impact.

Seven victims died in Downs Terrace, where a small parade of shops was decimated, 25 May 1943. (BHUF)

9	The point of impact of this bomb was about 400ft south-west from the west wall of Preston Road School. It then ricocheted around 900ft north-west, to explode and make a crater on the railway sidings. Three main line tracks were blocked from 12.30pm when the bomb exploded, until 18.55 on the same day. Four coaches and two goods wagons up to a distance of 45ft were damaged beyond repair. Rail tracks were torn up for a distance of approximately 75ft. Varying degrees of damage to coaches and goods wagons up to 100ft from the explosion. A 9-inch water main was fractured and the water supply was cut off for forty-eight hours. Repairs to the track were instigated almost immediately after the 'all clear' had been sounded.

Bomb No	Bombing information (raid of 25 May 1943) recorded by Sergeant Hilton of RAF Brighton (partial and edited)
10	The point of impact was on a two-storey dwelling house about 400ft south of the junction of Preston Road and Lovers Walk. The bomb ricocheted and exploded, making a large crater approximately 1,300ft north-west of the railway tracks and about 20ft south of the carriage repair shop. One brick roof-supporting pier was demolished and severe damage was caused to another pier. Both of these were at the open end of the shop. Severe damage was also caused to the west wall of the shop and extensive blast damage to glass roofs. In addition, a building used to repair and house Pullman cars was extensively damaged. Two Pullman cars approximately 25ft from the crater were completely wrecked. Five carriages were severely damaged, these being up to 40ft from the crater. Twelve suffered roof and blast damage to an approximate distance of up 150ft. The rail tracks were torn up in the vicinity of the crater. Workmen filled it in and the tracks were repaired the following day. A bomb which struck the steps at Lovers' Walk exploded in the Pullman Car works, doing considerable damage. Another fell on two empty trains standing close to the main line. Debris from the wrecked coaches was flung high over the chalk cutting and into the back gardens of the damaged houses in Stanford Road.
11	The point of impact for this bomb was the gasworks, 35ft north-north-east of No. 5 gasholder. The bomb ricocheted through this gasholder, causing a large fire and then entered No. 4 gasholder and exploded on its south side, 260ft south of the point of impact. No. 4 gasholder was completely destroyed, and severe damage was done to the 14in brick wall of the well on the south side of the container. A one-storey timber store with 14in brick walls and 97ft of frontage was destroyed. This stood 25ft south of No. 4 gasholder. Blast damage was caused to houses in the nearby streets to a distance of some 200 feet. The National Fire Service (NFS) were quickly on the scene.
12	The point of impact was the gasworks, Black Rock, and 22ft north of Valve House, just missing No. 5 gasholder. It then ricocheted through the Valve House wall, built of 14in brick, and travelled about 97ft before going through the roof on the south-west side, narrowly missing two workmen inside. It then passed over the storehouse and an old house: the storeman actually saw this bomb during its travels. It failed to explode and no further trace of it was found on land. All available evidence points to the fact of it having gone into the sea.

Bomb No	Bombing information (raid of 25 May 1943) recorded by Sergeant Hilton of RAF Brighton (partial and edited)
13	The point of impact of this bomb was the roof of No. 5 Cliff Road and approximately 400ft south-south-west from the junction of the main coast road and the Avenue, causing extensive damage to a semi-detached house. It then ricocheted onto a house 96ft to the south-west. From there it travelled on and exploded some 250ft further to the south-west at the base of Marine Gate. This was about 151ft east of Rifle Butt Road, causing major damage to the flats up to the eighth floor. These flats are steel framed with 9in brick outer walls and 4¼in division walls. The cement-rendered outer walls appear to have taken the full shock of the explosion well. Five two-storey houses in Rifle Butt Road, a distance of 200ft away, suffered heavy blast damage.

An early photo of Rifle Butt Road, showing a nearby gas holder. Five houses in the road sustained heavy blast damage in the attack on 25 May 1943. Minor damage had been caused to some of the properties at the end of June 1942. (Author)

Bomb No	Bombing information (raid of 25 May 1943) recorded by Sergeant Hilton of RAF Brighton (partial and edited)
14	This bomb scored a direct hit on the north-east side of the Marine Gate flats, approximately 242ft from the centre of Rifle Butt Road at a height of 42ft from the base. It passed right through the fourth storey. This caused extensive damage to three flats; the tail fins were found wedged in their wooden floors. After passing through the flats, it travelled across the main coast road and out to sea. No further trace of it was found.
15	This bomb landed on waste ground 129ft south-west of the junction with the main coast road and the Avenue. It then, about 90ft further on, ricocheted and hit a garage, totally destroying it. The bomb failed to explode. To the south-west of the garage it passed through the roof of a bungalow, causing severe damage to the roof and outer walls, ricocheted through the flats at Marine Gate and passed straight through. It next struck the roadway on the south side of Marine Drive about 190ft south of the flats and exploded. This caused a large crater and severed a 9in water main.
16	The point of impact was a bungalow on the south side of Cliff Road, 60ft west from its junction with the Avenue, causing very heavy damage to the roof and outer brick walls. The bomb then ricocheted 225ft south, hitting the ground 50ft from the eastern end of Marine Gate. It bounced and travelled a further 200ft to the edge of the cliffs, leaving a gap in the barbed wire entanglement as it passed through on its way to the sea, where it exploded.
17	The point of impact was the grassy area on the east side of The Avenue, approximately 110ft from the junction with Marine Drive. The bomb then ricocheted 43ft and hit a wall a glancing blow. This appears to have deflected a little to the south-west, for after travelling a further 500ft the bomb struck the south-eastern corner of Marine Gate close to the ground. It exploded at this point, causing severe damage to the flats on the first floor up to 30ft and over a 50ft x 43ft area. Here again the building appears to have taken the explosion very well. Blast damage was difficult to assess owing to the close proximity of the other exploded bombs. All the windows in the block were destroyed and severe damage was done to the inside walls, doors and personal furniture. Damage inflicted on the flats in a previous raid were still being repaired at the time of this incident.

MORE DEADLY VISITATIONS 203

Bomb No	Bombing information (raid of 25 May 1943) recorded by Sergeant Hilton of RAF Brighton (partial and edited)

Marine Gate, showing the point of entry of Bomb No. 17 and also the impact locations of Bombs Nos. 14 and 15. (TNA/Mary & John McKean)

18	This bomb fell on grass common land on the east side of Whitehawk Close, about 400ft north-north-west from Whitehawk Crescent. It then ricocheted 22ft across the roadway, causing noticeable damage up to the concrete surface and pavement flags. The bomb next struck a bungalow some 20ft away, causing heavy damage, especially to the roof and the north-east wall. Striking the bungalow roof, it ricocheted some 700ft south-west and hit a house in Maresfield Road, causing slight damage. The bomb finally exploded another 100ft south-west in allotment gardens, causing blast damage to roofs and windows in a 200ft radius. This area is now built up with dwelling houses. The crater caused by the explosion was partly filled in during the next few days.
19	The point of impact was the north-east side of the paint shop in the railway goods sidings. This was about 100ft from the south-east gable end and 15ft from ground level, badly damaging the wall.

Bomb No	Bombing information (raid of 25 May 1943) recorded by Sergeant Hilton of RAF Brighton (partial and edited)
19 (Cont.)	The bomb then ricocheted 80ft north-west onto the railway tracks, causing damage to one track. It continued its flight for further 500ft in a north-west direction, exploding on the railway track between a retaining wall and stationary goods wagons. This caused severe damage to the retaining wall and three wagons, while severe damage was also caused to three terraced dwelling houses on the north side and about 70ft of track. The damage to the houses was almost entirely due to blast and the wagons and the retaining wall appear to have taken a major part of the fragmentation. The crater on the permanent way was filled in during the following days.
20	The point of impact was the east side of the rail tracks and about 140ft north-west of the west wall of the locomotive works area adjoining Boston Street. The bomb then ricocheted apart, approximately 700ft north-west and exploded, making a crater on the railway tracks. This caused serious damage to the tracks, several yards of it being torn up. Other tracks were blocked by debris and several coaches suffered blast damage. Traction electricity cables were severed. The crater was filled in when track repairs began.
21	The point of impact of this bomb was the roof of a small dairy on the north-east side of Campbell Road, about 47ft from the junction with Argyle Road. This caused slight damage to the roof of the building. The bomb then ricocheted through a brick wall across the roadway, cutting a furrow in the tarmac surface. The bomb travelled on through a 12in stone-and-concrete wall and through the 9in brick cavity wall of a three-storey dwelling house, causing damage to its first-storey front wall. It then passed through the back window – a distance of 27ft from front to rear. The next ricochet took it to the old Baptist Hall, a two-storey brick-and-concrete building 61ft north-west of the dwelling house. The bomb passed right through the upper storey, a distance of 18ft, and then travelled a further 52ft before striking a pier of the railway viaduct. This was merely a glancing blow, causing only slight damage, but the impact appears to have deflected the bomb onto the next pier some 29ft to the north-west, where it exploded, completely demolishing the pier and two arches of the railway viaduct. This left sleepers and the railway tracks intact but without any support. Fragmentation marks found on the undamaged pier suggest that the bomb exploded at above-centre of the demolished pier. These brick piers are of a uniform size, 33ft long and 10ft thick. Blast damage to the neighbouring church and houses occurred to a distance of some 250ft.

Bomb No	Bombing information (raid of 25 May 1943) recorded by Sergeant Hilton of RAF Brighton (partial and edited)
	 *Sleepers and railway tracks suspended in mid-air (but soon repaired) by Bomb No. 21 on 25 May 1943.* (Author)
22	This bomb landed on the railway track 80ft south-east from the southern end of the carriage repair shop, causing a warp in one steel rail. The bomb seems to have been deflected at a steep angle but there was no evidence of it having struck anywhere between this point and Compton Road, where it made a direct hit on three-storey houses. This impact was 193ft north-west from the junction with Inwood Crescent on the north-east side of Compton Road, causing very serious damage. Four houses (two of them two-storeys) suffered severe damage. Blast damage, chiefly to roofs, tiles and glass, occurred to a distance of 250ft. One woman lost her life when her Morrison shelter was wrecked.

GASHOLDER DAMAGE IN THE TWIN TOWNS – SUMMARY AND NOTES

Following the attack, the raiders headed to Hove, where they attacked the gasholders before returning to their base in France. The wall of Container No. 8 was extensively ripped by cannon fire; this ignited the gas, which was lost. The loss of gas totalled 1.42 million cu ft.

In Brighton, the loss figure was 2.75 million cu ft. Containers Nos 4 and 5 were destroyed (Bomb No. 11 passed right through both before exploding). The gas was ignited and the entire contents were lost. Container No. 6 was split all round by cannon fire and its gas was ignited and all lost. The gas supply in both towns was resumed later the same day, although the plant at Black Rock was totally out of production due to Container No. 7 having been destroyed on a previous occasion. Repairs were undertaken immediately, with completion scheduled for 4–6 months thereafter.

RAILWAY DAMAGE – SUMMARY AND NOTES

Apart from the significant loss of life and damage to private property, this raid will no doubt always be remembered for the damage by Bomb No. 21 to Brighton's railway and rolling stock and, above all, to the London Road viaduct, a structure dating from 1846 and carrying the double track Brighton–Lewes and Brighton–Kemp Town line. Yet a temporary repair allowed trains to start using the viaduct again within twenty-four hours. Service was back to normal in less than a month. The arches were fully repaired in September 1943, although until then a 15mph speed restriction was enforced. Unnervingly, Preston Road could be seen by passengers through the trackside gaps between the sleepers where the brickwork had been blasted away.

Damage elsewhere (see Bomb No. 10 in the report) affected the main Brighton–London and Preston Park–Hove lines, various goods roads and sidings as well track to the Pullman car works. There was a loss of electric power to tracks and signals for a total of three hours and twenty minutes (it was restored at 15.45). The carriage sidings at Lovers Walk were cratered and severe damage was caused to the carriage washer road and Pullman shops. 'Down local', 'up' and 'down goods' roads, four sidings and the 'up siding' were blocked by debris. Several derailments occurred on various tracks. The electric main line was telescoped, and damage to rolling stock affected four coaches, fifty electric coaches (by bomb blast) and some goods wagons on the 'up' and 'down' roads to the station. Two Pullman cars were wrecked beyond repair and five were badly damaged, although possibly repairable, and twelve coaches were damaged to varying degrees. Considering the seriousness of the raid, the total loss of time through delays – fifty-three hours and thirty-seven minutes – was very modest indeed.

*

Turning again to the cost of this raid in human terms, we now honour those not previously mentioned who met their deaths as a consequence of it:

Killed in Down Terrace

BELL, David Keith (8) of 48 Freshfield Road, killed in a shop when a bomb struck a small parade of shops.
EATWELL, William Henry ('Billy') (11) of 4 Hallett Road, killed in a shop when a bomb struck a small parade of shops.
ELEY, Violet May (43) of 54 Down Terrace, killed in the debris of her confectioner's shop.
GOBLE, Florence Elizabeth (47) of 58 Down Terrace, killed in the debris of her grocer's shop.
GOBLE, John James (48) of 58 Down Terrace. Florence's husband, also killed in the couple's shop.
PINKSTONE, James Robert (48) of 52 Down Terrace, a member of the Brighton Home Guard. Had a butcher's shop at this address and died in the rubble of his premises.
SEBBAGE, Louisa Charlotte (58) of 23 Glynde Road, whose badly mutilated body was found among the debris in Down Terrace.

Killed elsewhere

BRAWN, Alexander (73) of 21a Chichester Place, killed in his home.
COCHRANE, Robert Allan (78) of 17 Chichester Place, seriously injured at his home address and rescued from the debris the following day. Died later that day at the RSCH.
CRELLEY, Violet (Retta Violet) (39) of 2 Park Crescent, died in the debris of her home.
DENBIGH, Kathleen Louisa (38) years of 26a Park Crescent, died in the debris of her home.

LLOYD, Mary Anne (52) of 24 Compton Road, died in the debris of her home.

PEARCE, Phillip John (48) of 14 Cheltenham Place, seriously injured at Brighton Station buildings and died later the same day at the Municipal Hospital, Elm Grove.

SHAKESPEARE, Percy (36), son of John Thomas Shakespeare, of 12 Maple Road, Priory, Dudley, Worcestershire. His body was found opposite Marine Gate.

SHEPHERD, Eliza (68) of 16 Rochester Street, died in the debris of 52 Eaton Place while visiting her sister, Lydia Shoosmith.

SHOOSMITH, Lydia (78) of 52 Eaton Place, died in the debris of her home.

SIMMONDS Emma (64) of 15 Chesham Road, died at her home.

THOMPSON, George Edward (43) of 9 Nuthurst Road, Whitehawk, killed in Arundel Road, near the junction with Whitehawk Road.

WALDER, Nellie Amelia (41) of 66 Twineham Road, Whitehawk, killed in Chesham Road.

Jean Hayler, née Eatwell (1936–), contributed a brief recollection of the loss of elder brother, Billy, to *Slobs and Slogs* [St Luke's Old Boys and St Luke's Old Girls], a collection of memories of former pupils of this Brighton school compiled by Doreen Waite, née Corbett (1932–):

> I can also remember Miss Winkworth and Miss Beaujard [teachers], who were both particularly helpful and supportive to me and the rest of my family when my brother, who was also a pupil at St Luke's, and a choir boy at St Luke's Church, was killed at the age of 11 by a German bomb which landed on the shops in Down Terrace on 25th May, 1943. I can still remember the events of that day as though it happened yesterday, and visiting the school last year brought home to me that but for the War, Billy could also have perhaps been present at that gathering.

Jean also contributed a longer account of her experiences to David Rowland's *Out of the Blue*.

David Knowles, author of *The Tree Climbers* (quoted from earlier), witnessed the raid of 25 May 1943 personally. He was aged 10 at the time and lived at 13 Sussex Square, Kemp Town. On the afternoon of the day in question, he had a dentist's appointment but had to attend school (Brighton College) in the morning:

> The lessons that morning seemed to go more quickly than usual, but my concentration wasn't particularly good as I was now somewhat preoccupied

again with the thought of the dreaded dental appointment that afternoon. At mid-day I was allowed to get ready to go home for lunch and an afternoon off school because of this appointment. […] I then […] started on my walk home along the Eastern Road – the time was approximately 12.15 pm.

I had got nearly as far as the Sussex County Hospital when everything seemed to happen at once. First the siren went; this stopped me in my tracks and I hesitated for a few seconds – wondering whether to seek cover in the hospital – an idea which I immediately dismissed because of my fear of hospitals, or carry on and run home – about half-a-mile away – or run back to school, only about two hundred yards away. Suddenly, there seemed to be explosions coming from all around me, and the sound of aeroplanes was almost deafening; I could also hear the guns on the seafront giving off a heavy barrage. In fact, you could say that – one minute it was nice and peaceful, and the next – all hell broke loose!

Under these circumstances, my mind was very quickly made up for me, and with 'my heart in my mouth' and extremely frightened, I ran as fast as my legs would carry me back to school, which was only a few seconds away at the pace I was going! I ran through the arch at the opening to the college on the Eastern Road, and almost ran into Mr Burstow, the assistant headmaster, who was standing just by the quadrangle, outside the entrance to Bristol House; he was shading his eyes with a book which he held in one hand, and was watching a couple of German aeroplanes flying straight over the college in the direction of the sports ground – another aircraft seemed to circle the school – but then flew off in an easterly direction. We didn't see any bombs dropped by these aeroplanes, but we heard some machine-gun fire, and we both saw the pilot in the one that circled over the school. We later found out that these were Focke-Wulf 190s. Mr Burstow, who had already grabbed me by the arm, hurried me into the school and down to the basement of Bristol House, which was used as a shelter. For several more minutes we could hear more bombs going off, some of these quite close to us, and the noise from all the Bofors guns along the seafront, was continuous and very loud.

The whole air raid was very frightening for all of us, and from what I can remember, the staff and some of the older boys did a very good job in comforting several of the youngest boys, who were crying and were very distressed. Eventually, the noise stopped and there was a tense sort of silence. We stayed where we were for about another ten minutes, and then, although I can't remember hearing it, we were told that the all clear had gone and that we could all return to the assembly room on the ground floor. I didn't know quite what to do, and asked Mr Stokes, the headmaster – telling him about my dental appointment; which at that time was obviously the least of anyone's worries; however, he went off to phone my parents, returning a few minutes later to tell me that everything was alright at home – which was a relief to me – and that I was to start walking back along the Eastern Road, where my mother would meet me halfway.

What hadn't been taken into consideration was that many nearby places had been hit by the bombs, and this included some of the Eastern Road area as well as numerous other nearby places, so, after David had got just past the Sussex County Hospital, he found that the police and ARP Wardens were blocking Eastern Road off. He could also see smoke coming from the direction of St Mary's Hall School. One of the policemen asked him where he was heading; David told him, and the policeman said he was to go down Chesham Place, a small road just nearby, and then along Rock Street and up into the square from there. He told the officer about his mother meeting him and was told that she would be informed at the other end, and would probably meet him in Rock Street. There was glass lying on the road and on the pavements in Chesham Place and there were floating bits and pieces of ash and matter in the air, and a strong smell of burning and smoke everywhere. He had noticed that Eaton Place, just nearby, had been bombed and that it was now closed by the police. The ARP and an ambulance were there as well as a small crowd of onlookers.

On turning into Rock Street, he immediately saw his mother and quickly told her about all he had seen since leaving the college; he also told her about Eaton Place being hit (this especially worried her as she knew some people who lived there, including one particularly good friend of hers so, holding his hand, she walked him to the bottom of that road where she was immediately reassured because she could see that her friend's house was undamaged and well away from the houses that had been hit). The damage at the bottom of the road looked terrible, and David could remember seeing one woman being carried on a stretcher. Another woman, with blood on her face, was walking beside her, holding her hand, and muttering over and over: 'God help us!' David's mother, not wanting him to see any more, clutched his hand even more tightly and they turned and walked back along Rock Street – here and there avoiding walking on piles of broken glass, and even walking onto the road just in time to avoid being hit by a pane of glass that quite simply 'fell to the ground' as they passed by.

We eventually arrived at number thirteen after stopping briefly to see smoke coming from the Arundel Road area and also that the gas works were once again on fire. Another thing we had noticed, after turning up from Rock

Street, was that there was a lot of activity going on near St Mary's Hall main school on the Eastern Road, and also quite a bit of smoke coming from the buildings. Amongst the rescue parties there, we saw several of the Lake Superior Regiment soldiers that we knew – they were in shirt sleeves and covered in dust – all of them looked grim and very determined.

In David's view, the raid had been

a planned attack on an area that looked from the air as a likely place where invasion preparations were building up – judging by all the equipment and vehicles that could now be quite easily seen – and these included the Bren-gun carriers and tanks of the Canadian Regiments and also those of the Lake Superior Regiment in and around Sussex Square. The square itself hadn't actually been hit, but parts of the Eastern Road nearby, and also some buildings at St Mary's Hall and houses at Eaton Place and Chichester Place were hit – with some fatalities. Arundel Road had been attacked again as had Marine Gate where there were casualties, but no fatalities. The gas works had also been hit again and this immediately resulted in the loss of a large amount of gas and left many people without the means to cook – and that included us! Many other areas in Brighton and Hove were also attacked in the ten minutes or so that this carnage took place in.

David agreed with Lieutenant Colonel George F.G. Stanley, the author of *In The Face of Danger*, that the Lake Superiors were superb during this crisis. They took part in both trying to gun down the enemy as well as helping in the mopping up and rescue activities that took place immediately after the raid. In Chapter XI, 'Straining at the Leash', the following account of the raid can be found:

Of all the raids upon Brighton, and they were frequent enough during these mid-years of the war, one of the most serious was that which occurred on May 25th. The German radio had announced several weeks previously, through the nasal, penetrating voice of William Joyce, Lord Haw Haw, the American-born Irishman who had left England to join the National Socialist party, that German planes would soon make it HOT for 'Worthington's circus'. And they did. Shortly after the noon hour had sounded, some twenty fighter-bombers, FWs 190, struck at Brighton. The vehicles of the Lake Superiors, Bren-gun carriers, trucks, cars, motorcycles, were parked in the streets and in the parking areas and there was no time to move them to shelter. For about ten minutes the German planes flew up and down, bombing and machine-gunning as they went. The area immediately adjacent to battalion headquarters was badly jarred and the building adjoining St Mary's Hall was damaged by a falling bomb. Headquarters' company at Arundel Place was also mauled by cannon and machine gun fire.

The men were at lunch when the raiders arrived, but no sooner did the planes depart than they went into action. The local ARP took some time to get organised, and it was a group of Lake Superiors under Sgt. C.J. Barnes who first began to dig the victims out of the ruins and the rubble. So feverishly did they work that, at St Mary's Hall, they managed to extract three casualties from the pile of jagged brick, crumbling plaster and broken glass, before the ARP men had arrived on the scene.

Similar incidents took place in other parts of Brighton as the officers took hold of the situation and organised rescue squads.

The work continued throughout the afternoon and well into the night. The following day a party under Captain Mackenzie was still digging. They unearthed an old man, 79 years of age, but still 'alive, and swearing a blue streak'. The civilian casualties were numerous [...] Neither soldiers nor civilians would readily forget the raid of May 25th, and the people of Brighton gratefully expressed their thanks for the help and friendly sympathy given them by the Canadian soldiers in their midst.

Continuing his recollections, David wrote:

As far as the rescue work is concerned, including searching for people buried under rubble and clearing up after the raid – I actually witnessed some of this, and also remember the bits and pieces I was told by my parents. I know that my father had a very high regard for the ARP and had friends and acquaintances who were members of it – he always said that they did 'a hell of a good job', and I remember that everyone was praised for their rescue work – British and Canadians alike. Concerning the damage at St Mary's Hall; back in the July of 1941, almost exactly a year after they had been closed down for the duration, the governors of the school declared their intention to re-open after the war, but the bomb that had fallen on the main school on the Eastern Road, had hit some terraced houses converted for school use, and this had some more far reaching consequences for the school.

He quotes a short passage from page 33 of *A Short History of St Mary's Hall, 1836–1992*:

Fate was to take a final hand in order to make the re-opening more difficult for on the 25th May 1943 a bomb fell on Hervey Terrace destroying the lodge, 227 and 229 Eastern Road and badly damaging the laboratory. This bomb may have been a blessing in disguise in the long term, for the old houses were quite unsuitable to form part of the school that was to arise when peace was finally restored. After the war it was decided to build 'Elliot House' to accommodate some sixty boarders on the site of the bombed houses in Hervey Terrace. By September 1951 the house was ready, and to start with occupied by twenty-two boarders. The old science laboratory that had also been damaged in the raid had been converted for use as a domestic science room and also came into use that September.

In the years to come there were times when David had nightmares about that raid, and would sometimes wake up, screaming out. It was always about the same incident during the raid – when he had run into Brighton College, where he was a pupil, and bumped into Burstow as the enemy planes circled above them – the difference being that, in the nightmare, the cockpit of one of the planes opened up and a German, with a horrible sneer on his face, leaned out of the aeroplane holding a bomb in his hands and chucked it down at them. At that point he would wake up!

After this horrific raid, the like of which would never be repeated with such intensity, Brighton was to enjoy a twelve-week period of respite. Then Whitehawk was bombed again.

Destruction in Whitehawk

Enemy aircraft were heard at 12.18am on Monday 16 August 1943, a couple of minutes after the sirens had alerted the residents. The machines were heading seaward after a raid and one dropped three bombs onto the estate. One landed on open ground to the east of Wilson Avenue, causing a large crater, another on playing fields to the west of Whitehawk Road, at the foot of Race Hill. These bombs caused relatively minor damage, apart from shattered roofs and windows.

The third bomb scored a direct hit on the church of St Cuthman at the junction of Lintott Avenue and Fletching Road. The white building, dating from as recently as 1937–38, was extensively damaged. Part of it collapsed due to the destruction of the roof and two outer walls, leaving just the tower standing. Inside, the beautiful organ and almost everything else was destroyed. Yet the large gilt crucifix behind the altar remained in position, unscratched. (It was taken away and eventually placed in the new church). A heavy belfry on the gable also survived. The vicarage, a few feet away from the church, suffered only slight damage to the roof and one or two cracked panes of glass. The vicar, the Reverend Chris Bryan, gave his story to the local press the next day:

> As I am a part-time warden, I was already dressed and coming down the stairs when the bomb fell. My wife was in the vicarage, which is only a few feet away from the north-west side of the church. We heard nothing at this time to suggest that the bomb had dropped within a few yards of us. You can imagine my consternation therefore when I opened the door and saw a heap of rubble where the church had stood.

One life was lost in this raid, that of ARP Warden, William Henry Hayler (49) of 122 Wiston Road, married with one daughter. He was not due to work that night but had swapped shifts as a favour for a friend in the Wardens' team. He died while writing out his report sheet in the church hall, which doubled as an Air Raid Warden's post. This took up about half of the hall and was turned to rubble, although somehow the other half was not badly damaged. William worked by day at the Allen West factory in Lewes Road, where war work was carried out, and was a keen gardener. After his death, two of his friends kept his allotment going and sold the produce to raise money for his widow, Jessie. On 23 September, a

St Cuthman's Church, Whitehawk, laid waste, 16 August 1943. (BHIB)

concert was put on at Whitehawk Boys' School by the Wardens and their friends to raise further funds for her and the Hayler family. The event was well attended and a fair amount of money was handed over to them shortly thereafter.

Yet some good came out of the ruins. Fred Netley (d. 11.6.20) remembered, in his book *Holy Oak – A History of Whitehawk and Manor Farm*, how nothing was allowed to go to waste:

> When the St Cuthman's Church was bombed, Civil Defence Workers were sent to the site to make it safe or to save any valuables that had not been destroyed. Anything that was re-usable was put to one side and the wood was given away to the local people for firewood, I read somewhere that the workers rationed it to one sack per family. Whether it was actually the case or not, I don't really know, but that is indeed what is most likely to have happened. So the little Whitehawk church still served the people even after being destroyed by helping to keep them warm, keeping in line with the wartime dictum; 'Waste Not, Want Not'. [...] Even in those times of shortages I remember that lovely warm fire with its welcoming glow reflecting around the room, particularly at dusk. Those logs, tar blocks, lumps of wood from bomb sites and screwed up newspaper supplementing the coal ration certainly kept us warm and cheerful in difficult circumstances.

Everything that was possible to pick up was salvaged by the vicar and his helpers early in the morning after the bomb fell. Regarding church services, it was arranged that these would temporarily be held in the vicarage, although by the following Sunday the congregation was established at St David's Hall in Whitehawk Avenue at its junction with Whitehawk Road. It had also been used before St Cuthman's was established.

Serious damage was caused in the vicinity of the church, and there were some lucky escapes. The *Herald* dated 21 August showed a damaged house with the caption: 'The occupants of this house – including three little children – had just taken shelter when a block of masonry from the church which was damaged during Monday's raid crashed through the side of the bedroom where they had been sleeping. They were all unhurt.'

It is comforting to know that the enemy plane which had dropped the trio of bombs was shot down by our ground defences when caught for a few seconds in searchlights.

St Cuthman's, which had been known as the Children's Church because money collected at Sunday school services all over Sussex helped toward its foundation,

St Cuthman's Church in ruins – another angle, with additional information. (Hawkins, E.A., Brighton (& Sussex) At War 1939-1945)

would not be rebuilt for several years. Sadly, its first vicar, the Rev. Francis Musgrave, was killed in August 1944 on chaplaincy service in France. The replacement church, designed by well-known Brighton architect John L. Denman, opened in 1952. The church hall was sold to the Community Association in 1982 and became the Valley Social Centre.

Unlucky Bonchurch Road

The last raid of 1943 took place nearly ten weeks after the attack on Whitehawk and the area most affected was Bonchurch Road, which lies east of Lewes Road and links Elm Grove and Hartington Road. Thankfully, nobody was killed.

At around 3.45am on Friday 22 October the residents of the road and the surrounding area had their night's sleep shattered by the sound of a diving enemy aircraft, one of a number crossing the Sussex and Kent coasts heading for London. Despite the additional noise of the sirens, some residents slept through the whole incident but most made a dash for their shelters. The target was thought to be the railway viaduct (again), part of which crossed Lewes Road near the junction with Upper Lewes Road.

Some residents of Bonchurch Road were injured when a 500 kg bomb fell on this cutting on the Kemp Town branch on the night of 21/22 October 1943. (BHUF)

Falling short of its target, the 500kg bomb landed on the railway track of the Kemp Town branch that ran behind Bonchurch Road and exploded on impact behind No. 79. Eleven people needed to be treated for their injuries, eight by first-aid teams and three in hospital – including a child injured when her bedroom ceiling fell on her. Rescue services commendably arrived within minutes and, with assistance from neighbours, were soon helping the injured. A welfare centre was set up and provided food and rest for those families rendered temporarily homeless.

Damage to property would have been greater had the high banks of the cutting not taken the worst of the blast, although houses in the immediate vicinity suffered and a number of roofs collapsed. Mrs Mabel Barnard of 91 Bonchurch Road said:

> I thought the plane had been hit and was crashing on us. I dived into the cupboard under the stairs and the whole house shook and seemed to sway backwards and forwards with the force of the explosion. A dense cloud of white dust made it impossible to see anything for a few minutes. My piano was lifted bodily across the room – it was a wonder it didn't play a tune.

Properties within a radius of half-a-mile were also damaged. Nearly all the rear windows of nearby Elm Grove School were broken and the school sustained a certain amount of roof damage. Recalling the terrifying event in *The Argus* of 21 January 2013, Kathleen Mears, then living in Peacehaven, said:

> The teachers put us under the desks where we were all chatting away merrily. I remember hearing the bullets hitting the ground outside. Our parents were banging on the door of the school trying to get in but they couldn't. Eventually a postman kicked the door down.

Windows were smashed and roof tiles and slates were broken in Seville Street and Upper Wellington Road. The Sunny Bank Laundry at 82–84 Bonchurch Road suffered very serious damage.

What eventually happened to the railway line? It used to cross Hartington Road on a bridge and then entered the deep cutting until it reached the northern portal of Kemp Town Tunnel. After the line's closure in 1971 much of the cutting was used as landfill then landscaped into the William Clarke Park (named after former railwayman and Brighton Mayor, William 'Nobby' Clarke). At its south-eastern side, the Park ends where it abuts play areas of Elm Grove Junior School.

Raids in 1944

Come 1944, enemy attacks of note numbered just three, one in February and two in March. The raid in February – on the 23rd – was the last serious one and the last to result in loss of life. There were eleven victims – seven were residents from the same road and one a visitor to it. Curiously, the area was the same as that where the first raid had taken place in July 1940 and the location of a subsequent attack.

On this cold, frosty night, a solitary enemy aircraft was caught in searchlight beams. Perhaps in an effort to escape, it released a string of high-explosive bombs and brought death, injury and damage to a number of streets, especially Bennett Road. Also hit were Arundel Road, Rugby Place and Eastern Road, as was Marine Gate (again). Part of Wilson's Laundry in Arundel Road suffered heavy damage, including to the staff canteen, and a gas main in that road was fractured and caught fire.

The Morrison shelter proved its worth in Bennett Road, where it saved the lives of the Burnett family of four at No. 19 and the Dinnages at No. 51, whose house was so badly damaged that it had to be demolished.

Damage to equipment in Wilson's Laundry, Arundel Road, Kemp Town, 23 February 1944. (BHUF)

The injured, of whom there were many, were conveyed in a fleet of ambulances and other vehicles to the RSCH, thankfully located nearby. Two first-aid posts treated the less serious cases on site.

No time was lost in repairing damaged properties, with gangs of workmen making a start shortly after 8am the next morning. An information office was set up for residents made homeless and provided assistance to those enquiring about injured relatives and/or friends.

The following residents died in this raid:

a) In or from Bennett Road:

BRADSTOCK, Rosina (60) of 1 Wilmington Parade, Patcham, injured at No. 68. She died the same day at the hospital.

LITTLE, Alfred Saunders (61) of No. 41, found dead in the front garden of his home.

MORLEY, Harry (39) of No. 35, a member of the ARP rescue service, at his home address. His wife (Kathleen) was badly injured but lived.

MORLEY, John Mervin (15) of No. 35, a member of the ATC, son of Harry. Was injured at home and died the following day at the Royal Sussex.

READING, Alfred (56) of No. 44, at his home address.

SHERLOCK, Edith Florence (61) of No. 24, at her home address. Wife of William Frederick Sherlock.

SHERLOCK, William Frederick (63) of No. 24, at his home address.

WEAVER, Edith Lucy (70) of No. 49, at her home address. Wife of Joseph Frederick Weaver.

WEAVER, Joseph Reginald (44), a Fire Guard of No. 49, at his home address. Son of Edith Lucy and Joseph Frederick Weaver.

b) Elsewhere:

BEADLE, William George (55) of 19 Rugby Place, at his home address.
WILLIAMS, Doris Caroline Lucy (23) of 246 Eastern Road, in Kemp Town.

*

The two raids which followed, in March 1944, were relatively minor affairs, resulting in only slight damage and no casualties.

On the 14th, residents living near the seafront heard the sound of low-lying aircraft shortly after 1am. Soon three clear and distinct explosions could be heard. Although the bombs landed in the sea a few hundred yards offshore, the blast from them damaged roofs and windows along the seafront – including the Metropole Hotel, which was being used for billeting troops – and shops and businesses in Western Road.

Just over a week later, on Wednesday 22 March, Brighton's last air raid occurred. It happened at 1.09am – almost exactly the same time as its predecessor. The sirens sounded and residents hurried to the shelters. Although the bomb fell on Nos 5 and 6 Old Farm Road, Patcham, damaging them substantially, it failed to explode. It did, however, leave a 21ft crater in the roadway and fractured the gas main and 9in sewer pipe. Two large, heavy manhole covers were lifted and hurled several feet. With local people promptly evacuated from their homes and the area cordoned off, the bomb was carefully rendered safe and removed.

A spectacular crash landing in St Nicholas' churchyard (Dyke Road in the background). The pilot of this ME 410, 24-year-old Richard Pahl, was killed when his machine was shot down on 19 April 1944 by a Mosquito of 96 Squadron over Brighton. His operator, 24-year-old Wilhelm Schuberth, baled out but was drowned at sea. (Royal Pavilion & Museums, Brighton & Hove/BHH collection)

CHAPTER 6

Seeing It Through
1943–1944

'Wings for Victory'

This was the name given to Brighton's major war savings initiative of 1943. The target set was £800,000 or the cost of 100 Whirlwind fighters – twin-engine, cannon-armed aircraft which, when they first flew in 1938, were one of the fastest combat aircraft in the world and the most heavily armed. The week set aside for Brighton's 'Wings for Victory' Week was that of 27 March to 3 April. During it, a Hurricane fighter stood in the Pavilion grounds as a reminder of the country's victory in the Battle of Britain and attracted a swarm of sightseers.

The event opened on Saturday 27 March with a pageant in the Dome, in the course of which an alert was sounded, but no one left the building. Later on, the Mayor announced that the aircraft which had caused the alert had been shot down.... Many visitors attended a free exhibition opened on the same day in the Corn Exchange at which numerous RAF items of interest were displayed, including bombs on which savings stamps could be stuck by the public and which, when covered with them and of course charged, would be dropped on Germany. The next morning, each of the Services was represented at Divine Service in the Dome and the subsequent church parade in the Pavilion grounds. Here Air Chief Marshal R.P. Mills and other officials and dignitaries took the salute, the march past being witnessed by many hundreds of spectators. A Gala Ball at the Regent was held on the Tuesday and a concert of Russian music was performed at the Dome on the Saturday. Another attraction was an action-packed amateur boxing tournament at the Dome on the 29th. During the week, stage and screen star Miss Winifred Shotter sold £1,045 worth of savings certificates at Bellman's; the store itself raised no less than £8,000. Mention should also be made of the splendid achievement by the village of Ovingdean, whose initial target had been £700, yet the total amount it subscribed was £4,121 – a feat indeed.

Not only did the 'Wings for Victory' Week achieve its target, but a last minute drive to 'make it a million' enabled the figure to be handsomely surpassed. The exact total realised was £1,041,803 – the cost of 130 Whirlwind fighters instead of the 100 originally aimed for.

Brighton Savings Committee poster announcing, on 27 March 1943, the opening of the 'Wings for Victory' event at the Dome on the following day. (BHG, 27.3.43)

Other savings and causes

Aid to Russia continued as a cause into 1943, with references to it appearing in the local press from April to October. On the poster advertising the Stalingrad Ball to be held on 9 April at the Regent Dance Hall, the full title of the cause was spelled out, namely the 'Brighton & Hove Effort for Mrs Churchill's Aid to Russia Red Cross Fund', with a side note: 'Supported by the Lord Bishop of Chichester'. Music was provided by the Lake Superior Regiment Dance Orchestra, the RAF Grand Hotel Dance Band, and others. Just six days later, an Anglo-Russian Dance, billed as 'an evening you will never forget', was put on at the Dome. The special late night was organised by Bellman's Helpy Club. At the same venue on 1 May, a successful concert was held at which the Mayoress made a moving appeal for funds. A specific appeal came in June from the Anglo-Russian Fellowship for support for a recently launched scheme to provide a British hospital in Stalingrad, whose estimated cost was £1,500. This amount was clearly only part of the picture, since it was stated at the 'Salute to Stalingrad' meeting at the Dome, held on 5 September under the auspices of the Fellowship and attended by the Mayor, that a sum of £66,000 towards the £75,000 aimed at providing the equipment and supplies of a new Stalingrad Hospital had been raised in Britain. Locally, steady support came from the Saltdean Fellowship, which in mid-August responded to an appeal in aid of the inhabitants of towns and villages recently liberated by the Red Army. At the end of September, mainly through a concert held at Telscombe Hall, the group made a contribution to the Comforts Fund for Women and Children of Soviet Russia. At around the same time, St Martin's church in the suburb held a retiring collection for Mrs Churchill's Aid to Russia Fund at its Harvest Festival (where among the gifts was a lemon from Sicily).

At the end of October, tickets were on sale in Brighton for another Stalingrad hospital dance on 11 November 'at the Dome or Bellman's'.

Funding for prisoners of war came to the fore during 1943. All proceeds from a Gala Concert at the Dome held on 27 February went to the Red Cross and St John Prisoners of War Fund. The event was graced by the presence of the Princess Royal and raised no less than £2,700. Another distinguished visitor was the Duchess of Norfolk who, in Red Cross uniform, visited Brighton and Hove on 22 April – a week before her own Regency Ball – at the Dome to receive cheques from the Zylo company totalling £257 towards the Prisoners of War Parcels Fund (Brighton and Hove were campaigning to raise £12,500 – the cost of 25,000 parcels). By early June, the Duchess's appeal had already raised £10,000. At the end of October, it was announced by the Fund's Executive Committee at the Golden Cross Hotel that the splendid efforts made in Brighton,

Another Dome event: Notice of the upcoming Stalingrad Hospital Dance to be held on 3 November 1943. (BHG, 30.10.43)

Hove and districts had resulted in the target not only being reached but exceeded by £400. Mention must be made of the extraordinary achievement by Patcham during its Entertainment Week (31 July to 7 August) of raising just over £480 for the Red Cross's fund. No fewer than 30,000 residents and visitors had supported the event.

Russia was not the only Allied country to receive support from Brighton. A 'Fighting French Week' was opened in early June 1943 at Stafford's Café, Western Road, when Lieutenant Colonel J.M. de Lagatinerie, the Chief Welfare Officer of the Fighting French Forces, voiced an appeal for support of the Association of Friends of the French Volunteers, which had more than 26,000 members in all parts of England and Scotland, and in just over two years had expended over £30,000 on welfare for the Fighting French, their wives and their families. The Association's immediate need was for clothing and for French books. Fighting French displays were held throughout the week at Bellman's, the Co-operative Store in London Road, Palmeira Stores, Plummer Roddis and at Stafford's itself.

Other causes for which funds were raised in 1943 included the Merchant Navy Comforts Service (light opera 'Merrie England' staged at the Theatre Royal, January), the Soldiers', Sailors', and Airmen's Families Association (Mayoral Garden Party, Royal Pavilion, June), the Royal Air Force Pilots and Crews Fund (variety show, Princes Hall, Aquarium, July), YMCA War Service (Saltdean Fellowship, November), Red Cross (Saltdean Fellowship, October and December), maintenance of own First-Aid Point and purchase of wool for comforts for the Forces (Saltdean Fellowship, December) and Lady Rawson's Merchant Navy fund (concert at the Royal Pavilion, December).

'Holidays at Home'

Brighton's success as a resort was mixed in 1943. An optimistic note was struck early in the year when Mr A.C. Miller, the President of the Brighton and Hove Hotels and Restaurants Association, described, at its annual meeting at the Old Ship Hotel in early February, as 'marvellous' the way in which the members had 'overcome their wartime difficulties'. The Mayor and Mayoress (and the Mayor of Hove) attended. Brighton's Mayor looked forward to the reopening of those establishments currently closed, admitting that most of them would require a great deal of redecoration and refurnishing when better times came. He had no real information with which to respond to the many enquiries he had been receiving about 'the ban', or defence area restriction.

All was revealed at the end of the month, when the Ministry of Home Security announced that the ban on pleasure visits to the coastal area between The Wash and the Thames and between Hastings and Littlehampton and to the Isle of Wight, which had been suspended until 1 March, would remain lifted until 1 April. So Brighton's door remained open – for another month at least.

This was a good time to implement 'Holidays at Home', a Government initiative to encourage people to take their holiday locally to take the pressure off the nation's rail network, give priority travel to military personnel, save fuel and keep up morale. A movement to ensure that Brighton should play its part in providing all the healthy outdoor recreation possible was set on foot in March with Councillor A.V. Nicholls as its sponsor. In his view, there was a great dearth of open-air attractions yet ample scope for the organisation of sports meetings, concerts and other fixtures in the parks, the Royal Pavilion grounds, and the public swimming baths and he had no doubt that the idea would appeal very strongly to residents obliged to stay at home. A Public Recreations Committee was appointed to carry out the project he sponsored.

Easter, which would be a good indicator of the success or otherwise of Brighton's subsequent holiday season, was unpromising, according to the *Gazette* edition of the holiday weekend (24–25 April):

> Despite the lifting of the visitors' ban there are few indications that the Easter Holiday will mean a 'boom' for Brighton and Hove, for though there has been a considerable influx of week-enders, the travelling restrictions have made the Government's 'stay at home' edict no idle warning. Those visitors who have already arrived have found little food awaiting them as no extra rations have been issued to hotels and restaurants by the Food Control authorities, and those who were wise brought their own rations to supplement any they might hope to obtain locally. There were no scenes at the Brighton Station reminiscent of ordinary holiday periods, and, although most of the London trains were crowded, the public seemed to have spread over their arrivals more than in the past, there being none of the 'last minute rush' invasion by day trippers. For the inhabitants it was definitely a 'Stay at Home' Easter, cinemas and other places of indoor entertainment being crowded. It was very much a case of the cupboard being bare in some quarters by the time Good Friday had arrived. The food shops had been swept clean by those who had visitors to cater for and another contributory factor was the usual housewife's fear of being 'caught short over the holiday period'. Supplies of liquor were none too plentiful either, as most of the licensees preferred to hold their dwindling stocks until the Easter Monday finale to a holiday which was definitely hallmarked as an austerity one.

Easter did, at least, bring one other blessing: the ringing of church bells (*Gazette*, 24 April).

On the administrative side of Holidays at Home, an Entertainments Committee of the Council was set up in mid-May and a month later an Entertainments Manager was appointed to organise the scheme. This was Fred White, whom the *Gazette* described as a 'well-known personality in entertainment circles in the town, who has spent a lifetime in the theatrical business, and has previous experience of municipal showmanship as manager of the Princes Hall and of the Dome'. Offices were opened on the old Publicity Department's premises at Royal York Buildings

While the *Gazette* expressed the view that 'it is useless to expect a large influx of visitors' at Whitsuntide, the twin towns did receive 'quite a fair number', despite travelling and other restrictions – further proof, if any were needed, 'of the appeal they continue to make, even under wartime conditions, to those in search of healthful relaxation' (*Gazette*, 19 June). Yet no extra travel facilities were offered to the public, nor did the Food Office sanction one extra ounce of rations for visitors.

The Holidays at Home programme included the erection of stages for concerts and entertainments in six of the town's parks: Preston Park, Queen's Park, the Sports Ground, Patcham, East Brighton Park, Moulsecoomb Wild Park and Whitehawk Sports Ground, as well as the Pavilion Lawn. Professional concerts were to be given in these parks six days a week, with the concert parties going from one park to another from Monday to Saturday. At other times, the stages were available to any local organisation that could make effective use of them, with the various districts arranging their own shows.

All programmes were stepped up during the special holiday week at the end of June/beginning of July. Community singing, always found to be popular, was provided for and there were paddle boats on the lake at Queen's Park for the children. The Sussex County Amateur Athletic Association promoted a sports meeting in Preston Park and the Sussex County Amateur Swimming Association organised a swimming gala at the North Road baths. The Brighton Parks Lawn Tennis Association arranged tennis matches and a tournament, while the Brighton Philharmonic Society, for its part, offered to cooperate in the arrangement of summer concerts. An inaugural Holidays at Home show was given at the Dome on 28 June and the Greyhound Stadium organised a horse and donkey show and gymkhana, the 'Big Show', to be held on 2 August.

A month later came the Summer Bank Holiday. On 31 July, the *Gazette* enthused:

> For many people this will be the happiest August Bank Holiday for four years. The dramatic events in Italy and the success of the Allied Forces in Sicily have given us all cheerful hearts. There is a feeling of optimism that we have really turned the corner at last, and without indulging in any speculation about victory being 'Just around the corner' there is reasonable justification for this happy spirit.

The invasion of the two towns began some days before the holiday weekend, with hundreds of visitors coming in each day. All the leading hotels had been booked up weeks earlier and those smaller hotels and boarding houses which had remained open throughout the war period were also fully booked and could have let their rooms several times over. Daily events for visitors staying beyond the weekend were scheduled for the week commencing 2 August – 8 August.

Bank Holiday crowds arriving at Brighton Station on 30 July 1943. (BHG, 31.7.43)

Planning for a new initiative, 'Blackpool Week', quickly followed. Further to an approach from Councillor Nicholls and a visit by a Brighton deputation, the Lancashire resort, enjoying a normally prosperous season thanks to its location, agreed to extend a helping hand to battlefront Brighton by staging a week of entertainment here in the week beginning 4 October. This would be a fitting finale to the Holidays at Home campaign and, even better, Blackpool was footing the bill.

The ban reintroduced

Before that Week, however, Brighton endured – albeit temporarily – the re-imposition of 'the ban', viz. being designated part of the Defence Area. Roads leading to various local areas had been carrying exceptionally heavy military traffic for some time previously and army movements by rail on an equally large scale had also been taking place. Some lines could soon be barred to civilians. Very large numbers of Dominion and US troops had reportedly been moved into various localities, occupying new barracks and additional quarters were still being constructed. An official notice stated that non-residents and those not in the affected areas for approved purposes 'will be well advised in their own interests to leave'. Those purposes were: visits to parents, children, wives or husbands, and to near relatives who were ill or over 70, or in an institution; weddings or funerals of relatives; and visits for purposes of treatment. Notices posted in the area also stated that identity cards would have to be carried and produced on demand by all persons. Vehicles and pedestrians would be obliged to follow the directions of the civil and military police and troops on duty and might be prohibited altogether from using certain roads at certain times. The carrying of cameras, telescopes and binoculars without a special permit would be forbidden. An additional notice signed by the General Officer Commanding in Chief stated that no persons other than residents or those having a permit could make use of the roads. Queues of applicants for permits formed at the Town Hall but many went away disappointed, so rigorous were the conditions. At the same time as holidaymakers were leaving, there was an influx of war workers, evidently bent on a last fling at the seaside before the ban was imposed again.

Immediately following the posting of the ban notices, all hotels and boarding-houses had to notify visitors of the necessity for their departure by midnight on Monday, 23 August, when the restriction became effective. Non-residents were given eight days to leave. Early the next morning, all the railway stations in the banned area, and all the roads leading into the boroughs,

Railway passengers being asked to produce their identity cards on arrival in the restricted area. (BHG, 21.8.43)

were placed under special police vigilance, and no one was allowed in without the closest scrutiny of identity card and papers. Holidaymakers left Brighton in droves, 'in an exodus the like of which has not been seen before during the present war' (*Gazette*, 21 August).

Just as during earlier periods of imposition of the ban, cases of infringements were heard by local magistrates, including that of 42-year-old Joseph Harris, found guilty of making use of a certain highway although not a resident of the area and, worse, of assaulting a police constable while in the execution of his duty. He was sentenced to one month's hard labour on the first charge and one month's hard labour on the second, the two months to run consecutively. Arrivals of visitors by rail immediately doubled in number compared with the corresponding days of 1942.

Yet as early as mid-September, there was talk of the ban being lifted 'following the completion of the amphibious exercise in the Channel' (*Gazette*, 11 September) and in fact the newspaper reported in its issue of 25 September that the ban was 'lifted last week'.

'Blackpool Week'

'Blackpool Week' went ahead as planned, opening on Monday 4 October. Alderman Percy Round, the Mayor of Blackpool, and his civic party were publicly welcomed at the Imperial Theatre in North Street on that day by our own Mayor (Councillor B. Dutton Briant), who had held an informal reception for the official delegation earlier in the day in the Mayor's Parlour. The Red Rose of Lancaster was worn in many buttonholes at the Norfolk Hotel on the 7th, when the Lancastrian Society of Sussex entertained the Blackpool delegation together with representatives of Brighton and Hove civic life. Among other points made there by an appreciative Mayor of Blackpool was his declaration that, 'The whole idea of the Week is to try and introduce fellowship between two leading health resorts of the country.' The productions which the northern resort transferred bodily to Brighton for the Week were the two successful shows, George Black's new revue 'We're All In It' with Wilfred Pickles of BBC fame heading a notable cast attracting nightly audiences of over 6,000 people, and Tom Arnold's broadcasting entertainment 'Happidrome', which had been having a successful season at Blackpool's Grand Theatre. The former was allocated to the Imperial Theatre and the latter to the Hippodrome. There were also displays by Blackpool's team of formation dancers (made up entirely of war workers who had obtained special leave of absence to appear here) and dancing competitions at the Regent, Sherry's and the Dome, plus recitals on the Dome organ at 3pm daily by Blackpool's ace organist, Horace Finch, recitals which were relayed to the Pavilion grounds. Finch also gave short recitals during the evening programmes at the Regent, Savoy and Astoria cinemas.

Blackpool Council subsequently told the *Gazette* that it was unanimous in its appreciation of the value of the Week and in the belief that the lead given by these two important holiday resorts should be followed by all other holiday towns in preparation for the post-war demands of a holidaymaking public.

CRIME

Crimes by Canadians

Crimes of all kinds continued to be committed in Brighton during the war years. Sadly, it was not uncommon for our Canadian cousins to appear in the news in this connection.

A tragic drama unfolded outside the SS Brighton leisure complex in West Street on the night of 16 February 1943. It involved 21-year-old Canadian dispatch rider Victor Eric Gill, a married man, and his girlfriend, Ivy Eade. During the blackout, the attractive daughter of a hairdresser from Camelford Street was shot in the Stadium car park. Immediately after the shooting, Gill rode on his motorcycle to the police station under the Town Hall and gave himself up. Eade had met Gill when working in a Brighton café in 1942 and had become his regular girlfriend, despite having been told about his wife and adopted family. When she fell pregnant by him, he wanted to marry her and tried to obtain a divorce. The girl had, however, been friendly in the meantime with another Canadian soldier, Private Stanley Morey, and a mutually affectionate relationship had developed between them. Gill had become jealous and confronted Eade in the long bar at the Sports Stadium. Following a fierce argument, during which she called him names and he slapped her, he took her outside and shot her with his service revolver. She was found dying from a bullet wound in the centre of her forehead. Although still breathing, she died in the ambulance on the way to the County Hospital. At the Sussex Assizes at Lewes in March, Gill pleaded not guilty to murder. The defence argued that he had suffered such provocation that he had lost control of his actions. The jury unanimously found him not guilty of murder but guilty of manslaughter and he was sentenced to six months' imprisonment.

In April, a captain in a Canadian unit named John Braden, 31, was sentenced to six months' hard labour at Brighton Borough Bench on each of two charges of unlawfully wounding Arthur Evelyn Paul Ellis and Margaret Ellis, the terms to run concurrently. Braden had pleaded guilty. On 13 February, the officer, who had been drinking, approached the couple, who were walking on King's Road with their daughter, and, claiming to be a security officer, asked to see their identity cards. Both Mr and Mrs Ellis tried to reason with him, Mrs Ellis saying, 'You are a Canadian Officer; don't let the Canadians down.' Braden, however, who was swinging a bottle, said, 'I will shoot you all', and struck Mrs Ellis on the head, knocking her down. Mr Ellis and his daughter, aged 19, assisted her to her feet, and they then went to their home which was nearby. Braden followed them and knocked Mr Ellis down with the bottle. When Ellis got up, Braden forced him into the hall and again struck him with the bottle, which broke. He then pushed him out into the garden and eventually into the basement area. Mrs Ellis and her daughter had meanwhile gone into the front room on the first floor of the house, where they opened the window and screamed for the police. An RAF sergeant and a policeman came up, and Braden was arrested. He was later horrified to learn what he had done and not only apologised but paid a substantial sum by way of compensation for his dreadful actions. He forswore alcohol, which a doctor declared had caused the Canadian's delusional insanity. At his trial, Braden, for his part, claimed that he had no recollection whatsoever of what had happened. His Commanding Officer stated that the accused had discharged his military duties satisfactorily and his conduct as an officer had been beyond reproach. In the following month, due in part to Arthur Ellis confirming that Braden had done all he could to make amends, Braden had his sentence quashed and was bound over in the sum of £5.

A few cases made the newspapers in the summer. In one, 21-year-old Canadian soldier, George Buhnia, was said to have 'gone from hotel to hotel collecting what trinkets he could find'. He was brought before the Borough Bench on 3 May, by which time the whole of the property he had stolen had been recovered. Drink was also to blame in this case (in the three days before the thefts he had spent £4 on liquor in one lunchtime session). The credit balance of $249 in his pay-book showed, however, that there had been no need for him to have committed the offences. He was sentenced to three months' hard labour – one month for each of the three charges on his charge sheet.

In another assault case, two Canadian soldiers, Glen Richie (21) and Frederic Charles Borrett (31) were charged on remand at Brighton Borough Bench with inflicting grievous bodily harm upon George Arthur Healey, a window cleaner, of 51 Edward Street. The three men had walked up Edward Street after leaving the Little Globe public house at 10.30pm on 24 April, and the soldiers assaulted Healey in Chapel Street, so severely that he was hospitalised for six days. Richie admitted assault in response to Healey behaving improperly towards him and was sentenced to two months' hard labour. Borrett denied committing any assault and was discharged.

Canadian soldier Maurice Kenneth Wilson (21) was remanded on bail on 1 June, charged with being drunk and disorderly in Hamilton Road and assaulting Police Inspector Joseph Henry Lawry while in the execution of his duty on 31 May. Lawry was not expected back for duty for at least another month, being required, as a result, to attend hospital regularly on account of a fractured joint on the right hand. Wilson was fined £10 on the assault charge and was allowed a month in which to pay.

A rather milder offence was committed by 23-year-old Canadian soldier Roderick Lothian, who had been remanded in December on a charge of attempting to steal the goods of James G. Nicoll, a poultry farmer, of Falmer Road, Rottingdean. He again came before Brighton Bench on the 4th and was fined 40*s*. Lothian had been caught in the chicken run and said he wanted some eggs.

The worst crime to have been committed by Canadian servicemen was perpetrated in the blackout on the evening of 29 November 1943 in Kemp Town. The three young female staff were just about to close the doors at the business where they worked and complete their accountancy of the day's money transactions when two young soldiers entered the premises, having arrived in a stolen jeep. One of them showed a Sten gun and said 'Don't move, sisters', while the other closed the office door and then jumped over the counter and filled his pockets with all the notes in sight plus the silver cash available. The haul amounted to £500 in £1 notes and about £7 in silver. The men then fled, hijacking an ammunition lorry equipped with a mounted machine-gun to make good their escape.

Despite diligent research, no reported sequel to this case could be traced by this author in the local press.

Canadian soldier Leo Alfred Coffie, aged 23, married, was sent to prison for a month with hard labour on 9 February 1944 on two charges of theft. The first charge related to a handbag and its contents, valued at about 30*s*, the property of Doris Elizabeth Haines; the second also concerned a handbag and contents, belonging to Ellen Ramsey, whose total value was given as £3. An officer of his unit described Coffie as a good soldier, declaring: 'There is nothing of this nature on his conduct sheet, and we were all very much surprised about it.'

Crimes by British servicemen

Crimes were sometimes committed by our own servicemen. Among those perpetrated in 1943 and 1944 were those set out below.

Neil Joseph MacKeil, aged 25, was charged that on the night of 4 March 1943, he broke into and entered the residence of Charles John Jackson in Brighton and stole various articles worth in total £15 4s. 7d. He was sentenced to two months' imprisonment. A sentence of three months' hard labour was served on Harold Smith, 32, who, purporting to be a watchmaker, sold a watch and alarm clock valued at £6 belonging to Violet Lavinia Halpin, and a wrist watch, valued at £1 10s, belonging to Amelia Rose Leech. Both ladies lived in Nevill Road, Rottingdean. On 10 June, William Peter Coen, 39, and Ronald Francis Tugwell Robinson, 30, broke into 8 Preston Road, a branch of the International Stores, and stole £35 14s 8d. It was stated at their trial that Coen had 'a shocking record and was a public danger'. He was imprisoned for five years. Robinson was sentenced to twenty-one months' hard labour.

Two cases were reported in the *Gazette* in November 1943. In the first, Leslie Smith, 29, a soldier, was committed for trial by Brighton Borough Bench on charges of wounding Mrs Violet Cook, coincidentally of 51 Edward Street, and breaking and entering 'The Knoll', Ovingdean, and stealing money and articles valued together at £30. At the Quarter Sessions in April 1944, he asked for other charges to be taken into consideration. However, he flatly refused to disclose the whereabouts of the stolen property on the grounds that it would give away a well-known 'fence'. It emerged that only £1 had been recovered out of £240 worth of property stolen. Detective Inspector Collyer wanted to be able to say something in Smith's favour but could not do so. The prisoner was sent to prison for two years with hard labour.

Leslie Joseph Scruby, 28, pleaded guilty at Brighton Quarter Sessions on 29 December 1943 to two charges of breaking and entering. In the first, which took place on the night of 9 December, the soldier was unlucky. Mrs Elizabeth Agnes Sims, the occupant of the house, in Upper North Street, heard a noise from a room on the floor above her bedroom. When she went to investigate, she saw Scruby standing on the landing, and when she asked him what he was doing there, he tried to push past her. Showing remarkable courage, the woman struggled with him down two flights of stairs and when Scruby tried to leave through the front door, she put the latch down. In answer to her screams, her husband and another man who had been in a basement room came to her assistance and Scruby was detained. The second charge against the defendant was that of breaking and entering premises in Kensington Place and stealing an overcoat and cigarette case, valued at £2 15s.

Scruby's wife did not now want anything more to do with him. Oddly, his adjutant gave him an excellent character in the Army and Sir Charles Doughty KC even said: 'I believe there is some good in you.' Yet the man had, since being an absentee from the Army, committed forty-four other offences of larceny, involving property to the total value of £60, of which only £6 10s worth had been recovered. Alhough Scruby had been frank with the police, he would not assist them with regard to the recovery of the property. Two days later, however, when the miscreant again appeared before the Recorder, a police officer stated that prisoner had given information which had led to the recovery of two rings. Sentencing was postponed until the end of the Sessions to give Scruby an opportunity of showing his repentance by telling the police what he had done with the stolen goods. He was bound over for twelve months in his own recognisance of £5.

The holder of what the Bench described as someone with 'a terrible record', William McIntosh Shields, aged 40, a soldier, was sent to prison for six months with hard labour on the same day as Scruby's first hearing. Shields admitted having attempted to steal 15s, the contents of an offertory box at the Church of St John the Baptist, Brighton. At his request a further offence, concerning thefts from St Bartholomew's, Portsmouth, was taken into consideration. It emerged that while the priests of the Kemp Town church were having their lunch, the alarm bell connected with the offertory box rang, and Shields was found standing by the box. Prisoner, an absentee from the Army, had twenty-one convictions recorded against him. What was worse, the Chairman (F.J. Wellman) mentioned, when announcing the sentence, that at different courts Shields had asked for over 140 cases to be taken into account. 'It is shocking', he added.

A soldier alleged to have acclaimed Germany as 'the finest nation in the world', appeared before Brighton Magistrates on 19 July 1944 to answer three charges: one of being drunk and disorderly in North Street the day before, and two with assaulting Detective Constable Arthur Frederick Leggatt and Special Sergeant Frederick Charles Carter. The accused was Dennis McLaughlin, 35, and he pleaded guilty to each charge. He said the infamous words in conversation with two customers in a hotel in North Street. In response to a question, he affirmed that Hitler could save Europe. One of the two policemen called to the scene overheard McLaughlin say: 'Hitler is going to be the saviour of the world. He is the only man worth fighting for.' The soldier then assaulted both officers outside the hotel and a third who attended the fracas. McLaughlin later claimed that he was the one who had been assaulted. He was sent to prison for three months on each of the charges of assault, the sentences to run consecutively. The charge of drunkenness with disorderly conduct was taken into consideration.

Crimes by local civilians

Among the crimes committed by civilians, the case of 47-year-old John Dorgan overshadowed all others in 1943. He and his wife, Florence Elizabeth Agnes, 60, lived in a basement flat at 8a Madeira Place, shared with their lodger, Charles Fyfe. The Dorgans had married in 1927 but it had not been a happy union. Dorgan had served, and been injured, in the First World War. After the war he had worked in various pubs and hotels in Brighton. By 1943, however, he was unemployed and becoming desperate for money. On 29 July, he began selling off personal possessions and items of furniture from the flat.

On 31 July, Charles Fyfe, who had been away for a couple of days, returned to Madeira Place and noticed that various items were missing. He went to his room to change and, looking under the bed for another pair of shoes, discovered Florence's body. The post mortem examination, carried out by Dr L.R. Janes, confirmed that she had been strangled. Death was recorded as having occurred on the previous day. Dorgan was arrested at 7.30pm outside the Queen's Head pub. He told the officers: 'I have done the old woman in. I have done it properly this time.' Apparently Florence had caught him stealing her belongings in order to sell them and a row had ensued. He had told her to 'shut up', but she would not be silenced. Dorgan's trial was held in Lewes on 2 December 1943. The defence of temporary insanity was not accepted and he was hanged at Wandsworth on 22 December.

Holding a position of responsibility is never a guarantee of blameless conduct, as the case of Benjamin Webb clearly illustrates. A Senior Air Raid Warden, of Old Shoreham Road, Brighton, Webb was sentenced to twelve months' hard labour on 28 September 1943 after being found guilty of three charges of obtaining money by false pretences with intent to defraud residents in their homes. F.J. Wellman, the presiding magistrate at Brighton Bench, declared: 'This is a serious case. You, as Senior Warden, going round to the homes of these poor people and abusing your position is one of the most despicable cases of fraud we have had in this Court for a long time. You must realise by now what suffering you have caused to these people.' The magistrates granted an application for five other charges – three similar ones of defrauding by false pretences and two of larceny – to be taken into consideration. Webb had served during the First World War in the RNVR and later with the Coldstream Guards and the Essex Regiment. Yet two previous convictions were recorded against him.

Juveniles misbehaving

Unruly behaviour by young people was sometimes a cause for concern in the war years, although on paper 1942 had seen significant improvement in this area over the previous year. The Annual Report of the Brighton Probation Officers stated that there had been a reduction of more than 30 per cent in the number (147 against 210) of children and young people brought before the magistrates in 1942. The officers attributed this reduction to 'the intensive drive, during the past twelve months or more, in the Youth Movement'. People living in the Queen's Park area in July 1943, however, would have had a different perception of young people. Writing in the 17 July issue of the *Gazette*, 'Gazetteer' commented on 'a state of things that ought to have been dealt with long ago', stating:

> Why this very charming park should be handed over practically without restriction to the young bandits and others not so young who make it their happy hunting ground, I really do not know. Before the first and only [Holidays at Home] concert was held there the platform was smashed up and had to be reconstructed.

Gangs of children had been making a general nuisance of themselves in the park and ruined the event. A wild rush of children swamped the enclosure and clambered over seats when the Jolly Good Company Concert Party was making its debut. Although the day's performances were carried through, the entertainment was spoilt. Despite their efforts, the ARP Wardens acting as ushers for the show had been unable to control the unruly group. Small wonder that the idea of holding Holidays at Home concerts in the park had to be abandoned. Even before this episode, there had been many complaints about the behaviour of juveniles there, as seats had been damaged, shrubs uprooted, and gangs of youths had run wild, making the area a place to be avoided. Before the war, several park keepers had managed to exercise some control over the activities of the youngsters, but lack of manpower made it impossible for the few men now responsible for the park's appearance to control the hooligans infesting what was once one of Brighton's most attractive open spaces.

Sadly, parks will always be targeted by undisciplined youths. On 22 April 1944, the *Herald* published a letter from 'Indignant', who had written:

> May I point out the vandalism that has occurred in Preston Park? Since war broke out, every window in the cricket ground stand and sports pavilion has been wilfully smashed. Some three or four weeks ago this was all repaired and painted. Yet within two weeks the largest plate glass window in the stand has been deliberately smashed in two or three places.

Nonetheless, it was reported by the Probation Officers in 1944 that there had been a reduction in serious breaches of the law in the borough, at least by juveniles, during 1943 compared with the previous year, so the downward trend was continuing. Against this, however, there was an increase of forty-seven in the number of young people who had to answer to summary offences, the biggest increase being in cases of damage. Yet this was often the result of horseplay and warlike games, often due to the amount of spare time the children had on their hands. An analysis of the cases showed that the total number of boys appearing before the magistrates was 194, of whom eighty-two were charged with indictable offences as against eighty-six in 1942, and 108 had to answer to summary offences as against sixty-one the previous year. Thirteen girls came before the magistrates, a decrease of six on 1942.

Despicable thefts by person(s) unknown

Regardless of Britain being at war, there were (and would always be) perpetrators of deeds which were shameful beyond words. Here are two random instances just from 1944. In the first, attention was drawn to the heartless behaviour of an unknown individual by the victim herself, a Mrs Joan Muddell, in a letter dated 14 October to the *Herald*. She lived at 'Richmond', 27 Withdean Court Avenue, Brighton:

> SIR. – Early this year my husband, a sergeant pilot in the RAF, was killed on active service. On his memorial stone in Patcham Churchyard a replica in bronze was fixed as a last tribute to the memory of a gallant airman who lost his life in the service of his country. This token remained for five weeks only before some unknown person wrenched it out of the stone to which it was riveted and stole it. Should this person happen to see this letter I would like to remind him that, by this action, he is robbing those who fought and died that he might live in comfort and freedom. This point will undoubtedly worry the thief little, but the widow of this airman waits for the day when she can trace him and see that he gets due reward for his vile act – the reward which so many widows and mothers would like to see meted out to him.

The lady's late husband, Walter Howard Muddell, had died on 5 March at the age of 22. He had flown with the Royal Air Force Volunteer Reserve, established in 1936. Many of its members from Brighton lost their lives during the conflict

Thefts from allotments were, by contrast, a regular yet frustrating annoyance. Indeed, the *Evening Argus* dated 20 January 1944 claimed that they 'cause the police greater trouble and anxiety than many more serious crimes'. Officers (occasionally victims themselves) were without doubt doing their very best to trace the perpetrators wherever possible and, by making an example of the culprits, helping to curtail this type of crime. The number of complaints from the public received at Brighton Police Station was actually 'exceedingly small'. This was down to most of the victims probably reporting incidents to the Parks and Gardens Committee and not directly to the police. The proof of this was that the complaints came mainly from those districts which had not joined the Allotment Police Patrol scheme. When the war had started, there were more allotments and fewer police to guard them. In view of this situation, R. Howell, Allotments Superintendent, had suggested a scheme to the Chief Constable for special allotment police. He had proposed that men should be chosen, interviewed, and have their records checked by the CID. If found suitable, they could be sworn in as Special Constables, solely for allotment patrolling. The Chief Constable approved the idea, but when it was suggested to the various Allotment Associations, only those of the Lower Roedale and Hollingbury sector and the Tenantry Down sector joined (the Moulsecoomb, East Brighton, Rottingdean and Patcham Associations had yet to do so). The results spoke for themselves: in the former two sectors there had been no complaint of theft, while in the various other districts there had been several. Brighton was in fact the only borough in the country to have its own patrols. The forty-eight hours per month put in by the Specials were voluntary and took the place of firewatching.

The feature in the paper on the pilfering nuisance quickly led to a letter from inevitably named 'Allotment Holder', in which it was asked:

> Can the despicable allotment thieves be rounded up? In December I lost some eight or ten grown cabbages. Previously I had had stolen spade, fork, rake, hoe and water can. Cabbages etc. were taken from the next allotment. These allotments do not possess lock-up shanties. Up till now I have not been able to trace the people responsible for depredations and would like to find them. The publicity you have given to allotment pilfering may be the means of doing some good in helping to bring the thieves to justice.

Food production, 1943–44

Back in February 1943 when launching the 'Dig for Victory' campaign, Robert Hudson, the Minister of Agriculture, urged that although the number of pre-war allotments had been nearly doubled, more were needed. 'Some local authorities', he said, 'are doing good work but others are not doing so well.' A *Gazette* reporter, anxious to establish that Brighton was not included in the latter category, contacted R. Howell, whose official title was Superintendent of the Corporation Allotments, and from him learned that the number of allotments being worked was 6,248, as against the pre-war total of 2,600 or so. A survey in 1942 had shown that these produced 7,500 tons of food. Including smallholdings, food crops totalled 9,500 tons and if private allotments were taken into account the total was 13,500 tons. The Superintendent stated:

> Brighton has definitely done better than the majority of towns. There is not one piece of ground vacant that is fit for producing food. Where you see vacant ground it is not suitable for cultivation because the chalk is right on the surface. There is no more land available except at such a distance that would-be allotment holders can't get to it, especially in these days when everybody is so busy and transport is restricted.

Maximum production from the land was still needed even at this late stage of the war, as confirmed by the Minister who declared, in a message to the opening of the West Riding of Yorkshire's 'Dig for Victory' campaign, 'The war is going well, but from the point of view of food it is still at a very desperate stage.'

Doris Williams of Falmer recalled that in early 1943, with the Army well established at Stanmer, a decision was made to form an Army Agricultural Unit to grow crops in an area stretching from Stanmer to Ditchling Beacon and Lewes Racecourse. Most of that farmland was then under army occupation after the evacuation of Stanmer village and farms in the parish in the previous year. Much of it was by then overgrown and neglected. After its reinstatement, vast quantities of fertiliser were needed to keep it in good heart with a place to store the sacks. The Victoria Room at Stanmer – once the scene of many social events arranged and enjoyed by people from Stanmer and Falmer before the war – became a store for hundreds of bags of fertiliser which filled the room.

Appreciation for land workers was shown in Brighton on 15 October 1943. Nearly sixty of them, including many WLA (Women's Land Army) girls, who had brought in Brighton Corporation's wartime crops were entertained to a 'harvest home' at the Royal Pavilion, when an informal dinner was given by Councillor H.B. Hartnell (Chairman of the local Sub-committee of the East Sussex War Agricultural Committee). This gesture was made to recognise the efforts which had turned derelict land into fertile acres and which had produced 300 tons of wheat, 200 tons of oats, over 60 tons of beans and peas and 40 tons of pure sugar from beet that year.

By September 1944, East Sussex had enthusiastically responded to the call for greater production, as over 4,000 acres of former downland were now

This advert for Clensel 'root stimulant and pest eradicator' hammers home the 'Dig for Victory' slogan. (EA, 8.1.44)

growing good crops. Much of the difficult work of clearing problem areas had been achieved by a battery of Fordson tractors with general-purpose ploughs. Bushes and gorse had been uprooted by chains attached to the upper spokes of the tractors' rear wheels. The East Sussex Local War Agricultural Committee had had to teach 'scratch' labour to do the work, since no trained tractor drivers were available. A photo published in the *Gazette* dated 23 January 1943 showed a tractor ploughing Brighton Corporation land at Brapool [*sic*] which a few weeks

Three Polish sailors recuperating in the Patcham district stacking wheat on the Brangwyn Estate with Councillor H.B. Hartnell. (BHH, 19.8.44)

earlier had been covered with gorse and small trees. The job of branch slashing and clearing was still being carried out by hardy members of the WLA, who also worked the three-furrow ploughs drawn by heavy tractors. The land – some 35 acres in extent – adjoined the London Road near Patcham.

Labour was always badly needed and, where available, gladly provided. As in previous years, schoolboys from Varndean School were again running their own Agricultural Service Camp in August 1943 in the Mayfield district and proving to be of valuable help to farmers. While in camp the lads received double rations, the same as farm workers.

Agricultural work could actually be a holiday in itself. An editorial in the *Herald* dated 29 April 1944 pointed out:

> We can take relaxation from our own jobs by undertaking another which will give us healthy if strenuous occupation. The Sussex War Agricultural Committee is again appealing for adult workers in the harvest fields during

Over 60 agricultural camps in the southern and eastern counties were accepting volunteers (over 100,000 were wanted) to help on the land. The East Sussex camps were in Rye, Lewes and Haywards Heath. (BHH, 10.6.44)

the coming summer. Here is work of national importance which yet affords that change of occupation which is the best form of holiday. From May 1 until the final harvest is gathered in next September, work awaits all those who are willing to assist the country in this way.

A few days later, the *Evening Argus* lent its voice in support:

Hundreds of thousands of part-time volunteers did nobly last year helping farmers in the evenings, at week-ends and at other times. This assistance was of the utmost importance, and volunteers are urgently needed again in many districts. [...] There is hardly a direction in which non-combatants can help more effectively the national war effort than this one.

Food exhibitions

It was not only gratifying but instructive (for example, as regards rations) for the townspeople and visitors to see the results of local food production efforts. Such displays often took the form of town centre exhibitions, the primary one in 1943 being entitled 'Off the Ration', organised jointly by the Ministry of Agriculture and the Ministry of Information and opened by Earl Winterton. It was held from 21 April to 15 May in the Royal Pavilion grounds, the Art Gallery and the Pavilion Theatre to show how self-help could be applied in producing 'off the ration' food and was the largest venture of its kind ever to be held locally. The methods suggested were the cultivation of allotments and the keeping of poultry, rabbits, pigs, goats and bees. All these ways of helping the country – and ourselves individually – were illustrated, with practical demonstrations being supplemented by film exhibitions, talks and displays of photographs. Experts were in attendance to give advice to enquirers. The local arrangements for the exhibition were in the hands of the Council's Wartime Food Committee, led by Councillor J. Horton-Stephens.

Among the exhibitions in September 1943 was the Food Production Exhibition held by the Brighton Equitable Co-operative Society at York Place Schools on the 18th. Entries numbered 620, exceeding the 1942 figure by no less than 200. Following the civic opening of the show, the Mayors of Brighton and Hove were conducted around the exhibition by E.A. Humbling, the Chairman.

A year later – on 9 September 1944 – a Food Production Exhibition was held in the Corn Exchange, one week before the Co-operative Society's in York Place Schools, and opened by the Mayor (Councillor B. Dutton Briant).

The Mayor of Brighton (Councillor B. Dutton Briant), accompanied by Commander Campbell of the BBC's Brain Trust, leading the official party on a tour of the 'Off the Ration' exhibition stalls. Inset is Lord Winterton, MP, who opened the exhibition. (BHG, 24.4.43)

The attractive features included a fruit preserving section for women, an inter-society competition (for the Brighton Allotments Cup), and sections for wartime gardeners. In Section A, there were classes for residents in Brighton, Hove, Portslade, Southwick and Shoreham, while Section B was for members of allotment societies in the borough. Section C was open to all allotment-holders and wartime gardeners who had not won more than two first prizes in any show. Music at the show was provided by the Patcham Boys' Brass Band.

On the 27th and 28th of that same month, the Royal Sussex County Hospital held its two-day Michaelmas Fayre and Horticultural Show at the Dome. In messages from Robert Hudson, Minister of Agriculture, and Mrs Hudson, read at the opening, Brighton was urged to keep the home food production front going, as more food than ever would be needed after the war. This was the view also expressed in the message from C.H. Middleton, the popular broadcaster, when he told the crowds, 'Keep the spade busy a little longer.' He described the event as 'one of the finest shows I've seen this year'. The nearby Royal Pavilion was the venue of the fayre, which, with its interesting handicraft exhibition, was well patronised.

Poster advertising the Co-operative Society's 1944 Food Production Exhibition. (BHH, 9.9.44)

A week later, a Domestic Front Exhibition was opened at the Brighton Electricity Showrooms, Castle Square. It ran for seven days and stressed the important part which the housewife had played in the war effort. The opening ceremony was presided over by the Mayor (Councillor B. Dutton Briant), who stated that Brighton was one of the first places to have a food advice centre. The event was organised by the Brighton Domestic Front Committee, in collaboration with the Ministries of Education, Information, Food and Fuel, members of local women's organisations, and the Board of Trade.

D-Day, the great crusade

The largest seaborne invasion in history took place on 6 June 1944 (D-Day) when Allied craft – with massive aerial support – headed for selected Normandy beaches as a first step towards the liberation of Europe. The amphibious landings were preceded by extensive aerial and naval bombardment and an airborne assault – the landing of 24,000 American, British, and Canadian airborne troops shortly after midnight.

Contributor Eileen Shilling recalled (in *D-Day – Brighton Remembers*) how the summer of that year had been a strange mixture of everyday life and a massive military presence:

> In early June the town was packed with soldiers, many of them Canadians, on one day and the next day they were gone. After the casualties of the Dieppe raid, few of our brave Dominion allies expected to survive the D-Day invasion.

Planning for Operation Overlord, as it was codenamed, had begun in 1943. In the months leading up to the invasion, the Allies conducted a substantial military deception, codenamed Operation Bodyguard, to mislead the Germans as to the date and location of the main Allied landings. Local resident Pam Piercey even believed she had received a decoy postcard:

> It was not until June 2004 and the TV coverage of the anniversary celebrations of D-Day that I realised that our invading forces had, in fact, departed from Hampshire and not from Kent. This made me wonder if I had been selected to receive a decoy postcard.
>
> Apparently, the powers that be had gone to great lengths, including the employment of a famous author, to create the illusion that the forthcoming landings would take place at Calais and that large invasion forces were assembling in Kent. I suddenly saw most of the military forces departing from Kemp Town so we realised something was about to happen. Just before D-Day I received a picture postcard from Sandwich in Kent. It was from a Canadian soldier I had met briefly while doing some voluntary canteen work. Being intensely patriotic, with the slogan 'careless talk costs lives' imprinted on my mind, I thought he was an idiot, particularly as I had a very German sounding name – SUHR – so like the River RUHR in Germany. (I am, in fact Danish). […] My British-born Danish father had fought for England in the First World War and was heavily involved in voluntary ARP work in the current conflict.

The beginning of the end for Hitler's Europe. (The Allen West Story)

A few days after D-Day, I received a phone call from the Canadian soldier. He had been wounded and was being sent back to Canada but wanted to see me to say goodbye. He said he was a bit of a mess as he had lost the sight of his left eye and been burned all down the left side of his face. It all seemed to have happened so quickly, within a few days in fact. I met him in the Old Steine at Royal York Buildings as I cycled back to work. He promised to contact my sister in New York to say we were OK. This he did, but although she invited him to dinner, he never turned up.

Eileen Shilling recorded a specific memory of the overseas troops:

My mother worked at the Bath Arms. Just before D-Day, there seemed to be tension amongst the troops in Brighton. The Canadians in particular seemed to know that something was about to happen, and they tried to have as good a time as possible. Many of them were selling anything of value to get extra money. The landlord of the Bath Arms bought a watch from a Canadian soldier who had it for his 21st birthday. After the war, the soldier contacted him to ask if he still had it. He had, and was pleased to be able to return it.

Also in *D-Day – Brighton Remembers*, Betty Wells recalled:

Nearly all the houses on the seafront had been requisitioned for the army and navy. We had a curfew and you had to have a special pass. Everybody in the town had an idea that something was brewing, because of the build-up of foreign troops. We had French Canadians, Polish airmen, Polish navy, the RAF and some Americans in the town. We were looking forward to D-Day. There was a sense of activity, but at the same time life went on just the same for those living at home. We already had gun emplacements on the seafront, at the back of the Downs and behind the hospital. [...] Tanks were parked at Preston Park, Preston Barracks or on the Downs. The lorries were parked in the streets under trees, and the drivers and a few other ranks would sleep under them at night.

I had a flat in Freshfield Road and the lorries were parked up and down the road. One night I returned home late and tripped over a soldier who was sleeping on my pathway.

There was extra activity amongst the air-raid wardens. They had extra duties and seemed to understand what was going on. Everybody talked about D-Day, though not outright, because of the posters saying 'Careless talk costs Lives'. In Shoreham there were tank landing craft – something was afoot.

Pupils at Varndean Boys' School noted in early 1944 that strange shapes (later learned to have been the components of the artificial Mulberry harbours) could be seen moving up and down the Channel; on the morning of 6 June all was revealed because the whole length of the horizon was lined with ships and craft of every description.

Tadeusz Stellar, another contributor, told how he had escaped from Poland and arrived in England in 1940. He had joined the army, but as there had been very heavy casualties in the RAF they asked for volunteers, whatever the rank, to learn to fly. He was bored with his job in Dundee so he volunteered. After training in Blackpool, he came down to Brighton to the Hotel Metropole which was occupied by the Polish Air Ministry. He went to Canada for training in bombing and navigation. Early in 1944, 305 Squadron was sent to Harrogate for special training on Mosquitoes, twin-engine fighter-bombers which could fly very low.

Before D-Day the crews' job was to fly to the French coast to bomb the launch sites of the Doodlebugs. Just before the end of May 1944 they stopped flying and were briefed about Normandy and their Sector 10.

In the Conclusion to *D-Day: Brighton Remembers*, the compiler points out how, in the spring of 1944,

> Brighton became an armed camp and a restricted zone. Troops were billeted on families or lodged in requisitioned property. Parks and open spaces were filled with encampments, military vehicles and supply dumps. [...] Anti-Aircraft guns were scattered round the town to guard against air attacks.

Commandos practising an amphibious landing on Brighton beach in 1944. (IWM H36107)

Tanks 'waterproofed' for D-Day being tested in the big static water basin in Preston Park. (BHIB)

Barry Hilsom recalled, in *SHELTERED LIVES – Ditchling Road School, The War Years*, that

> Brighton was full of Canadian soldiers in readiness for D-Day. This was very exciting for us and I can clearly remember the roads around Preston Park being full of tanks.

R.G. Layzell, another contributor to *D-Day: Brighton Remembers*, also recalled seeing those tanks:

> I was born in Havelock Road in 1940. My father was in the army. My mother used to take me across the park [Preston Park] to visit my grandmother at West Hill. The park was used as a collection point for army vehicles, hidden under the trees. At the bottom of the park, nearest to London Road, was a large water tank used for testing the tanks. They were waterproofed for the D-Day landings. Just before D-Day the tanks left Preston Park, I remember them driving past the house during the night.

The Argus, in its 'Argus 135' Supplement dated 30 March 2015, told its readers:

> Shortly before D-Day in 1944, [...] the Queen Mother visited Sussex to inspect Grenadier Guards stationed at Hove. Everyone knew an Allied invasion was in the offing but little was known of when, where or indeed how.

The family of resident Betty Field suddenly knew everything:

> We lived at the bottom of Freshfield Road, in a tall rambling house between two Southdown bus garages. My father worked for the bus company. The night prior to D-Day he had been on Home Guard duty at the garage. He came in very early at about 5am very excited, and woke my mother and me. 'Come outside and have a look,' he said, 'it's all happening.' One side of Freshfield Road is tree-lined, and beneath all the trees were tanks, guns, jeeps and troops. I recall that for such a mass of men and ammunition it was strangely quiet. The tanks had camouflage nets over them, and the soldiers' uniforms were camouflaged too. The whole length of Freshfield Road was full of soldiers all well hidden under the trees. My father crossed the road to speak to them, but he was interrogated by someone in authority. 'Did we have a telephone?', 'Was my father likely to leave the house that day?' I think they thought he was a spy. (From *D-Day – Brighton Remembers*)

The thunderous aerial armada in the small hours of 'The Day' left nobody in any doubt as to the *Argus*'s 'when', 'where' and 'how'. Local historian Clifford Musgrave vividly described the scene in his *Life in Brighton:*

> One morning it was seen that the concentrations of tanks and lorries had disappeared and the houses where troops had been quartered were empty. A few days later, at 2.30 in the morning of 6th June 1944, Brightonians were awakened by a loud continuous roar overhead far surpassing the noise of any of our earlier 1,000-bomber raids, and watchers from windows, from the seafront and the streets saw the dark shapes of the immense fleet of bombers, fighters, transport-planes and gliders silhouetted against the moonlit sky as they passed over the coast towards France. Many of them, bombers and fighters, passed and re-passed again and again as the morning wore on, and across the water was heard the dull rumble of gunfire and bombing. It was D-Day: the invasion of Europe had begun.

The *Herald*, for its part, recorded the wonder with which one local resident witnessed the scene:

> It was a marvellous sight and experience watching them go out. I got out of bed about half-past two. Transport planes and gliders were passing out towards the sea. They were very low, and I could see the gliders silhouetted in the moonlit sky. I said to my wife, 'This is It; the Invasion has started.' Later, as it was getting light, I watched great lines of heavy aircraft on their way, counting over 250 from where I was. I watched also the aerial transports returning as the morning advanced.

R.G. Layzell remembered waves of aircraft going over on D-Day. He thought – correctly – that some of them must have been towing gliders because he started to draw pictures of planes then started drawing them towing each other. Wave after wave went over. He remembered his mother saying she'd never seen so many planes together before.

Schoolchildren might hear an announcement of the incredible news on the school's public address system, as young Ken Francis did at Ditchling Road School:

> Even in those days we had school broadcasts and I remember that the loudspeaker was a large square one in a light colour wood. I remember hearing about the D-Day invasion at about 11am on June 6th 1944 when the school's broadcast was interrupted. A broadcast was also interrupted a few weeks later when the Allies invaded the South of France. (From *SHELTERED LIVES – Ditchling Road School, The War Years*)

Local schoolteacher Helen Roust made the following entry in her diary (published as *Brighton's War*):

> School at 8.30am before I called my register, Miss Stubbs told me that the beginning of the invasion had been announced on the 8am news. It has been a most exciting day. We listened to the news at school at 10am and then later at 12 midday. It was a solemn moment. Planes have hummed all day. At 6pm, we heard that the operations were proceeding according to plan, and at 9pm the King spoke. It was a short (but very good) speech urging the need for prayer. 9pm news also told us that our troops were already several miles inland in N. France. We heard recordings of all stages of this vast undertaking and also the voices of Eisenhower and 'Monty'. It was not over until 9.50pm. It is Marion's birthday today and we will always remember the day she was two years old.

There was something of a lull following the initial mighty wave; the *Herald* commented at the weekend that the roar of the night and early morning of Tuesday had been followed by an uncanny quiet which seemed to continue for hours. People wondered, but there was no mistake. Then the roar in the sky restarted, as squadron after squadron of heavy bombers flew over the towns and over the coast, while squadrons of attendant fighters circled round and round. In the early evening the great procession of transport planes restarted too, pouring troops across the stretch of sea into the breach made on the other side. A correspondent, who for an hour or more stood in a garden watching the procession of great planes, recalled seeing them in the distance like great blobs against the red and gold of the evening sun. They came over and seemed to lumber awkwardly across the sky. They came, passed, and returned in relays. It was, he declared, unforgettable.

Tadeusz Stellar had been in one of the countless aircraft very early that Tuesday morning. His flying time had been 2am and he and his crew had sat playing cards with their glasses on so that their eyes got adjusted to the dark. The other flyers had returned saying how easy it had been to find the targets and how successful they had been. Tadeusz's plane had to fly between Normandy and the Channel Islands, exactly ten miles from each coast so that they would be out of range of the guns. They spent three hours flying around looking for targets in what proved to be a difficult operation. Armed with contour maps of Normandy, they provided information for other troops because they could fly so low and see troops and supply movements. 'We were not heroes, we had a job to do. We did it.'

'*D Day: Invasion Has Begun*' was the headline plastered across the *Evening Argus*'s first edition of D-Day. The night staff of the paper had, we are told in the 'Argus 135' Supplement of 30.3.15, been working frantically to make sure the people of Sussex were up-to-date by the early morning. The main story provided the first draft of the historic day. The front cover also carried General Eisenhower's stirring pre-invasion speech to those involved and reported that the message had been read to all the men before they embarked on the conquest of Europe.

A cautionary note, however, was struck in the *Herald* on 10 June:

It is, however, very necessary that we should restrain this feeling that victory is just round the corner. [...] We shall succeed. Indeed, having set ourselves this task, there can be no turning back. Millions of oppressed people in Europe are looking to us for succour, and we will not fail them. But let none imagine that because we have a footing in Hitler's Europe the battle is over. [...] We shall achieve victory. We shall release Europe, and we shall beat Germany into unconditional surrender. This is the message of 'D-Day' – the day of deliverance – and we shall not halt or pause until we have accomplished that which we have set our hands to do!

A bomb aimer in one of Bomber Command's Halifaxes sent to strike behind the enemy's lines on D-Day night was a young Brightonian, Flying Officer Alan J. Robson, the elder son of Mr and Mrs W.E. Robson of Dyke Road. He left a graphic account of the vital part played by the huge force of aircraft on their first visit to the invasion coast, where road and railway junctions and bridges were attacked at various critical points. All the attacks, each of which was made by a strong force, were designed to block and delay the reinforcements which the enemy must be expected to bring up by every possible means of transport. He had expected to see a lot of the Luftwaffe, but in fact none of the crew in this attack saw any fighters at all. 'When our gunners realised that there were no fighters after us they trained their guns on the ground hoping to get a shot at some ground targets. They were looking for an enemy supply train, and were very disappointed when they did not get one.' Away to port, star shells were going into the sky, and he saw a couple of big fires going strong. Then he had to concentrate on his bombing. The target indicators seemed to be very well placed, and he felt that he ought not to miss, but before long the bright target indicators disappeared in the explosion of the bombs.

Clifford Musgrave recorded the immediate aftermath of D-Day as witnessed by Brighton townspeople:

> A day or so later a grim indication was given of the drama that was being enacted on the opposite coast when an empty landing-barge, blasted by explosions, was washed ashore at Brighton. Soon the first batch of wounded arrived at Brighton hospitals, followed in a little while by the first German prisoners, who were put to work filling air-raid shelter-trenches in the parks, or sent to neighbouring farms to help with the harvest.

Two days after D-Day, Helen Roust noted that there was still aerial activity:

> I awoke at 6.50 a.m. to a steady, light roar. Fortresses (I believe) were passing over in large numbers. They looked like large flies in the sky. I got out of bed and had a grandstand view from the bathroom window. Planes have been passing by all the time I have been writing this. I listened to the War Report No. 3 this evening and heard accounts from men who had travelled with the airborne troops and in gliders. Some of the wounded men spoke too. I took a hot water bottle to bed with me.

The compiler of *D-Day – Brighton Remembers* commented:

> For several weeks after D-Day, Brighton was reminded of the war by the German V1 (Buzz Bomb) offensive, the blackout and the coastal defences which kept people off the beaches. However by the late summer of 1944, the V1 launching sites in Northern France were captured in the Allied advance

Clearing beaches of mines. (BHIB)

and slowly peace returned to Brighton. In September, blackout restrictions were lifted on private houses and half-power street lights went on. That autumn began the difficult and dangerous task of clearing the beaches so they could be opened to the public again.

CHAPTER 7

Victory Year 1945

Features of the opening weeks of the year of victory included celebrations to welcome the New Year and make it a memorable time for the town's children, the disbanding of a number of local units, the occasional return of Brighton's servicemen from various theatres of war, on leave or permanently, and steps towards reinstating Brighton as a resort (especially by way of access to the beaches and the improvement of the seafront).

New Year celebrations

On New Year's Day 1945 itself, a happy crowd of boys and girls, children of members of the Brighton Division, Sussex Police Force, enjoyed a New Year party at the Royal Pavilion arranged by the Police Athletic Association. Two days later, over 100 small children of members of the forces who were on active service or prisoners of war enjoyed a delightful, albeit belated, Christmas party at St Michael's Church Hall in Victoria Place, a treat arranged by Mrs Z. Galloway, Chair of the Regency Ward Branch of Brighton and Hove Conservative Association. Toys from the laden Christmas tree, plus a 3*d* piece, were distributed among the children after their festive tea.

The very next day, no fewer than 500 boys and girls from Brighton and Hove, conveyed by a fleet of buses, were guests at the Brighton and Hove Greyhound Stadium, courtesy of its Director, Charles Wakeling. Following a sumptuous feast, prepared and served by 150 or so helpers, a number of entertainers delighted the children. Prominent guests included the Mayors and Mayoresses of Brighton and Hove and the Deputy Chief Constable of the Sussex Police Authority (Captain W.J. Hutchinson). At the same time, a giant children's party was in full swing in the Parish Hall of St Peter's Church, courtesy of the Ward Labour Party Association. The highly successful entertainment included games, community singing and antics by clowns. Since the numbers proved too many to be accommodated in the hall, arrangements were made for the youngsters to have tea at the café of the Brighton Equitable Co-operative Society. The sight of several hundred children lustily singing their way along London Road halted traffic and caught the attention

Children's party time in a large hall. (Royal Pavilion & Museums, Brighton & Hove)

of passers-by. Some of the youngsters who did not have coats were conveyed by taxi. During the plentiful tea, the children were waited on by members of staff of Bellman's, the nearby department store. The Labour Party also entertained some 400 children at their London Road and Elm Grove headquarters a week later.

Other parties during the month included one held at the Royal Pavilion on the 11th, hosted by No. 1 Division of Brighton's Wardens' service. This event was for adults, who enjoyed dancing to the band of HMS *Vernon*, a whist drive

Their duties over, Home Guard members raise their glasses in celebration. (Chris Horlock collection)

and various contests plus refreshments provided by the WVS. All receipts in excess of expenditure were donated to charity. The Wardens were not yet stood down, unlike some other units such as the Home Guard's 39th GPO Battalion, who had held a stand-down dinner and concert on 6 January at the Co-operative Restaurant in London Road, or the Civil Defence Guards, who would celebrate their stand-down – also at the Pavilion – on the 24th.

Entertainment and sport

The festive season would not, of course, have been the same without a pantomime and what could have been better than one on ice? *Snowflake and the Penguins* was hugely enjoyed by children and adults alike at the Sports Stadium on New Year's Day itself. Skating sessions for the public were regularly held at that venue in the afternoons and evenings, with a special children's session on Saturday morning. Ice hockey matches featuring, for example, the Sussex Tigers versus the Canadian Army, were a regular fixture. Another spectator sport still allowed during those times was racing every Saturday afternoon at the Greyhound Stadium in Nevill Road, Hove, and football at the Goldstone Ground. Here the Albion enjoyed triumphs and reverses, one of the latter being the unfortunate loss of their leadership of Group Two in the qualifying round of the Football League South Cup on 24 February when they were defeated 4-2 by Brentford. (This was nothing compared with the all-time worst defeat for the club – 18 goals to nil – at the hands of Norwich City on Christmas morning 1940).

Cinema entertainment did much to raise spirits. Early in the year, the immensely amusing *He Snoops to Conquer* starring George Formby teamed with Robertson Hare was showing at the Regent. Later in the month came a complete contrast in the form of the documentary film *Western Approaches*, shown at the Savoy. It told the story of the Atlantic convoys, its authenticity being assured by its cast of serving officers and men of the Allied Navies and Merchant Fleets. Before the preview of the film on 22 January, Brighton's Mayor took the salute from a section of the naval contingent. Marines and Wrens then saw the dramatic production as guests of the management. Almost a month later, a party of British, American, Australian and New Zealand airmen watched *Winged Victory* at the Regent. Practically the entire cast of this tribute to America's airmen were actually members of the Air Force. At this venue also, the servicemen watched the production as guests of the management. In early May came another film with a war theme, *Hotel Berlin*, starring Faye Emerson, Helmut Dantine and Raymond Massey. Based on a novel by Vicki Baum, it was

The circus came to town at the end of March, providing spectacular entertainment for young and old. (SDN 29.3.45)

described by the *Sussex Daily News* as 'a grim drama of the life of a fugitive from the tyranny of the Gestapo and the torture of Dachau concentration camp'. Its release was rushed by Warner Bros. to coincide with the Russian and Allied drives on Berlin.

Plays were well patronised. The audience at the Theatre Royal were able to escape from the war at New Year by watching Noel Coward's *This Happy Breed*, the story of the working class Gibbons family between the wars; in contrast, *Desert Rats*, starring Richard Greene, vividly brought the Western Desert to Brighton at its world premiere at the theatre in the following month. Its author, Colin Morris, had served in North Africa and knew his subject. He appeared in uniform after the production to acknowledge its enthusiastic reception, paying tribute in a brief speech to the cast and the producer, Henry Sherek.

Comedy shows always raised people's spirits – and who better to entertain the town than Brighton's own Max Miller, a regular performer at the Hippodrome, the venue where Vera Lynn was singing twice nightly in February? Music was always popular, hence the rousing reception given in January to the United States Army Air Forces Band, which was making a goodwill tour of this country. Geraldo and his band visited Brighton for the first time on 14 February when they played to a packed dance hall at the Dome. They had rushed down from a session in London to make what was only their third dance hall appearance that year and had to return immediately afterwards.

Worthy Funds

There was, of course, only a limited amount of money which families and individuals could spend on entertainment. Apart from having to meet their own needs, they were frequently called upon to assist either the war effort in general or specific local causes. Among the latter were funds to benefit our troops, such as the Army Benevolent Fund and the Prisoner of War Fund, and even a foreign country (Poland), while medical charities needing help included the Royal Alexandra Hospital for Sick Children (which benefited greatly at the end of May 1945 – the war by then over – from an Empire Day Fair opened by the Duchess of Devonshire) and the Queen's Nurses, for whom a successful Flag Day was held early in that month. The local press regularly featured appeals (often in poster form) urging the townspeople to contribute savings towards the prosecution of the war, particularly bearing in mind the final great efforts to be made. The generosity of Brightonians was demonstrated by the grand total of their savings reaching no less than £17,087,127 by 6 January 1945.

A resort reborn

This was the year of Brighton's rehabilitation as a resort. The first steps towards preparing the seafront for enjoyment by the townspeople and visitors were taken from mid-January, when the local press reported on the relaying of paving stones over a whole expanse of the Promenade near the Peace Statue. At its meeting on 22 February, the Council announced that a portion of the beach (that part between the Hove boundary and a little to the east of the West Pier) would soon be opened. This at least was a start. The popular Undercliff Walk from Black Rock to Saltdean was to be reopened on the same date – 10 March. In addition, the through road to Rottingdean along Marine Parade, which had been blocked between Chichester Place and Arundel Road, was to be reopened on the Monday following the meeting, 26 February. Excitement at the news of the beach's reopening was, however, dampened when its postponement was announced a short time later due to the military authorities being unable to give a clearance certificate which satisfied the Committee. The beach had to be absolutely safe for the public.

In March, scores of men and vans – starting at the western end of the stretch of beach scheduled for reopening – were hard at work between the two piers disposing of unnecessary and obsolete paraphernalia. Up on the Promenade, the familiar cry of 'Tickets Please!' was once again heard during the weekend of the 17th–18th, when scores of deckchairs were brought out for the first time in five years. By the end of the month, the clearance workers' labours culminated in the long-awaited beach reopening. The event, on Saturday 24 March, was marked by a civic ceremony at which Brighton's Mayor, Councillor A.V. Nicholls performed the opening before a great crowd of spectators. For many youngsters their paddle in the sea was the first in their lives.

Visitors would now be arriving in force but would, as the Mayor pointed out, have to ensure firm bookings for their accommodation. Brighton's hotels had suffered greatly during the war and were continuing to do so. At the annual meeting of the Brighton and Hove Hotels and Restaurant Association which had been held on 6 February at the Old Ship Hotel, the delegates trusted that 'every effort would be made to impress upon the Government the absolute necessity of the early de-requisitioning of hotels and boarding houses if the main industry of the locality is to be re-established within a reasonably early period.' Clifford Hindle of the Old Ship pointed out that the town had only 20 per cent of its normal accommodation for visitors and remarked: 'people are clamouring and scolding and calling some of us quite rude names because we can't fix them up.' Another delegate observed that Hastings and St Leonards were, by contrast, advertising that they had plenty of accommodation.

The Easter weekend of 1945 fell on April 1–2, during which the immense crowds in Brighton approached pre-war levels. Every train arrived at the station well loaded, traffic to the town was very heavy and at Pool Valley there were long queues for Southdown buses. Entertainment venues did record business and hundreds waited outside restaurants and the ice cream parlours. Many of Brighton's souvenir shops did their first real business for five years. The Whitsun weekend of 19–20 May saw Brighton thronged again, with the *Sussex Daily News* reporting that the 'reopened beaches were black with holiday-makers'. But before then, a momentous event would take place – VE Day.

VE Day, 8 May 1945

When it came, this long-awaited day to celebrate victory in Europe began as something of an anti-climax, here and across the nation. In London, the crowds gathered in Whitehall, around Buckingham Palace and in the West End from early on. Londoners felt somewhat aggrieved that they had been able to hear accounts of the German surrender on the radio and read factual reports on

A patriotic quartet take home their decorations from a Brighton store in preparation for the victory celebrations. (*SDN*, 8.5.45)

it in the papers but had still had to wait for the official announcement before celebrating.

In Brighton, too, peace came in a way that had not been anticipated; instead of a spectacular announcement, the news filtered through via the newspapers and the BBC through the Ministry of Information instead of the Prime Minister. The *Sussex Daily News* recorded 'a listlessness in the proceedings of the populace', adding that, 'With nothing in particular to do, they did nothing in particular. They seemed to have no aim in life until the Prime Minister spoke and the local proclamations were made at the close of the afternoon.' There was some purposeful activity in the morning, however, when laying in a stock of eatables was the prime concern of many, resulting in queues forming. Otherwise, there were no crowds in the streets for the greater part of the day. Scenes on the Front, however, left no doubt that the day was a holiday. In the town, fireworks – hitherto banned – were let off and colourful flags and bunting gave a festive appearance to the streets, large and small. Some of the displays – particularly that at Hannington's – were particularly striking.

Street parties were held everywhere, with reports published by the *Evening Argus* of celebrations at the following locations: Buller Road, Firle Road, Guildford Street, Islingword Place, Kensington Place, May Road, Newhaven Street, Nuthurst Road, Park Street and Queen's Gardens. An amateur film of VE Day events by one Winston Robinson recorded, mostly in colour, street parties

A joyful party in Gordon Road, Brighton. (Chris Horlock collection)

Woodingdean children celebrating VE Day in the garden of the Downs Hotel, Woodingdean. The children's fancy dress garden parties continued for many years after this particular event. (Peter Mercer collection)

attended by the Mayor and Mayoress in Eldred Avenue, Patcham, New England Street, Vere Road, Blaker Street, Tillstone Street, Carlton Hill (Milner Flats), Newmarket Road and Kimberley Road, as well as decorated buses and a fair which the Mayor arranged to be held in East Brighton Park. The film is viewable online (see Bibliography and Further Reading – Films). On a later date, he is captured in a *Sussex Daily News* photo playing the piano at a street celebration when touring the various festivities across the town with the Mayoress and US servicemen.

At 2.45pm on the great day, fifteen minutes before Churchill's long-awaited Proclamation of Peace in Europe, Mayor Nicholls broadcast the following message to the public of Brighton:

> Today brings to a successful end the efforts of our boys and our girls who have slain the greatest menace the world has ever known. We older folk have added in full measure our humble efforts to help in every way possible. Our exertions, preparations and sacrifices are well-known to us all and have touched every home, almost without exception, in our town. We thank God

The crowd which assembled to listen to the proclamation of victory from Brighton Town Hall on 8 May 1945. (Royal Pavilion & Museums, Brighton & Hove)

today they have not been in vain. So, today we rejoice and smile, many of us through our tears, that freedom and peace have once more been saved for civilization.

Following the speech, music was relayed until, at 3pm, the Prime Minister was announced. Silence reigned as his stirring message was delivered. Cheers then greeted his words, and many joined in singing the National Anthem. As 6pm approached, the crowds overflowed from Bartholomews into East Street to listen to the Mayor's official proclamation of the cessation of hostilities from the lower balcony at the north-east corner of the Town Hall.

His Worship was greeted by a fanfare from the Royal Sussex Cadets' Bugle Band, followed by *Sussex By The Sea* played by the 15th Sussex (Brighton) Home Guard Band. With his words relayed on the town's loudspeakers, he then quoted in full the speech which the Prime Minister had made earlier, adding:

It is not fitting that I should seek to embellish the speech of the greatest master of words […] but I have thought that on such an occasion, the like

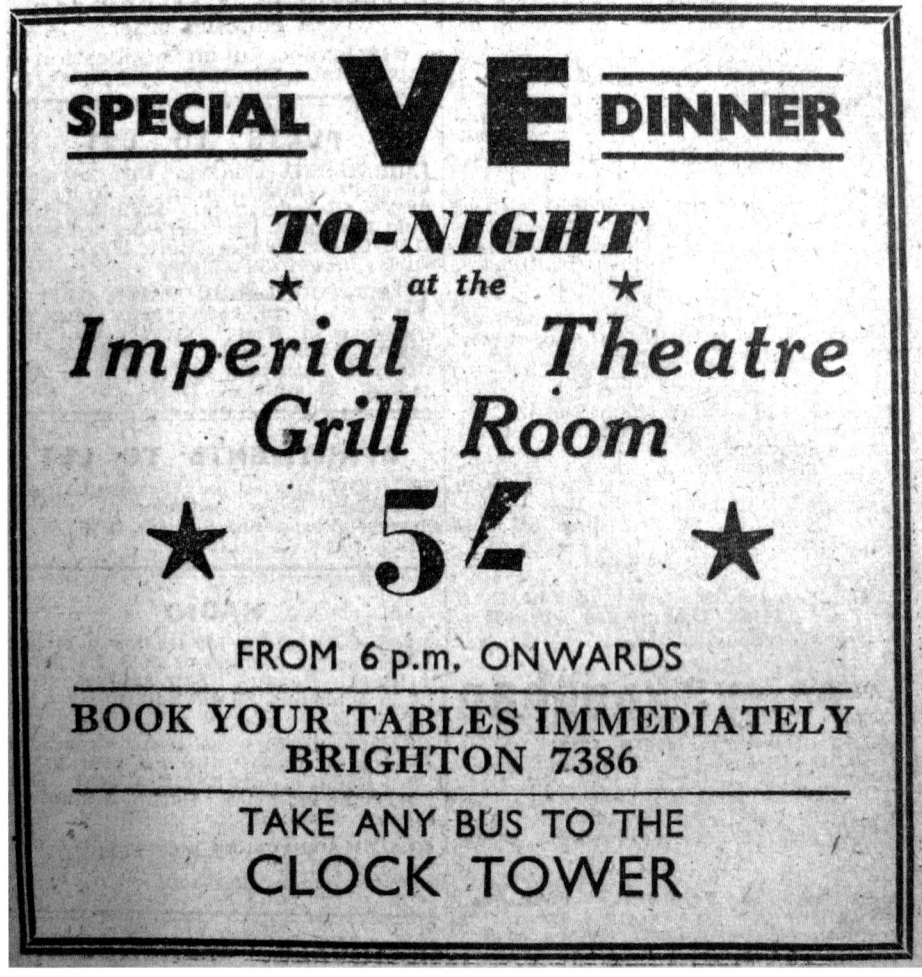

Advertisement for a commemorative VE Day dinner at the Imperial Theatre, North Street. (SDN, 9.5.45)

of which no one living has ever known, nor is likely to know again, I, your Mayor, should appear before you, so that together we may hear the words of thanksgiving to Almighty God for our great deliverance from mortal peril that my Chaplain, Canon James, is about to speak […].

The Mayor then stepped back and his place was taken by Canon T.J. James MC, who suitably addressed the crowd and led them in the Lord's Prayer. His listeners then stood to attention and sang the National Anthem. At the conclusion of this simple ceremony, the crowds dispersed to fulfil the wishes of the Mayor that they should all have a pleasant and happy evening. Already the fair arranged by him was being enjoyed by children in East Brighton Park. The dance halls, approp   'ely decorated, were soon full although most of the townspeople decided that the way to enjoy themselves was to tour the decorated streets. At 9pm a crowd of close on 3,000 people gathered once again in and around East Street and North Street to hear the King's speech, in which profound gratitude and heartfelt relief were expressed that, in this 'great deliverance', the 'dreadful shadow of war has passed far from our hearths and homes in these islands.' At the Dome that evening, a Civic Victory Ball arranged by the Mayors of Brighton and Hove (the latter was Alderman A.H. Clarke) under the management of Fred White was a very successful function which raised £300 or so for the Brighton and Hove 'Thank You' Fund to All Services. The amount was supplemented by over £19 from a collection made among the dancers.

Huge crowds of revellers gathered on the seafront, their enthusiasm making the day one which would long be remembered. Yet something was missing, according to one G.E. Wilmshurst of Hythe Road, who complained in a letter to the *Sussex Daily News* of being amazed at the apathy, lack of thought and imagination of Brighton Corporation in connection with the celebrations:

> Thousands of people on the Sea Front on Tuesday paraded past an empty bandstand: if a band could be obtained for an hour at the Town Hall, surely it could have been engaged for two or three hours for the people's pleasure in this same bandstand.
>
> The Corporation are renting premises in London at £3,000 per annum to boost the town; here was an opportunity at a fraction of the cost to do the same thing. By providing clean healthy recreation and entertainment for our own folk there would be no lack of visitors to the town.
>
> And why not a Victory parade and thanksgiving service in Preston Park, when thousands of people would have gathered to render their heartfelt thanks to God for our great deliverance, and for the fact that our old country has once again been in the van for freedom and righteousness. People of all Churches and of none would be delighted to have the opportunity of expressing their pent-up thankfulness.

Thanksgiving

Services were held in Brighton's churches during VE Day itself, but the town's United Service of Thanksgiving at the Parish Church of St Peter was postponed until noon the next day. It was a deeply impressive ceremony. The service was preceded by, and linked with, a Solemn Eucharist of Thanksgiving at St Bartholomew's at which the vicar (the Rev. D.D.A. Lockhart) was the celebrant, flanked by the Rev. J.G. Tiley (vicar of St Paul's) the deacon and the Rev. B.J. Scott (vicar of St Michael's) the sub-deacon. Many other clergy were present at the Mass. The choir was a composite one drawn from several churches, including St Peter's. When it ended, a procession was formed which made its way to St Peter's singing the hymn *Praise to the Lord, the Almighty, the King of Creation*. Brighton's

This young girl made sure she took her Union Jack along with her to the Chapel Royal for her family's personal thanksgiving. (SDN, 9.5.45)

Mayor and Mayoress, seated with the Deputy Chief Constable for Sussex (Captain W.J. Hutchinson), were in the large congregation. At the church door, the procession was met by the Rev. J.D.C. Fisher (Priest-in-charge) with other clergy. Triumphal music pealed from the powerful organ as choir and clergy passed up the nave to the chancel. The already large congregation was now swollen by people who had come with the procession from St Bartholomew's so the church was not only crowded to its utmost but a great many would-be worshippers were unable to gain admittance. Canon James' sermon was preceded by the singing of a verse of the National Anthem. In his address, he listed those points for which thanksgiving was to be offered to Almighty God, concluding with a reminder that the war in the Far East had still to be won and asking for prayers that God's blessing might rest on the Allied Forces engaged in that struggle. The final, and deeply moving, act of thanksgiving was the *Te Deum*, fervently sung to simple Anglican chants by the whole congregation.

Victory Parade

Four days later, on Sunday 13 May, Brighton's Victory Parade took place. A military band formed by units of the Brighton Home Guard played cheering

Civil Defence Wardens pass the saluting base. (BHIB)

music during the wait for it to start. All the Services, watched by thousands of spectators, then marched from Madeira Drive to Preston Street via King's Road, passing the saluting base in front of the Old Ship Hotel where Brigadier K.E.S. Stewart MC, Commander of the West Sussex Sub-District, took the salute in the company of the Mayor, members of the Town Council, their families and friends, and other prominent personages. Leading the parade was the Naval Cadet Band, preceded by two police motorcycle riders. Directly behind the Band marched Major J.C. Milner TD, Parade Marshal, representing the Army, Captain Norman Grace, representing the Navy, and Squadron Leader Baird, representing the Royal Air Force. All three took their places at the saluting base. The various Services then marched past, namely the men of the Navy, representatives of many leading British regiments, accompanied by members of the Canadian Army, followed by a very strong contingent of the Home Guard (although officially disbanded, having been stood down on 3 December 1944, they turned out to take their rightful part in the victory parade), the Air Forces of the Commonwealth, the women of the ATS, the WAAF and the WRNS. Then came the Observer Corps, the Land Army, the men and women of the NFS, the Police Force and the Civil Defence, the WVS and all the auxiliary nursing services. To all, a debt of heartfelt gratitude was owed.

It's over

Our story concludes with an apt quotation from the slim, largely pictorial, volume entitled *Brighton & Hove in Battledress, 1939–1945*, written by D.L. Murray and published by Brighton Herald Ltd in 1946 for the Brighton and Hove War Memorial Fund:

> May 8th, 1945. I was in a bus slowly making the ascent of the steep hill behind the station. Across the railway lines below, the panorama of Brighton stretched in soft afternoon sunshine. On the conductor's platform was gracefully poised one of those 'clippies' who had guided us through so many black and noisy nights in the last six years. A woman sitting by the doorway bent forward and asked her a question. She nodded. 'Yes,' she said. 'Unconditional surrender. Came through about an hour ago.' No one spoke. We jogged on, and got out at our various destinations. That was that.

APPENDIX 1

The Book of Remembrance

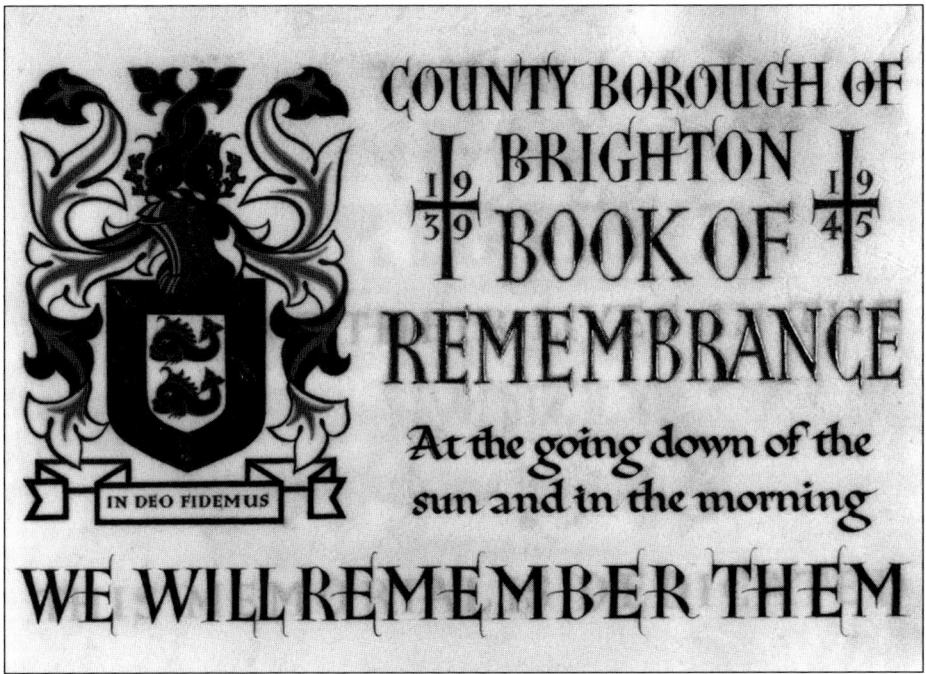

On Tuesday 11 November 1952, a service of dedication was held at St Peter's Parish Church, Brighton when a Book of Remembrance to commemorate those who lost their lives in the Second World War was unveiled. The project was commissioned by the Town Council and executed under the direction of Ernest Arthur Sallis Benney, Principal of Brighton College of Art. The pages of the book were designed, written and illuminated by his eldest son, Derek Benney, and the blue leather binding with its gold tooled decoration was designed and executed by William Matthews.

Until September 2016, the Book of Remembrance was kept in a glass case in St Peter's Church. This author, during research for the present volume, was given access to the book and took his own digital photos of its pages. He proposed that The Keep, the county archive centre at Falmer, north of Brighton, might be a more suitable home for such an important manuscript and set the ball rolling for its transfer there to join the other archives of the parish. It is in the care of the conservator but digital images are available on computers in the Reference Room at The Keep. (PAR 277/7/8/3)

It is a beautiful example of calligraphy and lists in alphabetical order the names of 968 servicemen, servicewomen and civilians from the parish killed between 1939 and 1945. Brighton College of Art was involved in many aspects of war work, including designing posters for the Ministry of Information and Women's Voluntary Service and producing maps for the RAF and it seems appropriate that they should have been so closely involved in the production of this Roll of Honour.

The list was compiled by Lieutenant Colonel C.H. Madden. A veteran of the First World War, in which he was almost blinded, Madden was a committed campaigner for the welfare of ex-servicemen. During the Second World War he was one of the first leaders in what was to become known as the Home Guard. Sadly, he did not live to see the dedication ceremony of the Book. He was killed in a plane crash on a mountainside in Sicily in early 1952 on his way to visit his daughter in East Africa.

The recorded names comprise those of 209 civilians and 759 service personnel.[1] Space does not permit the listing of the latter, but an analysis reveals that of those who gave their lives, by far the largest number (242, or 31.9 per cent) served with the RAF and 148 (19.5 per cent) with the Royal Navy, including Reserves. These two branches between them therefore accounted for just over half of all service fatalities.

Below is provided the Book's listing of the civilians who lost their lives in the conflict, a listing which exceeds the generally received/official (Commonweath War Graves record) figure of 198 casualties sustained by Brighton. Twelve names are included in the official list but not in the Book.[2] Names specific to the Book are marked in the following listing with an asterisk.

---

1. It should be noted that forty-four names in the listing are designated as 'Service not known'.
2. Ernest Joseph Burnet-Smith, Arthur Fenner, John William Gibbs, Peter Arthur Idle, Michael Patrick Kohane, David McAllister, Agnes Robertson (of Seaford but died in the RSCH), Agnes Smith, Harold Stone, Doris Tucknott, Herbert William Tucknott, and William George West (the Book does, however, record an Ernest West).

Civilian Deaths Recorded in the 1952 'Book of Remembrance'

Aldet*, Ahmed Georges
Allwright, Robert William
Avis, Annie
Bagot*, Alan
Bailey, George
Baldwin, Stanley
Ball, Frederick
Barker, Frank William
Barrett*, Doris Ivy
Bartley*, Ellen Emma
Barton-Tales, Edith Emily
Beadle, William George
Bell, David Keith
Berry*, Freda Mary
Bettesworth, Florence Emily
Betts, Arthur Thomas
Betts, Mildred Mary Cecilia
Blackwell, Jane
Borrow, Sydney Roy
Bowles, Stanley Albert
Boyling, Arthur George
Bradstock, Rosina
Brashill, Lillian Mary
Brawn, Alexander
Brown, Edward Clark
Burkinshaw, Charles
Burkinshaw, Charlotte
Calcraft, Rupert Harold
Cassler, Brenda
Cassler, Edith
Cassler, Natalie
Cassler, Nathan
Castledine*, Harold William George
Chapman, Alfred
Chapman, Iris Lilian
Chubb, William Henry
Clancy, Josephine Trisslie[3]
Coatman, Elizabeth
Coatman, Henry Joel
Cochrane, Robert Allan
Colbourne Bernard David
Coles*, Walter Weston Voyle
Cordier, Joan Mary
Cotton, Caroline
Crelley, Retta Violet
Crowley, James
Danegan[4], Alma Madeline
Davies, Ivor David
De Witt, Marion Eleanor Harriett
Denbigh, Kathleen Louisa
Drinkwater*, William Harold
Dudeney, John
Duplock, Monica Mary Ann
Duran, Julia
Dyer, Stephen William
Eade, James Henry[5]
Eade, Lucy
Eade, Muriel Gwendoline

---

3. 'Trissie' in official records.
4. 'Dannigan' in official records.
5. 'James Arthur' in official records.

Eatwell, William Henry
Eley, Violet May
Everett, Monica
Everett, Susannah Mary
Faith, Lilian Bertha
Fenson, Ronald
Fenson, Rosemary
Ford, William
Freeman, Agnes Florence Mary
Frew*, Alexander James
Gander, Albert
Glyde, Emily
Goble, Florence Elizabeth Mary
Goble, John James
Grinstead, Kenneth
Hardwick, Rosetta Alice
Hardwick*, Ruby Newman
Hargreaves, Ettie
Harris, Freda
Harris, Ivy Elizabeth
Harris, Susan
Hayler, William Henry
Holford, Lawrence William
Hook, Anne Teresa
Hook, Edith May Kathleen Agnes
Hylden*, Henry
Inman, Nora
Jones, David Thomas
Jones, Leonard Henry

Langley*, Lila Alice
Leadbeater, Anthony Vincent
Leech, Louisa Kate Maud
Little, Alfred Saunders
Lloyd, Mary Anne
Loftus, Nellie Irene
Lynes*, Margaret Yorath
Macdonald, Joseph Hilton Salvage
Marchant, Johanna
Martin, Harry
Maskell, Charles Hackney
Mason, Edith Ellen
Mawby, Charlotte Gabrielle[6]
May, Henry
Mcallister, David
Mckay[7], Hugh Miller
Mechen*, Sarah
Mepham, Arthur
Mitchell, Bertha Matilda
Morley, Arthur
Morley, Harry
Morley, John Mervin
Morley, Mabel Florence[8]
Newgeritz, Verena Mary Elizabeth
Newman, Ruby Emily
Norman*, William Charles
Norris, Jane Maria
O'Connell, Eileen Florence
O'Connell, Eileen Mary

---

6. 'Claudette Gabriel' in official records.
7. 'Miller-Mackay' in official records.
8. 'Frances' in official records.

Ockenden, Leslie Albert
Orme, Edith
Paine, Charles
Paine, Margaret Louise
Parr, Eliza
Parsons, Eliza
Patterson, Ian Robert
Payne, Mary Louisa
Peacock, Annie Eliza
Pearce[9], Philip John
Perkins*, Florence Margaret
Perry, Joan Constance
Perry, Rita Joan
Pinkstone, James Robert
Pullen, Violet Louise
Reading, Alfred
Rennie, Elizabeth Ann
Reynolds*, Alma Madeline
Richardson, Alice
Richardson, George Noel
Richardson, Mary Elizabeth
Ridout, Freda Mary
Rogers, Violet
Rosenzweig, Lilian Jean
Rush, Alan James
Rush, Margaret Lilian
Rush, Yvonne
Sawyer, Francis James
Sayers, Eliza Lydia

Sayers, Jose Clara
Sebbage, Louisa Charlotte
Shakespeare, Percy
Sharp, Mary Elizabeth
Shepherd, Eliza
Shepherd, Francis Joseph
Shepherd, Mercy Florence
Sherlock, Edith Florence
Sherlock, William Frederick
Shoosmith, Lydia
Shorrocks, Florence Augusta
Shorter, Cecil Reginald
Siddall, Charles Harry
Simmonds, Emma
Sinden, Jane
Smart*, Florence
Smithyes, Rosalie
Southon, Harriett[10] Elizabeth
Stone, John Alan Warren
Stops, Minnie
Stops, Susan Wakefield
Sturgess, Pamela Violet
Stuttaford, Frank Peter Hugo
Sulley, Ernest George
Sulley, Rosina Mary
Swain, Herbert
Thomas, Joyce Alma
Thompson, George Edward
Ticehurst, Robert Ernest

---

9. 'Phillip' in official records.
10. 'Harriet' in official records.

Tickner*, William
Tootell, Emma
Townend, Lydia Boardman Shuker
Tucker, Albert Edward
Tucker, Ernest Edward[11]
Tucker, Maude Charlotte Mary
Varney, Lena
Varney*, Frank Ernest
Vincent, Nellie
Walder, Nellie Amelia
Walker, Ronald William Noah
Wallis, Audrey Winifred
Wallis, Robert Arthur
Wallis, Rose Evelyn Emily
Warnett, Ellen Mary
Watson, John
Weaver, Edith Lucy
Weaver, Joseph Reginald

Welfare*, Edward
Wells, George
Wells, Sydney George
West*, Ernest
White, Philip Rampton
Wickens, Julia Emily
Williams, Doris Caroline Lucy
Williamson, Maria
Wood, Annie Sophia
Wood, George
Wood, Mary Marjorie
Wood, Ronald
Wright, Maria
Young, Alfred Arthur
Young, Doris Mary
Young, Elizabeth
Young, Frederick

Total = 209

Readers interested in the location of local memorials should use the link to the Imperial War Museum website (*iwm.org.uk*) and within it access 'Brighton' in the War Memorials Register. Ostensibly limited to the town, it does contain references to some located elsewhere (e.g. New Brighton, Surrey, etc.).

The imposing building in Queen's Road pictured below was built in 1849 and served as the Brighton, Hove and Preston Dispensary until the early 1930s. After the war, we are told in the booklet *Brighton & Hove in Battledress 1939–45*, it was

> purchased by the voluntary contributions of the townspeople of Brighton and Hove as a memorial to all those men and women who took part in the l939–45 war. The premises are to be equipped as permanent headquarters for

---

11. 'Edward Ernest' in official records.

Churchill House in Queen's Road, intended to stand as a memorial to servicemen and -women after the war but long since demolished. (BHIB)

the many regimental associations and ex-Service organisations which care for those who fought in our wars.

Regrettably, the building was eventually acquired for commercial use (by Eagle Star Insurance) and demolished in the 1960s for the erection of new offices.

APPENDIX 2

Local Industrial Production

A number of local manufacturing facilities made an important contribution towards Britain's wartime industrial output.

Allen West founded the electrical engineering firm of that name in 1910. During the First World War it manufactured armaments and other military items in addition to its electric motor control business (see this author's *Brighton in the Great War* published in 2016). A new factory at East Moulsecoomb was completed just before the Second World War on ten acres of land purchased from Brighton Corporation. A second factory was completed in 1940.

During the war, staff numbers grew from approximately 2,000 to 4,500, many of whom were women working part-time.

The company became involved in the manufacture of radio transmitters and receivers and played a significant part in the development of radar equipment. Self-contained radar trailers, which soon proved their value, were manufactured under conditions of the utmost secrecy, as was equipment for long-range detector units which gave timely warning to RAF Fighter Command and made it possible

Allen West's East Moulsecoomb site in 1940. (The Allen West Story)

Demonstration of Allen West radar trailer on Brighton Sea Front, 1945. (Author)

for the enemy to be intercepted many miles from the coast. Allen West equipment considerably facilitated the sinking of the German battleship *Scharnhorst*, a fact officially acknowledged by the Admiralty in one of many letters of appreciation of the company's services. The company's engineering skill was also closely involved in the construction of control gear for the famous 'Pluto' petroleum line and for the fog dispersal scheme known as 'Fido'.

When the Germans introduced the magnetic mine as one of their 'secret weapons', Allen West was called upon to supply apparatus for experimental work by Admiralty engineers. Development work was involved, but designs were put in hand immediately and, in view of the extreme urgency, production was commenced before the designs were complete. Over 2,000 British and Allied vessels were rendered immune to the magnetic mine, and a large number of oscillators and gear for dealing with another enemy menace, the acoustic mine, were supplied. Many mines laid in enemy waters and parachute mines were of Allen West manufacture. The company also made equipment for the control of the mine network protecting ports at home and abroad.

Midget submarines and 'human torpedoes' (which figured in many daring exploits, including the sinking of the 10,000-ton cruiser *Bolzano*) had essential parts of their mechanism made by Allen West in Brighton. In an official letter to the company on behalf of Admiralty Special Operations Branch, it was stated: 'I have not heard of a single failure of the mechanism when on operations, which is satisfactory, and I am very grateful for your help and suggestions in making the device a success.'

The Allen West shops produced a remarkable variety of other service equipment during the war, such as that needed for the electrical firing of tank cannon, aero-engine testing, cold storage plants, air-sea rescue apparatus, and equipment for the amenity ships, or 'floating pubs', for the Far East.

For the Admiralty alone, more than 100,000 starters, controllers and resistances for electric motors and 1,250,000 pattern articles of various types were supplied during those years, and it was the company's proud claim that probably every naval ship had on board some essential apparatus produced in the Allen West factories.

In a remarkable achievement, the company also supplied the pierheads used in the construction of the prefabricated invasion harbour, code-named 'Mulberry', accommodating our little ships in connection with D-Day. Each contained, from the very first experimental model, a control mechanism on which Brighton men and women had toiled secretly day and night.

Regrettably, a tragic event occurred in the vicinity of the production site in 1941. War Reserve PC Lawrence Holford was on duty in the Lewes Road area on 30 April and went to visit Allen West's gatekeeper, Stephen Dyer, in his hut in Natal Road. While there, two Beaufighters of 219 Squadron based at Tangmere collided and the engine of one of the aircraft crashed down onto the hut, killing both men. Sergeant Twidale managed to use his parachute and landed safely. The other crew members, POs Black and Holman and Sergeant Forster, were killed.

Other engineering enterprises contributed to the war effort. The machine tool company CVA (as it was known for much of the twentieth century) was founded at the end of the First World War and had its headquarters for over fifty years in Portland Road, Hove, near the bottom of what is now Olive Road. Its manufacturing expertise was used extensively towards the war effort and because of this the company expanded to a number of other sites in the Brighton and Hove area, such as on the north side of Bristol Road near the junction with Bedford Street.

The Talbot Tool Company, founded in 1940, just off Borough High Street next to Guy's Hospital, manufactured products essential to the war effort. Within two years, due to its perilous production site so close to London Docks, the family-owned business moved to a calmer location at the behest of the War Ministry. The new location, a large converted garage in King Street in the centre of Brighton, allowed the uninterrupted production of jig bushes and tooling parts for the Ministry of Aircraft Production. (Due to increasing sales after the war, larger premises were required and in 1946 the business moved to Roedale Road, Brighton. It survives today on the Hollingbury Industrial Estate on a site adjacent to that of KDL Precision Engineers Ltd, which it took over in 1958.)

Surprisingly, Brighton College played a part in wartime component production. A pupil's father, G. Rushton, ran his own engineering works and (crucially) was a wartime government contractor. Martin Jones' history of the school records that,

> he was prepared to give high quality lathes and to place contracts for die cast and machine tooled components if the College would convert its workshops into a munitions factory. Thus was born the Engineering Scheme. Rushton's machines were ready by March [1940] and work began that Easter holidays with 33 volunteer dayboys. To begin with, inevitable lack of skills led to reject rates of up to 90 per cent on orders. At that point a Junior School parent, H. Upward of the local Reliance Motor Works, stepped in. He offered supervision, training and better quality tools. That did the trick. Machining to an accuracy of 2.5 thousandths of an inch in aluminum, brass and steel, reject rates thereafter were never greater than 3 per cent, even when the factory was turning out 25,000 items per month.

Mention should also be made of the firm of H.J. Galliers Ltd, founded at the turn of the last century by an electrical engineer of that name. It operated for many years from premises at 32 St James's Street. Herbert James Galliers (1880–1952) was Mayor of Brighton in 1928/29 and prominent in civic affairs over a considerable period.

At individual level, Alan A. Saunders, managing director of a firm of builders' merchants in the town, was made Coordinator of Radio Production for the whole country, and was responsible for the production of radar sets and other detection

The Engineering Room, Brighton College. (Brighton College 1845–1995 by M.D.W. Jones)

Women on war work at H.J. Galliers Ltd., one of the many small, but highly-skilled, factories making munitions. (BHIB)

equipment. Early in the war he was told 400 submarine detector sets were needed. On his own initiative he ordered 4,000, which were quickly found to be of vital value.

Finally, the following post (reproduced with permission) to the 'My Brighton & Hove' website from Dennis Fielder dated 11 January 2014 is of relevance and interest:

> I worked at a garage in Beconsfield [sic] Road l/h side going out of Brighton, it was next to the Viaduct. This was in the late 50s or early 60s! One day the chap that owned it said – are you interested in seeing something unusual in your tea break? – so I said OK. We then went upstairs and to my utter amazement there before me was a small intact Munitions Factory. All the machinery was still there and the benches etc etc. Time had just stood still. And the guy told me he was in charge of it during the war and they had never bothered to take the machines away. Now I can't remember what the garage was called – it's a long time ago and I only worked there about six months. I have a couple of Kellys directories but can't find the garage name. He sold a few cars and had a service bay.

Bibliography and Further Reading

A: Newspapers, Periodicals & Miscellaneous Papers

Brighton & Hove Herald
Brighton & Hove Gazette
Sussex Daily News
Sussex Express
Evening Argus/(since 2002:) *The Argus*

B: Books

Allen West & Co. Ltd., *The Allen West Story*, Allen West & Co. Ltd., Brighton 1960
Allt, Tony & Robson, Brian, *Onward and Upward – York Place to Varndean 1884–1975*, Brighton, The Old Varndeanians Association
Argus, The, *Sussex Remembered – Pictures from the Archives of The Argus*, The Breedon Books Publishing Company, Derby, 2003
Betts, Derek, *Whatever Happened to Brighton's Tin School? The History of Balfour Primary School, 1905 to 1955*, Self-published, Brighton, 2015
Brown, Mike, *Evacuees – Evacuation In Wartime Britain 1939–1945*, Sutton Publishing Ltd, Stroud, 2000
Buckton, Henry, *Sussex at War Through Time*, Amberley Publishing, Stroud, 2014
Bullock, Albert & Medcalf, Peter, *Palace Pier, Brighton*, Sutton Publishing Ltd, Stroud, 1999
Burgess, Pat & Saunders, Andy, *Battle Over Sussex 1940*, Middleton Press, Midhurst, 1990
Burgess, Pat & Saunders, Andy, *Blitz Over Sussex, 1941–42*, Middleton Press, Midhurst, 1994
Burgess, Pat & Saunders, Andy, *Bombers Over Sussex, 1943–45*, Middleton Press, Midhurst, 1995
Butler, Chris, *East Sussex Under Attack – Anti-Invasion Sites 1500–1990*, Tempus Publishing, Stroud, 2007

Carter, Ray, *A History of Hollingdean*, Lewis Cohen Urban Studies Centre, Brighton, 1986
Chambers, Ken, *Brighton Diaries*, Hanover Books, Brighton, 2009
Cluett, Leslie G. (compiler), *Brighton And Hove Under Fire – Story of the Bombing Years, 1940–1944*
Collis, Rose, *Brighton Boozers*, Royal Pavilion, Libraries & Museums, Brighton & Hove City Council, Brighton, 2005
Cooksley, Peter, *The Home Front – Civilian Life in World War Two*, Tempus Publishing, Stroud, 2007
Cooper, B.K., *Rail Centres – Brighton*, Ian Allan Ltd, Shepperton, 1981
Crocker, Emma, *The Home Front in Photographs*, Sutton Publishing, Stroud, 2004
Crook, Paul, *Sussex Home Guard,* Middleton Press, Midhurst, 1998
d'Enno, Douglas, *Brighton Crime and Vice, 1800–2000*, Wharncliffe Books, Barnsley, 2007
Dallaway, Enid, *Sunshine, Sand and Sea*, New Horizon, Bognor Regis, 1980
Dennis, Teresa (compiler), *Brighton's War,* S.B. Publications, Seaford, 2005
Elliston, R.A., *Lewes at War 1939–45,* Alma Cott Publications, Eastbourne, UK, 1995
Foster, Christine (Ed.), *Coastal Reflections*, The Saltdean Community Charity, Saltdean, Brighton, 2018
Fyfe, Hamilton, *BRIGHTON – The Official Handbook of the County Borough of Brighton 1939–40,* Brighton Corporation Publicity Committee
Gardiner, Marjorie, *The Other Side of the Counter – The Life of a Shop Girl, 1925–1945*, QueenSpark, Brighton 1985
Gaston, Harry, *Brighton's County Hospital, 1828–2007,* Southern Editorial Services, Newhaven, 2008
Goodwin, John, *Defending Sussex Beaches, 1940–42,* Middleton Press, Midhurst, 2010
Grehan, John & Mace, Martin, *Battleground Sussex*, Pen and Sword Military, Barnsley, 2012
Harding, P., *The Kemp Town Branch Line*, Self-published, Woking, nd.
Hawkins, Ernest A., *Brighton (& Sussex) At War 1939–1945 –* A Pictorial Record from the Photographic Files of Ernest A Hawkins
Heater, Joyce, *Brighton College*, Tempus Publishing Ltd, Stroud, 2007
HM Government, Home Office, *The Protection of Your Home Against Air Raids*, London, 1938
Horlock, Christopher, *BRIGHTON – The Century in Photographs, Volume 1*, S.B. Publications, Seaford, 2000
Humphrey, George, *Eastbourne at War*, S.B. Publications, Seaford, 1998

Humphrey, George, *Wartime Eastbourne*, Beckett Features, Eastbourne, 1989
Hylton, Stuart, *Kent and Sussex 1940 – Britain's Front Line*, Pen & Sword Military Books, 2004
Jones, Lavender & Pollard, Jacqueline, *Hilly Laine to Hanover – a Brighton Neighbourhood*, Brighton Books Publishing, Brighton, 2008
Jones, Martin D.W., *Brighton College 1845–1995*, Phillimore & Co. Ltd., Chichester, 1995
Knight, John, *A Hap'orth Of Sweets – A Child's 1930s–40s,* QueenSpark Books, Brighton, 1998
Knowles, David J., *The Tree Climbers – A Childhood in Wartime Brighton*, Knowles Publishing, Rochester, 1998
Knowles, David J., *With Resolve with Valour: Volunteers of WWII on the Home Shores*, Knowles Publishing, Rochester, 2002
London Road Social History Group, *LONDON ROAD – Brighton's First Suburb*, Brighton 2010
Longstaff-Tyrrell, Peter, *Barracks to Bunkers – 250 Years of Military Activity in Sussex*, Sutton Publishing Ltd, Stroud, 2002
Lyons, Paul K., *Brighton in Diaries*, History Press, Stroud, 2011
Macdougall, Philip, *If War Should Come – Defence Preparations on the South Coast 1935–1939,* Spellmount, Stroud, 2011
Masterson, Olive, *The Circle of Life,* QueenSpark Books No. 18, Brighton, 1986
Mercer D. (Ed.), *Chronicle of the 20th Century*, Longman, London, 1988
Mercer, Peter; Holland, Douglas, *The Hunns Mere Pit: The Story of Woodingdean and Balsdean,* The Book Guild Ltd, Lewes, 1993
Mewett, Clifford, *Sussex at War 1939–45*, Pen & Sword Military, Barnsley, 2018
Middleton, Judy, *Yesterday in Brighton & Hove*, Amberley Publishing, Stroud, 2010
Miller, Edwin P., *St James's Street, Brighton, and Its Environs*, Pomegranate Press, Lewes, 2011
Minns, Raynes, *Bombers & Mash – The Domestic Front 1939–45*, Virago Press Ltd, London, 1980
Moore, Judy (compiler), Voigt, Ann (consultant ed.), *Memories of Roedean – The First 100 years,* S.B. Publications, Seaford, 1998
Murray, D. L., *Brighton & Hove in Battledress, 1939–1945,* Brighton, Brighton Herald Ltd, 1946 (for the Brighton and Hove War Memorial Fund)
Musgrave, Clifford, *Life in Brighton*, The History Press, Stroud, 2011
Netley, Fred, *Holy Oak – A History of Whitehawk and Manor Farm*, Phoenix News, Brighton, nd

Newman, Kevin, *Brighton & Hove in 50 Buildings,* Amberley Publishing, Stroud, 2016

Paul, Albert, *Hard Work and No Consideration – 51Years as a Carpenter-Joiner 1917–1968,* QueenSpark Books, Brighton, 1981

Readers' Digest Association, *Life on the Home Front*, Readers' Digest Association, London, 1993

Roles, John & Beevers, David, *A Pictorial History of Brighton*, The Breedon Books Publishing Company, Derby, 1993

Rowland, David, *The Brighton Blitz,* S.B. Publications, Seaford, 1997

Rowland, David, *Coastal Blitz,* S.B. Publications, Seaford, 2001

Rowland, David, *Out of the blue – The story of Brighton's worst air raid*, Finsbury Publishing, Peacehaven, 2003.

Rowland, David, *Spitfires over Sussex – The exploits of 602 Squadron,* Finsbury Publishing, Peacehaven, 2011

Rowland, David, *Target Brighton,* Finsbury Publishing, Peacehaven, 2002

Rowland, David, *War in the City – The Bombing of Brighton and Hove, Volume I,* Finsbury Publishing, Peacehaven, 2002

Rowland, David, *War in the City – The Bombing of Brighton and Hove, Volume II,* Finsbury Publishing, Peacehaven, 2007

Rowland, Richard, *A History of St Aubyns – 1895–2013*, WASP Printers Ltd, Peacehaven, 2015

Smith, Ethel, *Little Ethel Smith – Her Story Told by Herself*, QueenSpark Market Books, Brighton, 1992

Southern Railway of England, *Hints for Holidays in Southern Sunshine*, 1938 Edition, Official Guidebook of the Southern Railway, London, Waterloo Station, 1938

Stammer, O.W., *Letters To My Brother, 1940–1946*, nd [after 1982], printed by Carmichael, Brighton

Sussex Express and County Herald, The War in East Sussex, Lewes, 1945, reprinted 1985

Various *Brighton Behind the Front,* QueenSpark Books & the Lewis Cohen Urban Studies Centre at Brighton Polytechnic, Brighton, 1990

Various, *Catching Stories: Voices from the Brighton Fishing Community*, Brighton Fishing Community Project Team, QueenSpark Books, Brighton, 1996

Various, *D. Day – Brighton Remembers*, Lewis Cohen Urban Studies Centre, University of Brighton, 1994

Various, *Rose Hill to Roundhill: a Brighton Community*, Brighton Books Publishing, Brighton 2004

Various, *Sheltered Lives – Ditchling Road School: the war years*, Downs Junior School, Rugby Road, Brighton, 1995
Various, *The People's History of the Level*, Brighton & Hove City Council, Brighton [2014]
Visser, Nisse, *Will's War in Brighton*, CBS Green Man Publication, Burnham-on-Crouch, 2014
Waite, Doreen, *Slobs and Slogs*, London, Pen Press Publishers Ltd, 2004
Ward, Margaret, *Memories of Rottingdean 1920–1945*, QueenSpark Market Books, Brighton, 1993
Williams, Doris, *Turn Back The Years,* Xerographic Printing Services Ltd, Brighton, 1991
Williams, Doris, *Wartime Memories*, printed & typeset by Sussex University Printing Dept., nd
Wilsher, Kevin & Roberts, Stewart, *Brighton Tigers – A Story of Sporting Passion,* Kevin Wilsher, Brighton, 2020
Wilson, Pamela Sydney, *Life Was A Grand Hotel*, Book Guild Publishing, Brighton, 2008
Winter, Sheila, *Moulsecoomb Memories,* QueenSpark Books, Brighton, 1998
Wren, Tim, *Flying Sparks*, QueenSpark Book 33, QueenSpark, Brighton, 1998

C: Internet

archive.sussex.ac.uk/
bbc.co.uk/history/ww2peopleswar/
brightonmuseums.org.uk/
culture24.org.uk/
cwgc.org/
en.wikipedia.org
google.co.uk/
hansard.parliament.uk/
homestyle-online.co.uk/
images.brighton-hove-r pml.org.uk/
iwm.org.uk/history/
movinghistory.ac.uk/whitehawkhomefront/
museumcrush.org
mybrightonandhove.org.uk/
nationalarchives.gov.uk/
takeshelter.org.uk.gridhosted.co.uk/

telescoper.wordpress.com/
theargus.co.uk/
ww2.brightonmuseums.org/

The 1939 Register, a useful resource made available in November 2015, was taken on 29 September 1939 in order to issue identity cards and ration books. It can be accessed via Findmypast (www.findmypast.co.uk) or Ancestry (www.ancestry.co.uk).

D: Films

https://www.nwfa.mmu.ac.uk/blighty/indexBrighton.php
player.bfi.org.uk/free/film/watch-brightons-blitz-1940-online
screenarchive.brighton.ac.uk/collection/216/
screenarchive.brighton.ac.uk/detail/448/
screenarchive.brighton.ac.uk/detail/450/

Index

Accident(s), 52, 161
Admiralty, 12, 82–3, 87, *176*, 281–2
   First Lord of, 170
AFS (Auxiliary Fire Service), 33, 35, 93, 137, 156
Agriculture, 145
   Agricultural work, 72
Agriculture, Minister of, 73, 240–1, 246
   Ministry of, 74, 149–50, 245
Aid to Russia, 176, 179, 224
   see also Russia
Air Raid Precautions
   see ARP
   Air Raid Precautions Committee & Sub-committee, 24, 30, 56, 120
Air Raid Warden(s), *see* Warden(s)
Air raid(s) and warnings, 26, 31–2, 44, 50, 54, 59–60, 92, 94, 96, *97*, 103–104, 112, 117, 119, 125, 129, 131, 136, 140, 169, 180, 182, 187, 192–3, 207–209, 213, 215, 219–21
Air Training Corps, *see* ATC
Aircraft Production, Ministry of, 283
Aircraft, British, 255
   Beaufighter, 282
   bombers, 169
   Halifax, 255
   Hurricane, 35, 222
   Mosquito, 221, 250
   Spitfire, 135–6, 184, 193
   Typhoon Mk 1b, 193
   Whirlwind, 168, 222

Aircraft, German, 193, 209, 211, 213
   Dornier Do 217, 92, 96, 130, 134, 136
   Focke-Wulf 100 A4, 125
   Focke-Wulf 190, 187, 193–5, 209, 211
   Junkers, Ju 87/Stuka, 173
   Junkers Ju 88, 109, 136, *169*, 170
   Me 109, 120, 122, 136, 170
   Me 410, 221
   see also Luftwaffe;
   US: Flying Fortresses, 256
Airmen:
   American, 260
   Australian, 260
   British, 260
   New Zealand, 260
Aliens, enemy, 41, 56–8
   friendly, 56
Allen West, 28, 214, *281*, 281–2
Allied/Allied forces, 228, 248, 254, 256, 262, 271
Allotment(s), 73–4, 102, 116, 145, 147,149, 214, 239–41, 246
Ambulance(s), 63, 82, 93, 102, 117, 139, 164, 168, 210, 220, 232
   ambulance train, 37
America, 124
Anglo-German relations, 18
   Anglo-German Friendship League, 18
Anglo-Russian, 224
   Anglo-Russian Fellowship, 224
Anti-aircraft defence, 23, 25, 251

Aquarium, *26*, 75–6, 156, 226
Argus, The, 84, 100, 143, 156, 218, 252, 286
   see also Evening Argus
Armed Forces, 168
Army, British, 58, 68, 74, 78, 88, 160, 162, 236, 250, 252, 262, 272
Army, Canadian, 186, 260, 272
Army, French, 86
ARP, 16, 20, 23–4, 28, 30, 33–5, 52, 58–9, 61–2, *62*, 63, 88, 93, 102–103, 113–14, 117, 120, 131, 136, 139, 142, 158, 180, 189–90, 210, 212, 214, 220, 238, 248
   Headquarters, 21, 23, 33
Arundel, 155
ATC, 220
ATS, 63, *64*, 71, 272
Australia, 51
Austria(n)(s), 56–7, 195
Auxiliary Fire Service, *see* AFS
Auxiliary Territorial Service, *see* ATS

Ban, area entry, 156–7, 227, 231, *see also* Defence Area/Zone; Protected Area; Restricted Area
Bank Holiday, 228, *229*
Battle of Britain, 27, 65, 222
Belgian, 90
Bellman's (department store) 164, 168, 222, 224–5, 259
Berlin, 262
Billets/billeting, 16, 36–7, 39, 48, 50–1, 68, 161
Birch, Charles, Brighton Chief Fire Officer, 20–1
Bishop of Chichester, Bell, George, 13, 16–17, 19, 32, 57, 88, 178, 224

Bishop of Lewes, Hordern, Hugh M., 20, 103, 110, 179
Black Rock, 28, 46, 90, 122, 195, 200, 206
Blackout, 28, 31, 35, 41, 52, 54, *55*, 159, 234, 257
Blackpool Week, 229, 231
Blackpool, 162, 229, 231, 250, 263
Board of Trade, 247
Boats, fishing,
   Brighton, 82, 85, 87
   Hove, 87
Boats, pleasure, 82, 90
Bognor Regis, 121
Bomb(s), 19, 33, 43, 63, 93–4, 96, *101*, 103, *112*, 113, 116–17, 120–1, 123–8, 131, 133, 138, 161, 169, 187, 189–92, 194, 196, 198, 200–203, *203*, 204–205, 208–10, 213, *217*, 221–2, 255–6
   flying, V1 (doodlebug, buzz bomb), 148, 251, 256
   gas, 62
   high explosive, 62, 113, 115, 117
   incendiary, 21, 63, 94, 112–13
   oil, 109, 112–13
Book of Remembrance, 273, 275–8
Borough Surveyor, 31, 60–1, 184
Breeze blocks, 58
Brighton & Hove Albion, 33, 75, 260
Brighton and Hove Gazette, 48, 50, 58–9, 63–4, 67–8, 77, 79–81, 83, 90, 96, 102, 129, 135–7, 141, 144, 147, 150–1, 153–4, 156, 162, 164, 181–2, 227–8, 231, 235, 238, 240, 242, 286
Brighton and Hove Herald, 19–20, 24, 28, 32, 38, 76, 83, 157, 166, 174–5, 184–5, 215, 239, 243, 253–5, 286

Brighton Beach, 41, 83, 154, *251*, 263
Brighton Belle, 82
Brighton Bench, 156-7, 237
   see also Magistrates, Brighton
     Borough
Brighton Borough, 162
Brighton Corporation, 60, 93, 136,
   145, *146*, 150, 241–2, 269, 280
Brighton Equitable Co-operative
   Society Ltd, 74
Brighton Queen, 82
Brighton Services Club, 69
Brighton Station, 156–7, 206, 208,
   227, *229*, 264, 272
Brighton Town Council, 61, 120, 138,
   151, 153, 175, 227, 245, 263, 272–3
Brighton, 16, 18, 23, 25, 34–5, 37,
   39, 41, 43, 48, 50, *51*, 51–2, 56–8,
   60, 62, 64–5, 71, 77, 80–2, 88,
   92, 102, 109, 113–14, 118, 120–1,
   123, 126–8, 130, 133, 135–8, 140,
   141,143–7, 149, 150–1, 154–7, 160,
   162, 164–6, 168–9, 173, 175–82,
   184, 185, 187, 193–6, 206, 211–12,
   221–2, 224–7, 229, 231–2, 235,
   237, 239–41, 246–7, 251–2, 256–7,
   260, 262, *264*, 264–5, 271–3, 278,
   281, 282–3, 285
Brighton, East, 28, 195–6, 240
Brightonians, 253, 262
Britain, 12, 19, 42–3, 56, 74, 82, 224,
   239, 280
British Expeditionary Force (BEF), 67
British Legion, 18
Buchanan, Jack, 80
Burgess Hill, 155
Bus(es), 32, 38–40, 44, 46, 52, 60,
   93, 160–1, 173, 191, 252, 258, 264,
   266, 272

Brighton, Hove & District Omnibus
   Company, *53*, 69
Butter, 72, 74

Calais, 248
Canada, 51, 180, 186, 191, 193, 196,
   211–12, 249
Canadian(s), 232–3, 249
Chamberlain, Neville, 12–19, 42–3
Chancellor of the Exchequer, 162, 171
Channel Islands, 255
Channel, English, 86–7, 117, 122,
   125, 187, 193–5, 231, 250
Cherbourg, 173
Chichester, 18
Children, 36, 39–40, 44, 48, 50–1,
   127, 153, *188*, 188, 190, 215, 230,
   238, 258–60, 269
   see also Schoolchildren
Christmas, 28, 32, 50, 72, 138
Church, 54, 57, 95, 102, 114, 147,
   153, 177, 204, 214–15, 222, 270
Churches,
   All Saints, 126, 128
   Chapel Royal, *270*
   Dome Mission, 19
   Good Shepherd, 40
   Holy Trinity, 58
   Preston Old Church, 57
   St Andrew's, 58
   St Bartholomew's, 178, 270–1
   St Cuthman's, 187, 213, *214*,
     215, *216*
   St John's, Preston, 57, 116
   St John the Baptist's, 102, 236
   St Luke's (Queens Park Rise), 208
   St Luke's, Prestonville, 43
   St Mark's, 187
   St Martin's, 224

St Peter's, 7, 16, 62, 258, 270, 273
St Saviour's Mission, 128
St Wilfred's, 153
St Wulfran's, 144
Wesleyan, Preston Road, 187
Churchill, Lady Clementine's Fund for Russia, *177*
  see also Red Cross
Churchill, Mrs Clementine, 177–80
Churchill, Sarah, *78*
Churchill, Winston, 12, 67, 92, 111, 141, 266–7
Churchyard, St Nicholas', 221
CID, Brighton, 57
Cinema(s), 77, 96, 98, 102, 104, 170, 227, 260
  Academy, 158
  Astoria, 77, 173, 190, 232
  Essoldo, 80
  Odeon, Kemp Town, 77, 96, *97*, 100, 187, 193
  Odeon, West Street, 97, 158-9
  Prince's, 178
  Regent, 232, 260
  Savoy, 113, 158, 232, 260
  see also Theatre(s), Imperial
Circus Street, 21, 23, 33, 144, 187, 190
  see also ARP Headquarters
Civic Restaurants, 151, *152*
Civil Defence Comforts Fund, 180
Civil Defence Guards, 260
Civil Defence, 35, 62–3, *101*, 103, 108–109, 129, 136, 141, 169, 192, 215, 272
Civilian(s), 36, 92, *111*, 112, 154, 161, 193, 212, 229, 236, 274–8
Clinic, Municipal, 187, *188,* 188–9, 193
Clinic, school, Ditchling Road, 190

Clothing, 49
Coal, 74
Coldean, 147, 193
Colledge, Cecilia, 79, *80*
Commons, House of, 13, 43
Commonwealth War Graves, 274
Communal Feeding, 150
  see also Mass catering
Conservative Association, Brighton and Hove, 258
Co-Operative Party, Brighton (and District) Equitable, 78, 180, 245, *247*, 258
Co-Operative Store, 225
Corn Exchange, 13, 30, 151, 153, 156, 169, *169*, 173, 176, 222, 245
Court, Brighton Police, 46
Crime(s), 232, 234, 236, 239
Croquet, 75
Croydon, 49–50
Curfew, 158–60
CVA, 282
Cyclists, National Cyclists Union, 67
Czech, people, 17
  refugees, 78
Czechoslovakia, 12, 16, 78

Dachau, 262
Daladier, Edouard, 12
Dance halls, 269
  Regent Ballroom, *41*, 81, 179–80, 222, 224, 232
  Sherry's, 81, 158, 232
Dance(s), 32, *159*, 179
Dancers, 177
Dancing, 75, 231
Day, Frances, 54
D-Day, 248–56, 282
Defence Area/Zone, 154, *155*, 229

see also Ban, area entry; Restricted Area
Destroyer, 171
Devil's Dyke, 155
Dieppe, 186, 248
Dig for Victory, 73, 145, 149–50, 169, 240–1, *242*
Ditchling Beacon, 155, 241
Ditchling Road, 190
Ditchling, 19
Divisional Food Officers, 74
Dome, 17, 30, 159, *159*, 173, 176, 178–80, 182, 222–4, *225*, 227–8, 232, 246, 269
Dover, 14, 83
Downland/Downs, 24, 122, 146, *146*, 161, 241, 250
Drink, 233
Drunkenness, 236
Dundee, 250
Dunkirk, 82–8, *89*
Durham, 262
Dutton Briant, Councillor Bernard, 28, 33, 37, 56, 61, 145, 154
see also Mayor of Brighton
Dyke Road, 60, 90, 164, 255

East Street, *114*, 267, 269
East Sussex County Council, 49
East Sussex, 241
Eastbourne, 87, 159
Easter, 51, 79, 139, 156, 227, 264, 283
Eastern Road, 196–7, 200, 209–13, 219–20
Education, 49
Education, Ministry of, 247
Eggs, 72
Eisenhower, Dwight D., 254–5
Electricity, 74

Elm Grove, 52, 216, 259
Employment, 32, 72
 juvenile, 72
 unemployment, 32
England, 18, 58, 83, 123, 134, 147, 225
Entertainment, 75, 77, 158, 160, 225, 227–9, 258, 260, *261*, 262, 264, 269
Europe, 12, 248, 253, 255, 264, 266
Evacuation, 36–8, 46, 50–1
 Dunkirk, 85, *86*
Evacuee(s), 36, *39*, 40, 45, *45*, 46, 48–9, *51*, 95
Evening Argus, *41*, 48, 59, 68, 71-3, 75, 88, 149, 239, 245, 265, 286
 see also Argus, The

Falmer, 71, 161, 186, 241, 273
Far East, 176, 271, 282
Farmers, 70–1
Farmland, 71
Farms/farming, 69, 71–2, 144, 148, 160, 241
Feeding, 49
 see also Communal feeding
Ferring, 155
Film(s), 79, 123, 170, 178, 245
Fire Brigade, Auxiliary, 29
Fire Guard, 220
 Brighton College's, 138
Fire Station, Brighton Central, 58–9
Fire Watcher, 138, 193
Fire Watching, 138, 240
Firefighting, 24
Firemen, Brighton, 173
First Aid, 20, 30–1, 33, 63, 131, 136, 226
First World War, 56, 77, 88, 142, 186, 237, 248, 274, 283
Fishermen, Brighton's, 82, 84, 87

Fishing boats, Brighton, 88
Fishing Museum, Brighton, 88
Flag Day, 180, 262
Food, 72, 149, 153, 241
   advice centre, 247
   Control Committee(s), Brighton Council's, 72, 74, 245
   distribution, 69, 150
   Exhibition, 245
   Ministry of, 72, 74, 247
   Mobile Unit, 180
   Office(s), 74, 228
   Production, 73, 144, 240, 245–6
   shops, 41, 227
   waste, 146
France, 12, 16, 82–4, 86, 91, 130, 206, 216, 253
   northern, 256
   south of, 254
French, 86, 251
Friendship League, 19
Fruit, 147–8, 246
Fuel, household, 74
Fuel, Ministry of, 247
Fundraising, 162

Gas holder, 195, 201
Gas mask(s), 23–4, 28, 39, 44, 46, 58, 140–1, *141*, 144
   census, 28
   distribution, 28
Gas, 74
German(s), 18, 86–7, 91, 94, 102, 106, 120–1, 130, 134–5, 143, 148, 169, 186, 190, 208, 211, 213, 248, 256, 264, 282
Germany, 12, 17–19, 40, 42–3, 45, 57, 78, 86, 194, 222, 236, 255
Gestapo, 262

Gibraltar, 86
Goring, 155
Government, British, 12, 43, 52, 60, 71, 139, 153, 157, 162, 166, 182, 226–7, 263
Greyhound Stadium, Brighton and Hove, 228, 258, 260

Hampshire, 248
Hannington's (department store), 113–14, 265
Harvest(s)/harvesting, 71, 74, 161
Hassocks, 155
Hastings, 159, 226, 263
Haywards Heath, *244*
Health, Ministry of, 31, 37, *47*
Help to Russia Fund, 180
Hitler, Adolf, 12, 15–16, 78, 86, 162, 164, 175, 177, 236, *249*, 255
Hoare, Sir Samuel, Home Secretary, 20
Holidaymakers, 24, 41, 226, 228–9, 238
Holland, 90
Hollingbury, 143, 164, 240, 283
Hollingdean, 137
Home Front, 186
Home Guard, 65, 92, 137, 141–2, *143*, 144, 195, 207, 253, *259*, 260, 271–2, 274
   see also LDV
Home Office, 24, 29, 58, 137
Home Secretary, 56, 118–19
Home Security, Minister/Ministry of, 61, 154, 226
Horsham, 40, 147, 156
Horsted Keynes, 73, 147, *148*
Hospital(s), 37, 40, 54, 69, 85, 101–102, 106, 113–14, 126, 128, 180, 234, 256

Municipal (later Brighton General), 40, 104, 109, 128, 191, 208
New Sussex, 40
Royal Alexandra Hospital for Sick Children, 60, 262
Royal Sussex County/RSCH, 40, 44, 92, 96, 98, 102, 104, 112, 114, 118, 126, 131, 180, 193, 195–7, 207, 209–10, 220, 246, 274
Stalingrad, 224, *225*
Sussex Eye, 40
Sussex Throat and Ear, 40
Hotel(s), 28, 32, 56, 154–6, 160, 224, 230, 233, 236–7, 263
Downs Hotel, Woodingdean, *266*
Golden Cross, 224
Grand, 75
Homelands Private Hotel, 54
Metropole, 46, 75, 221, 250
Norfolk, 69, 159, 231
Old Ship, 19, 72, 226, 263, 272
House of Commons, 142, 147
Hove, 14, 16, 18–19, 31, 34, 41, 45, 50–1, 56, 64–5, 88, 92, 112, 120, 124, 126, 138, 144, 154–6, 158–9, 164, *166*, 169, 178, 181–2, 184–5, 187–8, 192, 195, 200, 206, 211, 224–5, 227, 231, 246, 252, 278, 283
Hurstpierpoint, 155
Hutchinson, Captain W.J., Brighton Chief Constable, 20, 38, 41, 44, 52, 56, 58, 65, 75, 149, 158, 240

Ice hockey, 75, *76*, 78, 260
Tigers, Sussex, 260
Ice rink, 78–9
see also Sports Stadium
Industrial production, local, 280
Infantry, Canadian, 186

Information, Ministry of, 180, 245, 247, 265, 274
Isle of Wight, 226
Italy, 228

Jews/Jewish, 18–19, 57, 78
see also Refugee Relief Council
Juveniles, 237–8

Keep, The, 273–4
Kemp Town, 54, 64, 68–9, 96, *97*, 98, 100, 118, 134, 139, 187, 195, *196*, 208, *217*, *219*, 234, 236, 248
Kent, 216, 248
King George VI, 92, 254, 269
Kristallnacht, 19

Labour Party/Association, Brighton, 162, 179–80, 258–9
Lake District, 51
Lancing, 155
Land Army/Land Girls, 71, *71*, 161, 272
Land workers, 71, 241
Landmines, 91
Le Havre, 86
League of Nations Union, 19
Leconfield, Lord (Lord Lieutenant of Sussex), 67, 69, 162
Leisure, 75
Level, The, 35
Lewes Road, 25, 62, 90, 104, *107*, 109, 111, 216, 282
see also Viaduct
Lewes, 237, *244*
Lighting, 74
Lindfield, 71
Littlehampton, 154, 226
Livestock, 72, 74, 160
see also Pigs

Local Defence Volunteers (LDV), 64–5, *66*, 67, 141
  see also Home Guard
London County Council (LCC), 38, 48–9
London Road, Brighton, 40, 60, 75, 101, 120, 128, 146, 156, 173, 175, 194, *194*, 206, 225, 243, 252, 258–60
London, 18, 37, 41, 48–50, 62, 69, 77, 79, 101, 127, 133, 138, 144, 153, 156–7, 206, 216, 262, 264, 283
Londoners, 156, 264
Luftwaffe, 256

Magistrates, Brighton Borough, 58, 63, 74, 76, 232–4, 236, 239
  see also Brighton Bench
Malta, 173
Marine Gate, 54, *121*, 122, 187, 195, 201–202, *203*, 211, 219
Mass catering, 150, 151
  see also Communal Feeding
Mayfield, 148–9, 243
Mayor of Brighton, 15, 17, 20, 29, 36–7, 52, 75, 77, 80, 88, 103–104, 109, 111, 133, 145, 147, 150–1, *152*, 164, 170–1, *171*, 173, 175, *175*–6, 177, 180, 182, 218, 222, 224, 226, 231, 245, *246*, 247, 258, 260, 263, 266–7, 269, 271–2, 283
Mayor of Hove, 15, 17, 20, 162, 171, 177, 226, 245, 269
Mayor's Fund, 17
Mayoress of Brighton, 80, 88, 111, 173, 177, 224, 226, 266, 271
Mayors (Brighton & Hove), 158, 170
Meat, 72
  bacon, 72, 74–5
  ham, 74
  pork, 74

Memorials, 278
Merchant Navy, 226
Milk, 72
  condensed, 75
Miller, Max, *69*, 79, 262
Montgomery, Bernard, 254
Moulsecoomb, 35, 40, 122, 137, 150–1, 240
  Moulsecoomb, East, 280, *280*
Munich, 12, 15–18
Munitions, 182, 184, 283, 285
  Munition Girls, 169
Mussolini, Benito, 12, 15

National Fire Service, *see* NFS
National Savings, 162, 166, 173
  Certificates, 162
  Committee, *165*, 166
National Service, 34
National Socialist party/Nazi(s), 18–19, 57, 78, 102, 136, 169, *170*, 211
  Nazi Germany, 78
New Year, 156, 258, 260, 262
New York, 249
New Zealand, 51
Newhaven, *85*, 87, 113
NFS (National Fire Service), 200, 272
  College, 64
Norfolk Square, 60, 115, 117–18, *119*
Normandy, 248, 251, 255
North Africa, 262
North Street 58, 80, 113, *114*, 231, 236, 269

Operation Dynamo, *see* Dunkirk
Operation Overlord, 248, *see* D-Day
Ovingdean, 28, 74, 129–30, 134, 137, 144, 193, 222, 235

Pantomimes, 32
Parks, East Brighton, 228, 266, 269
  Moulsecoomb Wild, 228
  Preston, 33, 112, 157, 206, 228, 238, *252*, 252, 269
  Queens, 90, 189, 228, 238
  Stanmer, 161, 186
Patcham, 16, 39–40, 136, 145, 164, 220–1, 225, 228, 239–40, *243*, 243, 246
Peace/peacetime, 12, 14, 33, 125, 151, 158, 213, 257, 265–6
Peacehaven, 218
Pier(s), 90, 263
  Palace, 90–1, 193–5
  West, 32, 77
Pigs, 145, 147, 182, 245
Pioneer Corps, 161
Poland/Poles/Polish, 40, 42–3, 57, 86, 250, 262
Police, 56, 58, 77, 93, 103, 118, 129, 133, 141–2, 149, 154, 156, 192, 195, 210, 230–1, 233–4, 236, 239, 258
  Police Station/HQ (Brighton), 56–8, 240
  police stations, 64
  see also Hutchinson, Captain W. J., (Chief Constable)
Portslade, 34, 46, 50, 65, 246
Preston Barracks, 250
Preston Circus, 128, 164, 173
  Fire Station, 144
Preston Manor, 34
Preston Road, 195, 200, 206, 235
Preston, Brighton, 111, 115, *115–16*, 156, 169
Prisoners of war, 224, 258; St John Fund, 224, 262
Protected area, 58

  see also Ban, area entry; Defence Area/Zone; Restricted Area

Queens Road, 66–7, 81, 113, 278, *279*

Racing, horse, 75
  greyhound, 75
Radar, 117
RAF, 68, 88, 111, 162, 180, 222, 226, 233, 239, 250, 260, 272, 274
  Fighter Command, 280
  Fund, 180
  RAF Brighton, 195–205
  Volunteer Reserve, 239
Rail/railway, 65, 120, 126, 187, *194*, 200, 203–206, 216, 226, 230, *230*, 231, 256, 272
  Kemp Town branch, 24, 33, *35*, 139, 218
  Southern, 63, 65, *66*, 76, 144
  Trains, 41, 58, 62
Rationing/ration books, 72, 74, 150, 153, 291
  rations, 245
Rawson, Sir Alfred Cooper, Brighton MP, 14, 88, 118
Recruitment, 68
Recycling, 145
Red Army, 224
Red Cross, British, 20, 40, 176–7, 180, 226
  International, 57
  see also Russia
Re-evacuation, 50
Refugee Relief Council, Brighton and Hove, Jewish, 19
Refugees, 19, 56
Regiments; Cavalry of the Line, 68
  Coldstream Guards, 237

Essex Regiment, 237
Infantry of the Line, 68
Royal Armoured Corps, 68
Royal Artillery, 23, 68
Royal Engineers, 68
Royal East Kent Regiment
   (Buffs), 68
Royal Observer Corps 129, 272
Royal Sussex, 68
Royal West Kent, 68
Regional Commissioner(s), 33, 103, 139, 154, 156, 159–60
Register, 1939, 291
Reserves, Naval, 274
Respirators, *see* Gas masks
Restaurants, 155
   British/Civic, 153
Restricted Area, *230*
Returnees, 50
RNVR, 237
Robertsbridge, 40
Roedean, 65
Rottingdean, 18, 33, 48, *71*, 75, 90–1, 120–1,129–31, *132–4*, 137, 170, 194, 234–5, 240, 263
Royal Air Force, *see* RAF
Royal Marines, 68, 260
Royal Navy
   British, 68, 82–3, 86, 88, 162, 171, 250, 272, 274
   Italian, 173
Royal Pavilion, 18–19, 21, 24, 33–4, 43, 50, 63–4, 87, *145*, 149–50, 162, 164, 170, *171*, 173, 175, *175*, 178, 180, 182, 222, 226, 232, 241, 245–6, 258–9
Royal York Buildings 227, 249
Russia, 176, 180, 224–5
   see also Red Army

Russia, Mrs Churchill's Red Cross Aid to Russia Fund, *177*, 177–9, 224–5
   Aid to Russia Week, 177
   see also Churchill, Mrs Clementine
Russian(s), 178–9, 182, 195, 222, 262
Rustington, 40, 155
Rye, 87, *244*

Saint-Valéry-en-Caux, 82–3, 85–7
Saltdean, 75, 130, 133, 135, 137, 147, 170, 263
   Fellowship, 224, 226
Saltdean, Ocean Hotel, National Fire Service College, 64
Salvage, 181-2, *183–4*, 184-5,
Salvation Army, *101*, 109, 128
Sandbags, 25, 26, 44, 58, 59, 126, 149
   Sandbagging/sandbag filling, 36, 58
Sandwich, Kent, 248
Saving(s), War, 162, 168, 170, 175, 181, 224, 262
   Campaign, 176
   Savings Committee, Brighton, 162, 166, *223*
   Savings Group(s), 164, *165*, 165, 175
School(s), 32, 38, 73, 113–14, 128, 131, 133, 170, 190, 192, 209, 254
   Balfour Primary, 52
   Brighton and Hove Grammar/ Brighton, Hove and Sussex Grammar, 138, 149
   Brighton College, 65, 73–4, 138, 148, 164, 174, 208–10, 213, *283*, 284
   Brighton College of Art, 169, 274
   Circus Street Board, 22, 190
   Ditchling Road, 189, 254
   Dorothy Stringer, 144
   Downs Junior, *39*

Elm Grove Junior, 218
Hollingdean Special School, 40
Intermediate School(s), 50, 94, *95*
Middle Street, 40
Moulsecoomb, 35, 40, *140*
Moulsecoomb School for Girls, 140
Patcham, 20
Pelham Street, 40
Preston Road, 199
Roedean, 26, pupils, *27*, 51
Rottingdean, 40, 131
School of Art, 169
St Aubyns, 131
St Luke's, 40, 208
St Mark's, 195, *196*, 197
St Mary's Hall, 196, 211–12
Varndean Boys, 27, 36, 49, 52, 73, 138, 146–8, *148*, 243, 250
Varndean Girls, 39
Warmdene, 39–40
Warren Farm, 40
Whitehawk, 40, 215
Whittinghame College, 40
York Place, 245, *247*
Schoolchildren, 37, 61, 150, 195, 254
Scotland, 225
Seaford, 40
Seafront, Brighton, 44
Searchlight(s), *23*, 23–4, 90, 219
Second World War, 176, 273–4, 280
Servicemen, *see also* Soldiers and Troops
  British, 234, 258, 260, 274, *279*
  US, 266, 274
Servicewomen, British, 274, *279*
Seven Dials, 60
Shelter(s), air raid, 31, 44, 58–60, 131, 137, 139, *140*, 189, 197, 209, 216, 221, 256
  Morrison, 192, 196, 205, 219

Shilling Fund, 64, 68-9
Ships,
  HMS *Cockade*, 176
  HMS *Kipling*, *168*, *171*, 172–6
  HMS *Renown*, 173
  HMS *Unbeaten*, 172–3
Shopbreaking, 54
Shore establishment;
  HMS *Vernon,* 259
Shoreham, 62, 155, 246, 250
Sicily, 228, 274
Siren(s), 34, 41, 90, 92, 109, 113–14, 125, 131, 187, 189, 194, 216, 221
Skating, 78, 260
Skylark, 83, *83*, 84, 88
Soldier(s), British, 103, 107, 129, 161, 192, 226, 235–6, 248, 253
  Allied, 82
  Canadian, 233–4, 248–50, 252
South Africa, 51
South Coast, 82
Southend, 162
Southern Railway, *see* Rail/Railway
Southwick, 34, 62, 92, 246
Soviet, Soviet Union, 16, 78
  see also Russia
Spain, 86
Spitfire Fund, 111, 180
Sport, 75
Sports Stadium/SS Brighton, 32, 78–9, 158, 232, 260
St Dunstan's, 180
St John Ambulance Brigade, 20, 40
St Leonards, 263
Stanmer, 71, 142, 160, 186, 241
Steyning, 155
Streatham, 127
Street parties, 265

Submarine, 285
  German, 173
Sudetenland, 12, 17
Sugar, 74
Supply, Ministry of, 182
Surrey, 50, 278
Sussex Assizes, 232
Sussex Daily News, 15–16, 28, 31, 39, 42, 44–6, 68, 70, 262, 264–6, 269, 286
Sussex Express, 286
Sussex Square, 24, 142–3, 208, 211
Sussex Territorial Army Association, 67-8
Sussex, 18, 33, 40, 151, 154, 162, 170, 181–2, 216, 228, 252, 255
  Sussex, East, 70–1

Tank Fund for Brighton, Hove, 180
Tanks, 161, 166, 170, *252*, 252–3
Telscombe Hall, 224
Territorial Army, 14
  headquarters, 14
Theatre(s), 77
  Hippodrome, 79, 158–9, 231, 262
  Imperial, 80–1, *81,* 178, 231, *268*
  Pavilion 245
  Theatre Royal, 32, 69, 77, 179, *179*, 262
Theft, 54, 234, 240
Town Clerk, Brighton, 88
Town Hall, Brighton, *29*, 35, 49, 58, *59*, 60, 87, 153, 157, 169, 182, 230, 232, *267*, 267
Trams, 181, *181*
Transport, public, 160
Trenches, *25*, 26, *30*, 31, 59–61, 140, 151, 190
  Trench-digging/ trenching, 25, 31, 35, *36*, 61, 136

Troops, 230, 251, 253, 255
  American airborne, 248
  Belgian, 82
  British, 82, 161, 262
  British airborne, 248
  Canadian, 161, 186
  Canadian airborne, 248
  Dominion, 229
  French, 82
  French Canadian, 250
  German, 42, 56, 62, 82
  Moroccan, 82
Tunbridge Wells, 63

Uckfield, 40
United States, 51, 229
USSR:
  see also Russia, 180

VAD(s), (Voluntary Aid Detachment), 38, 40
VE Day, 264–5, *266*, *268*, 270
Vegetables, 73, 146–7, 149
Vera Lynn, 262
Veules-les-Roses, 85–6
Viaduct, 62, 120, 187, 194, *194*, 204, 206, 216, 285
Vicar of Brighton, 88
Victory, 258, *264*, *267*, 269
  Victory Parade, 271–2

WAAF, (Women's Auxiliary Air Force), 147, 272
Wandsworth, 237
War Agricultural Executive Committee, 70, *146*, 147
  East Sussex, 241–3
War Effort, 168, 182, 247, 282–3
War Office, 68

War Weapons Week, 156, *168–9*
169–72,
War work, 214, 274, *284*
War, 15, 17–18, *22*, 26–7, 31–3, 35, 37, 40, *41*, 42–4, 48, 52, 62
declaration of, 58
War, Ministry of, 283
Secretary of State for, 64
War/wartime, 65, 67, 74–5, 96, 124, 126, 131, 136, 144, 149, 155, 162, *162*, *163*, 166, 170, 173, 184, 186, 189, 193, 196, 208, 213, 215, 226–7, 239, 241, 246, 258, 260, 269, *279*, 285
Warden(s), Air Raid, 20–1, 28, 33, 35, *35*, 58, 61–3, 90, 114, 119, 137, *137*, 138, 140, 158, 187, 189, 191, 210, 214–15, 237–8, 250, 259
Civil Defence, 271
Shelter, 136
Street, 136–7
Warship Week, *172*, *174–5*, 184
West Grinstead, 40

West Street, 78
Western Road, 46, 100, 113–14, 118, 157–8, 221, 225
Weymouth, 170
White Street, 104, *105*
Whitehawk, 26, 40, 140, 146, 150–1, 177, 208, 213, 216, 228
Wings for Victory, 176, 222, *223*
Withdean, 28, 68
WLA (Women's Land Army), 241, 243
Woodingdean, 48, 90, 126, 145, 147, 187, *266*
Works and Buildings, Ministry of, 185
Worthing, 23–4, 155–6, 159
WRNS (Women's Royal Naval Service), 260, 272
Wuppertal, 18
WVS (Women's Voluntary Services for Air Raid Precautions), 109, 114, 153, 181–2, 184–5, 260, 272, 274

YMCA, 226
Yorkshire, 52